# WHERE ARE THE LESSON FILES?

Purchasing this Classroom in a Book gives you access to the lesson files that you'll need to complete the exercises in the book, as well as other content to help you learn more about Adobe software and use it with greater efficiency and ease. The diagram below represents the contents of the lesson files directory, which should help you locate the files you need. Please see the Getting Started section for full download instructions.

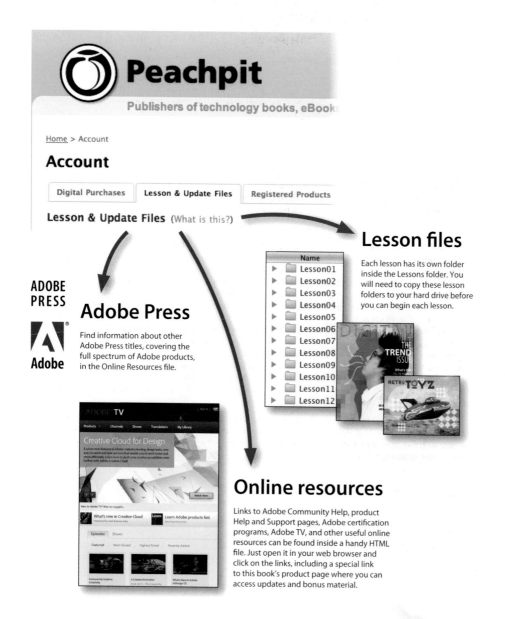

**Peachpit**

Publishers of technology books, eBooks

Home > Account

## Account

Digital Purchases | **Lesson & Update Files** | Registered Products

**Lesson & Update Files** (What is this?)

**ADOBE PRESS**

### Adobe Press

Find information about other Adobe Press titles, covering the full spectrum of Adobe products, in the Online Resources file.

Name
► Lesson01
► Lesson02
► Lesson03
► Lesson04
► Lesson05
► Lesson06
► Lesson07
► Lesson08
► Lesson09
► Lesson10
► Lesson11
► Lesson12

### Lesson files

Each lesson has its own folder inside the Lessons folder. You will need to copy these lesson folders to your hard drive before you can begin each lesson.

### Online resources

Links to Adobe Community Help, product Help and Support pages, Adobe certification programs, Adobe TV, and other useful online resources can be found inside a handy HTML file. Just open it in your web browser and click on the links, including a special link to this book's product page where you can access updates and bonus material.

# CONTENTS

**GETTING STARTED**     **1**

About Classroom in a Book.................................... 1

What's new in this edition.................................... 2

Prerequisites ................................................. 2

Installing Adobe Photoshop and Adobe Bridge.............. 3

Starting Adobe Photoshop................................... 3

Accessing the Classroom in a Book files...................... 3

Restoring default preferences .............................. 4

Additional resources ........................................ 5

Adobe certification ......................................... 6

**1   GETTING TO KNOW THE WORK AREA**     **8**

Starting to work in Adobe Photoshop ...................... 10

Using the tools .............................................. 14

Setting tool properties...................................... 21

Undoing actions in Photoshop ............................. 25

More about panels and panel locations..................... 29

Customizing the workspace................................. 32

Finding resources for using Photoshop ..................... 36

Review questions and answers............................. 38

**2   BASIC PHOTO CORRECTIONS**     **40**

Strategy for retouching .................................... 42

Resolution and image size .................................. 43

Getting started ............................................. 44

Straightening and cropping the image in Photoshop ....... 45

Adjusting the color and tone ............................... 47

Using the Spot Healing Brush tool ......................... 48

Using content-aware fill.................................... 52

# Adobe®
# Photoshop® CC

# CLASSROOM IN A BOOK®
The official training workbook from Adobe Systems

Adobe® Photoshop® CC Classroom in a Book®



Adobe Systems Incorporated, 345 Park Avenue, San Jose, California 95110-2704, USA



Adobe Press books are published by Peachpit, a division of Pearson Education located in San Francisco, California. For the latest on Adobe Press books, go to www.adobepress.com. To report errors, please send a note to errata@peachpit.com. For information on getting permission for reprints and excerpts, contact permissions@peachpit.com.

Printed and bound in the United States of America

ISBN-13: 978-0-321-92807-8

ISBN-10: 0-321-92807-5

9 8 8 6 5 4 3 2 1

Repairing areas with the Clone Stamp tool . . . . . . . . . . . . . . . . . 52

Applying a content-aware patch. . . . . . . . . . . . . . . . . . . . . . . . . 54

Sharpening the image . . . . . . . . . . . . . . . . . . . . . . . . . . . . . . . . . 56

Review questions and answers . . . . . . . . . . . . . . . . . . . . . . . . . . 59

**3 WORKING WITH SELECTIONS**        **60**

About selecting and selection tools . . . . . . . . . . . . . . . . . . . . . . 62

Getting started . . . . . . . . . . . . . . . . . . . . . . . . . . . . . . . . . . . . . . . 63

Using the Quick Selection tool . . . . . . . . . . . . . . . . . . . . . . . . . . 63

Moving a selected area . . . . . . . . . . . . . . . . . . . . . . . . . . . . . . . . 64

Manipulating selections . . . . . . . . . . . . . . . . . . . . . . . . . . . . . . . 65

Using the Magic Wand tool. . . . . . . . . . . . . . . . . . . . . . . . . . . . . 68

Selecting with the lasso tools . . . . . . . . . . . . . . . . . . . . . . . . . . 71

Rotating a selection. . . . . . . . . . . . . . . . . . . . . . . . . . . . . . . . . . . 72

Selecting with the Magnetic Lasso tool . . . . . . . . . . . . . . . . . . . 73

Selecting from a center point . . . . . . . . . . . . . . . . . . . . . . . . . . . 74

Resizing and copying a selection . . . . . . . . . . . . . . . . . . . . . . . . 75

Cropping an image . . . . . . . . . . . . . . . . . . . . . . . . . . . . . . . . . . . 77

Review questions and answers . . . . . . . . . . . . . . . . . . . . . . . . . . 79

**4 LAYER BASICS**        **80**

About layers . . . . . . . . . . . . . . . . . . . . . . . . . . . . . . . . . . . . . . . . . 82

Getting started . . . . . . . . . . . . . . . . . . . . . . . . . . . . . . . . . . . . . . . 82

Using the Layers panel . . . . . . . . . . . . . . . . . . . . . . . . . . . . . . . . 83

Rearranging layers. . . . . . . . . . . . . . . . . . . . . . . . . . . . . . . . . . . . 88

Applying a gradient to a layer . . . . . . . . . . . . . . . . . . . . . . . . . . 98

Applying a layer style . . . . . . . . . . . . . . . . . . . . . . . . . . . . . . . . . 99

Adding an adjustment layer . . . . . . . . . . . . . . . . . . . . . . . . . . . 103

Updating layer effects . . . . . . . . . . . . . . . . . . . . . . . . . . . . . . . 105

Adding a border . . . . . . . . . . . . . . . . . . . . . . . . . . . . . . . . . . . . 107

Flattening and saving files . . . . . . . . . . . . . . . . . . . . . . . . . . . . 108

Review questions and answers . . . . . . . . . . . . . . . . . . . . . . . . . 111

**5  CORRECTING AND ENHANCING DIGITAL PHOTOGRAPHS    112**

Getting started . . . . . . . . . . . . . . . . . . . . . . . . . . . . . . . . . . . . . . . . .114

About camera raw files. . . . . . . . . . . . . . . . . . . . . . . . . . . . . . . . . . .117

Processing files in Camera Raw . . . . . . . . . . . . . . . . . . . . . . . . . .117

Applying advanced color correction. . . . . . . . . . . . . . . . . . . . . .130

Correcting digital photographs in Photoshop. . . . . . . . . . . . .142

Correcting image distortion. . . . . . . . . . . . . . . . . . . . . . . . . . . . .147

Adding depth of field . . . . . . . . . . . . . . . . . . . . . . . . . . . . . . . . . . .150

Review questions and answers . . . . . . . . . . . . . . . . . . . . . . . . . . .158

**6  MASKS AND CHANNELS    160**

Working with masks and channels. . . . . . . . . . . . . . . . . . . . . . . .162

Getting started . . . . . . . . . . . . . . . . . . . . . . . . . . . . . . . . . . . . . . . . .162

Creating a mask . . . . . . . . . . . . . . . . . . . . . . . . . . . . . . . . . . . . . . . . .163

Refining a mask. . . . . . . . . . . . . . . . . . . . . . . . . . . . . . . . . . . . . . . . . .164

Creating a quick mask. . . . . . . . . . . . . . . . . . . . . . . . . . . . . . . . . . . .168

Manipulating an image with Puppet Warp . . . . . . . . . . . . . . . .170

Working with channels . . . . . . . . . . . . . . . . . . . . . . . . . . . . . . . . . .172

Review questions and answers . . . . . . . . . . . . . . . . . . . . . . . . . . .179

**7  TYPOGRAPHIC DESIGN    180**

About type . . . . . . . . . . . . . . . . . . . . . . . . . . . . . . . . . . . . . . . . . . . . . .182

Getting started . . . . . . . . . . . . . . . . . . . . . . . . . . . . . . . . . . . . . . . . .182

Creating a clipping mask from type. . . . . . . . . . . . . . . . . . . . . . .183

Creating type on a path . . . . . . . . . . . . . . . . . . . . . . . . . . . . . . . . . .187

Warping point type . . . . . . . . . . . . . . . . . . . . . . . . . . . . . . . . . . . . . .191

Designing paragraphs of type. . . . . . . . . . . . . . . . . . . . . . . . . . . .192

Working with type styles. . . . . . . . . . . . . . . . . . . . . . . . . . . . . . . . .194

Adding a rounded rectangle . . . . . . . . . . . . . . . . . . . . . . . . . . . . .199

Adding vertical text. . . . . . . . . . . . . . . . . . . . . . . . . . . . . . . . . . . . . .200

Review questions and answers . . . . . . . . . . . . . . . . . . . . . . . . . . .203

**8  VECTOR DRAWING TECHNIQUES    204**

About bitmap images and vector graphics. . . . . . . . . . . . . . . .206

About paths and the Pen tool . . . . . . . . . . . . . . . . . . . . . . . . . . . .207

Getting started . . . . . . . . . . . . . . . . . . . . . . . . . . . . . . . . . . . . . . . . .207

Using paths with artwork . . . . . . . . . . . . . . . . . . . . . . . . . . . . . .208

Creating vector objects for the background. . . . . . . . . . . . . . .217

Working with defined custom shapes . . . . . . . . . . . . . . . . . . . .222

Importing a Smart Object . . . . . . . . . . . . . . . . . . . . . . . . . . . . . . .227

Review questions and answers . . . . . . . . . . . . . . . . . . . . . . . . . .233

**9   ADVANCED COMPOSITING                                    234**

Getting started . . . . . . . . . . . . . . . . . . . . . . . . . . . . . . . . . . . . . . . .236

Arranging layers . . . . . . . . . . . . . . . . . . . . . . . . . . . . . . . . . . . . . . .237

Using Smart Filters . . . . . . . . . . . . . . . . . . . . . . . . . . . . . . . . . . . . .240

Painting a layer . . . . . . . . . . . . . . . . . . . . . . . . . . . . . . . . . . . . . . . .243

Adding a background . . . . . . . . . . . . . . . . . . . . . . . . . . . . . . . . . . .245

Automating a multistep task . . . . . . . . . . . . . . . . . . . . . . . . . . .246

Upscaling a low-resolution image . . . . . . . . . . . . . . . . . . . . . . .255

Saving the image for four-color printing . . . . . . . . . . . . . . . . .257

Matching color schemes across images. . . . . . . . . . . . . . . . . . .258

Stitching a panorama . . . . . . . . . . . . . . . . . . . . . . . . . . . . . . . . . .261

Finishing the image. . . . . . . . . . . . . . . . . . . . . . . . . . . . . . . . . . . .263

Review questions and answers . . . . . . . . . . . . . . . . . . . . . . . . . .267

**10   EDITING VIDEO                                          268**

Getting started . . . . . . . . . . . . . . . . . . . . . . . . . . . . . . . . . . . . . . . .270

Creating a new video project. . . . . . . . . . . . . . . . . . . . . . . . . . . .271

Animating text with keyframes . . . . . . . . . . . . . . . . . . . . . . . . . .275

Creating effects. . . . . . . . . . . . . . . . . . . . . . . . . . . . . . . . . . . . . . . .277

Adding transitions . . . . . . . . . . . . . . . . . . . . . . . . . . . . . . . . . . . . .284

Adding audio. . . . . . . . . . . . . . . . . . . . . . . . . . . . . . . . . . . . . . . . . .286

Muting unwanted audio . . . . . . . . . . . . . . . . . . . . . . . . . . . . . . . .287

Rendering video. . . . . . . . . . . . . . . . . . . . . . . . . . . . . . . . . . . . . . .288

Review questions and answers . . . . . . . . . . . . . . . . . . . . . . . . . .289

**11   PAINTING WITH THE MIXER BRUSH                           290**

About the Mixer Brush . . . . . . . . . . . . . . . . . . . . . . . . . . . . . . . . .292

Getting started . . . . . . . . . . . . . . . . . . . . . . . . . . . . . . . . . . . . . . . .292

Selecting brush settings . . . . . . . . . . . . . . . . . . . . . . . . . . . . . . . .293

Mixing colors. . . . . . . . . . . . . . . . . . . . . . . . . . . . . . . . . . . . . . . . . .298

Creating a custom brush preset . . . . . . . . . . . . . . . . . . . . . . . . . . 301

Mixing colors with a photograph . . . . . . . . . . . . . . . . . . . . . . . 303

Review questions and answers . . . . . . . . . . . . . . . . . . . . . . . . . 309

**12 WORKING WITH 3D IMAGES**      **310**

Getting started . . . . . . . . . . . . . . . . . . . . . . . . . . . . . . . . . . . . . . . 312

Creating a 3D shape from a layer . . . . . . . . . . . . . . . . . . . . . . . 313

Manipulating 3D objects . . . . . . . . . . . . . . . . . . . . . . . . . . . . . . . 314

Adding 3D objects . . . . . . . . . . . . . . . . . . . . . . . . . . . . . . . . . . . . 316

Merging 3D layers to share the same 3D space . . . . . . . . . . . 320

Positioning objects in a scene . . . . . . . . . . . . . . . . . . . . . . . . . . 321

Applying materials to 3D objects . . . . . . . . . . . . . . . . . . . . . . . 328

Lighting a 3D scene . . . . . . . . . . . . . . . . . . . . . . . . . . . . . . . . . . . 334

Rendering a 3D scene . . . . . . . . . . . . . . . . . . . . . . . . . . . . . . . . . 337

Review questions and answers . . . . . . . . . . . . . . . . . . . . . . . . . 340

**13 PREPARING FILES FOR THE WEB**      **342**

Getting started . . . . . . . . . . . . . . . . . . . . . . . . . . . . . . . . . . . . . . . 344

Creating slices . . . . . . . . . . . . . . . . . . . . . . . . . . . . . . . . . . . . . . . 347

Exporting HTML and images . . . . . . . . . . . . . . . . . . . . . . . . . . . 353

Using the Zoomify feature . . . . . . . . . . . . . . . . . . . . . . . . . . . . . 358

Review questions and answers . . . . . . . . . . . . . . . . . . . . . . . . . 363

**14 PRODUCING AND PRINTING CONSISTENT COLOR**      **364**

About color management . . . . . . . . . . . . . . . . . . . . . . . . . . . . . . 366

Getting started . . . . . . . . . . . . . . . . . . . . . . . . . . . . . . . . . . . . . . . 368

Specifying color-management settings . . . . . . . . . . . . . . . . . . 368

Proofing an image . . . . . . . . . . . . . . . . . . . . . . . . . . . . . . . . . . . . 369

Identifying out-of-gamut colors . . . . . . . . . . . . . . . . . . . . . . . . 370

Adjusting an image and printing a proof . . . . . . . . . . . . . . . . 372

Saving the image as a CMYK EPS file . . . . . . . . . . . . . . . . . . . . 374

Printing . . . . . . . . . . . . . . . . . . . . . . . . . . . . . . . . . . . . . . . . . . . . . 375

Review questions and answers . . . . . . . . . . . . . . . . . . . . . . . . . 377

**APPENDIX: TOOLS PANEL OVERVIEW**      **378**

**INDEX**      **382**

# GETTING STARTED

Adobe® Photoshop® CC, the benchmark for digital imaging excellence, provides strong performance, powerful image editing features, and an intuitive interface. Adobe Camera Raw, included with Photoshop CC, offers flexibility and control as you work with raw images, as well as TIFF and JPEG images. Photoshop CC gives you the digital-editing tools you need to transform images more easily than ever before.

## About Classroom in a Book

*Adobe Photoshop CC Classroom in a Book®* is part of the official training series for Adobe graphics and publishing software, developed with the support of Adobe product experts. The lessons are designed to let you learn at your own pace. If you're new to Adobe Photoshop, you'll learn the fundamental concepts and features you'll need to master the program. And if you've been using Adobe Photoshop for a while, you'll find that Classroom in a Book teaches many advanced features, including tips and techniques for using the latest version of the application and preparing images for the web.

Although each lesson provides step-by-step instructions for creating a specific project, there's room for exploration and experimentation. You can follow the book from start to finish, or do only the lessons that match your interests and needs. Each lesson concludes with a review section summarizing what you've covered.

# What's new in this edition

This edition covers many new features in Adobe Photoshop CC, such as conditional actions, which let you run different actions according to criteria you specify; editable rounded rectangles, which let you designate the curve for each corner of a rectangle separately, and edit them at any time; the Camera Shake Reduction filter, which reduces the blur that can occur with a handheld camera; and refinements to the Crop tool that give you greater control when you're cropping, straightening, and skewing an image. In addition, these lessons introduce you to using the Liquify filter as a Smart Filter, using Smart Objects with Iris Blur and other blur options in the Blur Gallery, intelligent upscaling, copying layer attributes to CSS code for use in web pages, and more.

This edition is also chock-full of extra information on Photoshop features and how to work effectively with this robust application. You'll learn best practices for organizing, managing, and showcasing your photos, as well as how to optimize images for the web. And throughout this edition, look for tips and techniques from one of Adobe's own experts, Photoshop evangelist Julieanne Kost.

# Prerequisites

Before you begin to use *Adobe Photoshop CC Classroom in a Book*, you should have a working knowledge of your computer and its operating system. Make sure that you know how to use the mouse and standard menus and commands, and also how to open, save, and close files. If you need to review these techniques, see the documentation included with your Microsoft® Windows® or Apple® Mac® OS X documentation.

To complete the lessons in this book, you'll need to have both Adobe Photoshop CC and Adobe Bridge CC installed.

# Installing Adobe Photoshop and Adobe Bridge

Before you begin using *Adobe Photoshop CC Classroom in a Book*, make sure that your system is set up correctly and that you've installed the required software and hardware. You must purchase the Adobe Photoshop CC software separately. For system requirements and complete instructions on installing the software, visit www.adobe.com/support. Note that some Photoshop CC features, including all 3D features, require a video card that supports OpenGL 2.0 and that has at least 512MB of dedicated vRAM.

Many of the lessons in this book use Adobe Bridge. Photoshop and Bridge use separate installers. You must install these applications from Adobe Creative Cloud onto your hard disk. Follow the onscreen instructions.

# Starting Adobe Photoshop

You start Photoshop just as you do most software applications.

**To start Adobe Photoshop in Windows:** Choose Start > All Programs > Adobe Photoshop CC.

**To start Adobe Photoshop in Mac OS:** Open the Applications/Adobe Photoshop CC folder, and double-click the Adobe Photoshop program icon.

# Accessing the Classroom in a Book files

In order to work through the projects in this book, you will need to download the lesson files from peachpit.com. You can download the files for individual lessons, or download them all in a single file.

Your Account page is also where you'll find any updates to the chapters or to the lesson files. Look on the Lesson & Update Files tab to access the most current content.

To access the Classroom in a Book files, do the following:

1 On a Mac or PC, go to www.peachpit.com/redeem, and enter the code found at the back of your book.

2 If you do not have a Peachpit.com account, create one when you're prompted to do so.

3 Click the Lesson & Update Files tab on your Account page. This tab lists downloadable files.

4 Click the lesson file links to download them to your computer.

5 Create a new folder on your hard disk, and name it **Lessons**. Then, drag the lesson files you downloaded into the Lessons folder on your hard disk.

# Restoring default preferences

The preferences file stores information about panel and command settings. Each time you quit Adobe Photoshop, the positions of the panels and certain command settings are recorded in the preferences file. Any selections you make in the Preferences dialog box are also saved in the preferences file.

To ensure that what you see onscreen matches the images and instructions in this book, you should restore the default preferences as you begin each lesson. If you prefer to preserve your preferences, be aware that the tools, panels, and other settings in Photoshop CC may not match those described in this book.

If you have custom-calibrated your monitor, save the calibration settings before you start work in this book. To save your monitor-calibration settings, follow the simple procedure described below.

## To save your current color settings:

1 Start Adobe Photoshop.

2 Choose Edit > Color Settings.

3 Note what is selected in the Settings menu:

  • If it is anything other than Custom, write down the name of the settings file, and click OK to close the dialog box. You do not need to perform steps 4–6 of this procedure.

  • If Custom is selected in the Settings menu, click Save (*not* OK).

The Save dialog box opens. The default location is the Settings folder, which is where you want to save your file. The default file extension is .csf (color settings file).

4   In the File Name field (Windows) or Save As field (Mac OS), type a descriptive name for your color settings, preserving the .csf file extension. Then click Save.

5   In the Color Settings Comment dialog box, type any descriptive text that will help you identify the color settings later, such as the date, specific settings, or your workgroup.

6   Click OK to close the Color Settings Comment dialog box, and again to close the Color Settings dialog box.

### To restore your color settings:

1   Start Adobe Photoshop.

2   Choose Edit > Color Settings.

3   In the Settings menu in the Color Settings dialog box, select the settings file you noted or saved in the previous procedure, and click OK.

# Additional resources

*Adobe Photoshop CC Classroom in a Book* is not meant to replace documentation that comes with the program or to be a comprehensive reference for every feature. Only the commands and options used in the lessons are explained in this book. For comprehensive information about program features and tutorials, refer to these resources:

**Adobe Photoshop Help and Support:** www.adobe.com/support/photoshop is where you can find and browse Help and Support content on Adobe.com.

**Adobe Creative Cloud Learning:** helpx.adobe.com/creative-cloud/tutorials.html provides inspiration, key techniques, cross-product workflows, and updates on new features. The Creative Cloud Learn page is available only to Creative Cloud members.

**Adobe Forums:** forums.adobe.com lets you tap into peer-to-peer discussions, questions, and answers on Adobe products.

**Adobe TV:** tv.adobe.com is an online video resource for expert instruction and inspiration about Adobe products, including a How To channel to get you started with your product.

**Adobe Design Center:** www.adobe.com/designcenter offers thoughtful articles on design and design issues, a gallery showcasing the work of top-notch designers, tutorials, and more.

**Resources for educators:** www.adobe.com/education and edex.adobe.com offer a treasure trove of information for instructors who teach classes on Adobe software. Find solutions for education at all levels, including free curricula that use an integrated approach to teaching Adobe software and can be used to prepare for the Adobe Certified Associate exams.

Also check out these useful links:

**Adobe Marketplace & Exchange:** www.adobe.com/cfusion/exchange is a central resource for finding tools, services, extensions, code samples, and more to supplement and extend your Adobe products.

**Adobe Photoshop CC product home page:** www.adobe.com/products/photoshop

**Adobe Labs:** labs.adobe.com gives you access to early builds of cutting-edge technology as well as forums where you can interact with both the Adobe development teams building that technology and other like-minded members of the community.

# Adobe certification

The Adobe training and certification programs are designed to help Adobe customers improve and promote their product-proficiency skills. There are four levels of certification:

- Adobe Certified Associate (ACA)

- Adobe Certified Expert (ACE)

- Adobe Certified Instructor (ACI)

- Adobe Authorized Training Center (AATC)

The Adobe Certified Associate (ACA) credential certifies that individuals have the entry-level skills to plan, design, build, and maintain effective communications using different forms of digital media.

The Adobe Certified Expert program is a way for expert users to upgrade their credentials. You can use Adobe certification as a catalyst for getting a raise, finding a job, or promoting your expertise.

If you are an ACE-level instructor, the Adobe Certified Instructor program takes your skills to the next level and gives you access to a wide range of Adobe resources.

Adobe Authorized Training Centers offer instructor-led courses and training on Adobe products, employing only Adobe Certified Instructors. A directory of AATCs is available at partners.adobe.com.

For information on the Adobe Certified programs, visit www.adobe.com/support/certification/main.html.

# 1 GETTING TO KNOW THE WORK AREA

## Lesson overview

In this lesson, you'll learn how to do the following:

- Open Adobe Photoshop files.

- View files in Adobe Bridge.

- Select and use some of the tools in the Tools panel.

- Set options for a selected tool using the options bar.

- Use various methods to zoom in on and out from an image.

- Select, rearrange, and use panels.

- Choose commands in panel and context menus.

- Open and use a panel in the panel dock.

- Undo actions to correct mistakes or to make different choices.

- Customize the workspace.

 This lesson will take about an hour to complete. Download the Lesson01 project files from the Lesson & Update Files tab on your Account page at www.peachpit.com, if you haven't already done so.
As you work on this lesson, you'll preserve the start files. If you need to restore the start files, download them from your Account page.

PROJECT: BOOK COVER DESIGN

As you work with Adobe Photoshop, you'll discover that you can often accomplish the same task in several ways. To make the best use of the extensive editing capabilities in Photoshop, you must first learn to navigate the work area.

# Starting to work in Adobe Photoshop

The Adobe Photoshop work area includes menus, toolbars, and panels that give you quick access to a variety of tools and options for editing and adding elements to your image. You can also add commands and filters to the menus by installing third-party software known as *plug-ins*.

In Photoshop, you primarily work with bitmapped, digitized images (that is, continuous-tone images that have been converted into a series of small squares, or picture elements, called *pixels*). You can also work with vector graphics, which are drawings made of smooth lines that retain their crispness when scaled. You can create original artwork in Photoshop, or you can import images from many sources, such as:

- Photographs from a digital camera or mobile phone
- Commercial CDs of digital images
- Scans of photographs, transparencies, negatives, graphics, or other documents
- Captured video images
- Artwork created in drawing programs

## Starting Photoshop and opening a file

**Note:** Typically, you won't need to reset defaults when you're working on your own projects. However, you'll reset the preferences before working on most lessons in this book to ensure that what you see onscreen matches the descriptions in the lessons. For more information, see "Restoring default preferences" on page 4.

To begin, you'll start Adobe Photoshop and reset the default preferences.

1 On the desktop, double-click the Adobe Photoshop icon to start Adobe Photoshop, and then immediately hold down Ctrl+Alt+Shift (Windows) or Command+Option+Shift (Mac OS) to reset the default settings.

If you don't see the Photoshop icon on your desktop, choose Start > All Programs > Adobe Photoshop CC (Windows) or look in either the Applications folder or the Dock (Mac OS).

2 When prompted, click Yes to confirm that you want to delete the Adobe Photoshop Settings file.

The Photoshop work area appears as shown in the following illustration.

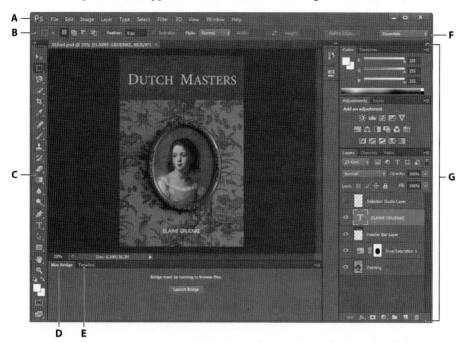

**A.** Menu bar
**B.** Options bar
**C.** Tools panel
**D.** Mini Bridge tab
**E.** Timeline tab
**F.** Workspaces menu
**G.** Panels

**Note:** This illustration shows the Windows version of Photoshop. The arrangement is similar on Mac OS, but operating system styles may vary.

The default workspace in Photoshop consists of the menu bar and options bar at the top of the screen, the Tools panel on the left, and several open panels in the panel dock on the right. When you have documents open, one or more image windows also appear, and you can display them at the same time using the tabbed interface. The Photoshop user interface is very similar to the one in Adobe Illustrator®, Adobe InDesign®, and Adobe Flash®—so learning how to use the tools and panels in one application means that you'll be familiar with them when you work in the others.

There is one main difference between the Photoshop work area on Windows and that on Mac OS: Windows always presents Photoshop in a contained window. On Mac OS, you can choose whether to work with an application frame, which contains the Photoshop application's windows and panels within a frame that is distinct from other applications you may have open; only the menu bar is outside the application frame. The application frame is enabled by default; to disable the application frame, choose Window > Application Frame.

On Mac OS, the application frame keeps the image, panels, and menu bar together.

3  Choose File > Open, and navigate to the Lessons/Lesson01 folder that you copied to your hard drive from the peachpit.com website. (If you haven't downloaded the files, see "Accessing the Classroom in a Book files" on page 3.)

4  Select the 01End.psd file, and click Open. Click OK if you see the Embedded Profile Mismatch dialog box.

The 01End.psd file opens in its own window, called the *image window*. The end files in this book show you what you are creating in each project. In this project, you'll finish the layout for a book cover.

**5** Choose File > Close, or click the close button on the title bar of the image window. (Do not close Photoshop.)

## Opening a file with Adobe Bridge

In this book, you'll work with different start files in each lesson. You may make copies of these files and save them under different names or locations, or you may work from the original start files and then download them from the peachpit.com website again if you want a fresh start.

In the previous exercise, you used the Open command to open a file. Now you'll open another file using Adobe Bridge, a visual file browser that helps take the guesswork out of finding the image file that you need.

**1** Choose File > Browse In Bridge. If you're prompted to enable the Photoshop extension in Bridge, click OK.

Adobe Bridge opens, displaying a collection of panels, menus, and buttons.

**2** Select the Folders tab in the upper left corner, and then browse to the Lessons folder you downloaded onto your hard disk, so that the Lessons folder appears in the Content panel.

> **Note:** If Bridge isn't installed, you'll be prompted to install it when you choose Browse In Bridge. For more information, see page 3.

**3** Select the Lessons folder, and choose File > Add To Favorites.

Adding files, folders, application icons, and other assets that you use often to the Favorites panel lets you access them quickly.

**4** Select the Favorites tab to open the panel, and click the Lessons folder to open it. Then, in the Content panel, double-click the Lesson01 folder.

Thumbnail previews of the folder contents appear in the Content panel.

**5** Double-click the 01Start.psd thumbnail in the Content panel to open the file, or select the thumbnail and choose File > Open.

The 01Start.psd image opens in Photoshop. You can leave Bridge open or close it; you won't need it again in this lesson.

## Using the tools

Photoshop provides an integrated set of tools for producing sophisticated graphics for print, web, and mobile viewing. We could easily fill the entire book with details on the wealth of Photoshop tools and tool configurations. While that would certainly be a useful reference, it's not the goal of this book. Instead, you'll start gaining experience by configuring and using a few tools on a sample project. Every lesson will introduce you to more tools and ways to use them. By the time you finish all the lessons in this book, you'll have a solid foundation for further explorations of the Photoshop toolset.

## Selecting and using a tool from the Tools panel

The Tools panel is the long, narrow panel on the far left side of the work area. It contains selection tools, painting and editing tools, foreground- and background-color selection boxes, and viewing tools.

● **Note:** For a complete list of the tools in the Tools panel, see the Appendix, "Tools panel overview."

You'll start by using the Zoom tool, which also appears in many other Adobe applications, including Illustrator, InDesign, and Acrobat.

1   Click the double arrows just above the Tools panel to toggle to a double-column view. Click the double arrows again to return to a single-column Tools panel and use your screen space more efficiently.

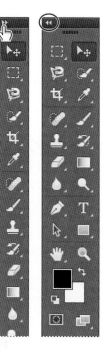

2   Examine the status bar at the bottom of the work area (Windows) or image window (Mac OS), and notice the percentage that appears on the far left. This represents the current enlargement view of the image, or zoom level.

3   Move the pointer over the Tools panel, and hover it over the magnifying-glass icon until a tool tip appears. The tool tip displays the tool's name (Zoom tool) and keyboard shortcut (Z).

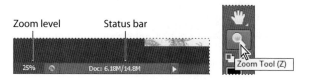

Zoom level  Status bar

4   Click the Zoom tool (🔍) in the Tools panel, or press Z to select it.

5   Move the pointer over the image window. The pointer now looks like a tiny magnifying glass with a plus sign in the center of the glass (🔍).

6   Click anywhere in the image window.

The image enlarges to a preset percentage level, which replaces the previous value in the status bar. The location you clicked when you used the Zoom tool is centered in the enlarged view. If you click again, the zoom advances to the next preset level, up to a maximum of 3200%.

7   Hold down the Alt key (Windows) or Option key (Mac OS) so that the Zoom tool pointer appears with a minus sign in the center of the magnifying glass (🔍), and then click anywhere in the image. Then release the Alt or Option key.

Now the view zooms out to a lower preset magnification, so that you can see more of the image, but in less detail.

● **Note:** You can use other methods to zoom in and out. For example, when the Zoom tool is selected, you can select the Zoom In or Zoom Out mode on the options bar. You can choose View > Zoom In or View > Zoom Out. Or, you can type a new percentage in the status bar and press Enter or Return.

**8** If Scrubby Zoom is selected in the options bar, click anywhere on the image and drag the Zoom tool to the right. The image enlarges. Drag the Zoom tool to the left to zoom out.

When Scrubby Zoom is selected, you can drag the Zoom tool across the image to zoom in and out. Scrubby Zoom is available only if Use Graphics Processor is enabled in the Performance panel of the Photoshop Preferences dialog box. (Choose Edit > Preferences > Performance or Photoshop > Preferences > Performance to open the dialog box.)

**9** Deselect Scrubby Zoom in the options bar if it's selected. Then, using the Zoom tool, drag a rectangle to enclose the area of the image that includes the oval painting and the red crosshairs.

The image enlarges so that the area you enclosed in your rectangle now fills the entire image window.

You have now used four methods with the Zoom tool to change the magnification in the image window: clicking, holding down a keyboard modifier while clicking, dragging to zoom in and out, and dragging to define a magnification area. Many of the other tools in the Tools panel can be used with keyboard combinations and options, as well. You'll have opportunities to use these techniques in various lessons in this book.

## Selecting and using a hidden tool

Photoshop has many tools you can use to edit image files, but you will probably work with only a few of them at a time. The Tools panel arranges some of the tools in groups, with only one tool shown for each group. The other tools in the group are hidden behind that tool.

A small triangle in the lower right corner of a button is your clue that other tools are available but hidden under that tool.

1  Position the pointer over the second tool from the top in the Tools panel until the tool tip appears. The tool tip identifies the Rectangular Marquee tool (⬚), with the keyboard shortcut M. Select that tool.

2  Select the Elliptical Marquee tool (◯), which is hidden behind the Rectangular Marquee tool, using one of the following methods:

- Press and hold the mouse button over the Rectangular Marquee tool to open the pop-up list of hidden tools, and select the Elliptical Marquee tool.

- Alt-click (Windows) or Option-click (Mac OS) the tool button in the Tools panel to cycle through the hidden marquee tools until the Elliptical Marquee tool is selected.

- Press Shift+M, which switches between the Rectangular and Elliptical Marquee tools.

3  Move the pointer over the image window, to the red cross positioned above and to the left of the portrait.

When the Elliptical Marquee tool is selected, the pointer becomes cross-hairs (+).

4  Click the upper left red cross, and drag the pointer down and to the right to the lower red cross to draw an ellipse around the frame, and then release the mouse button.

An animated dashed line indicates that the area inside it is *selected*. When you select an area, it becomes the only editable area of the image. The area outside the selection is protected.

You'll learn more about making different kinds of selections and adjusting the selection contents in Lesson 3, "Working with Selections."

## Applying a change to a selected area

In most cases, you'd change the area within the selection. But in this project, you want to change the color of the wallpaper without affecting the painting. To do that, you'll need to invert the selection, so that everything *but* the painting is selected in the image.

Selected    Unselected
(editable)  (protected)
area         area

▶ **Tip:** The keyboard shortcut for this command, Ctrl+Shift+I (Windows) or Command+Shift+I (Mac OS), appears by the command name in the Select menu. In the future, you can just press that keyboard combination to invert a selection.

1 Choose Select > Inverse.

Although the animated selection border around the oval frame looks the same, notice that a similar border appears all around the edges of the image. Now everything in the image is selected except the area within the oval. The unselected area (the painting) cannot be changed while the selection is active.

2 In the Adjustments panel, click the Hue/Saturation icon to add a Hue/Saturation adjustment layer. The Hue/Saturation options appear in the Properties panel.

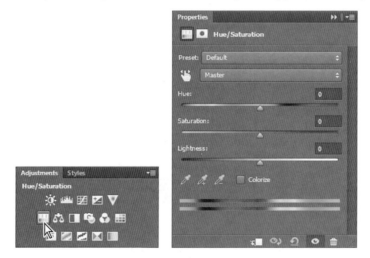

3 In the Properties panel, select Colorize. Then change the Hue value to **200** to adjust the color in the selected area.

The wallpaper color changes to shades of blue.

**4**  In the Layers panel, click the eye icon next to Selection Guide Layer to hide the red guides. (If the Layers panel isn't open, click its tab or choose Window > Layers.)

Layering is one of the fundamental and most powerful features in Photoshop. Photoshop includes many kinds of layers, some of which contain images, text, or solid colors, and others that simply interact with layers below them. You'll learn more about layers in Lesson 4, "Layer Basics," and Lesson 9, "Advanced Compositing."

**5**  In the Layers panel, examine the Hue/Saturation adjustment layer.

Adjustment layers let you make changes to your image, such as adjusting the color of the wallpaper, without affecting the actual pixels. Because you've used an adjustment layer, you can always return to the original image by hiding or deleting the adjustment layer—and you can edit the adjustment layer at any time. You'll use adjustment layers in several lessons in this book.

**6** Choose File > Save As, name the file **01Working.psd**, and click OK or Save.

**7** Click OK in the Photoshop Format Options dialog box.

You've just completed your first task in Photoshop. The wallpaper now matches the blue bar at the top of the book cover. You'll make another adjustment to the color later in the lesson, but first you'll add the author's name.

# Zooming and scrolling with the Navigator panel

The Navigator panel is another speedy way to make large changes in the zoom level, especially when the exact percentage of magnification is unimportant. It's also a great way to scroll around in an image, because the thumbnail shows you exactly what part of the image appears in the image window. To open the Navigator panel, choose Window > Navigator.

The slider under the image thumbnail in the Navigator panel enlarges the image when you drag to the right (toward the large mountain icon) and reduces it when you drag to the left.

The red rectangular outline represents the area of the image that appears in the image window. When you zoom in far enough that the image window shows only part of the image, you can drag the red outline around the thumbnail area to see other areas of the image. This is also an excellent way to verify which part of an image you're working on when you work at very high zoom levels.

# Setting tool properties

When you selected the Zoom tool in the previous project, you saw that the options bar provided ways for you to change the view of the current image window. Now you'll learn more about setting tool properties using context menus, the options bar, panels, and panel menus. You'll use all of these methods as you work with tools to create a colored bar with the author's name.

## Using context menus

*Context menus* are short menus that contain commands and options appropriate to specific elements in the work area. They are sometimes referred to as "right-click" or "shortcut" menus. Usually, the commands on a context menu are also available in some other area of the user interface, but using the context menu can save time.

1  Select the Header Bar Layer in the Layers panel so that it's the active layer.

2  Select the Eyedropper tool (✐) in the Tools panel, and then click the oval frame to sample a brown color.

You'll use this color to create a colored bar for the author's name.

3  Select the Zoom tool (🔍), and zoom in on the area below the blue title bar.

4   Select the Rectangular Marquee tool (⬚), hidden beneath the Elliptical Marquee tool (◯), and then select a rectangular area overlapping the blue title bar and the wallpaper beneath it.

5   Select the Brush tool (✎) in the Tools panel.

6   In the image window, right-click (Windows) or Control-click (Mac OS) anywhere in the image to open the Brush tool context menu.

Context menus vary with their context, of course, so what appears can be a menu of commands or a panel-like set of options, which is what happens in this case.

7   Select the first brush (Soft Round), and change the size to **65** pixels.

8   Paint the selected area until it's fully painted. Don't worry about staying within the selection; you can't affect anything outside the selection as you paint.

9   When the bar is colored in, choose Select > Deselect so that nothing is selected.

## Setting tool properties in the options bar

Next you'll use the options bar to select the text properties and then to type the author's name.

1   In the Tools panel, select the Horizontal Type tool (T).

The buttons and menus in the options bar now relate to the Type tool.

**2** In the options bar, select a font you like from the first pop-up menu. (We used Myriad Pro, but you can use another font if you prefer.)

**3** Specify **15 pt** for the font size.

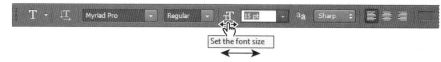

▶ **Tip:** You can place the pointer over the labels of most numeric settings in the tool options bar, in panels, and in dialog boxes in Photoshop to display a "scrubby slider." Dragging the pointing-finger slider to the right increases the value; dragging to the left decreases the value. Alt-dragging (Windows) or Option-dragging (Mac OS) changes the values in smaller increments; Shift-dragging changes them in larger increments.

You can specify 15 points by typing directly in the font-size text box and pressing Enter or Return, or by scrubbing the font-size menu label. You can also choose a standard font size from the font-size pop-up menu.

**4** Click once anywhere on the left side of the colored bar, and type **Elaine Gruenke.**

The text is the same color as the bar you typed it on. You'll fix that next.

## Using panels and panel menus

The text color is the same as the Foreground Color swatch in the Tools panel, which is the brown color you used to paint the bar. You'll select the text and choose another color from the Swatches panel.

**1** Make sure the Horizontal Type tool (T) is selected in the Tools panel.

**2** Drag the Horizontal Type tool across the text to select the full name.

**3** Click the Swatches tab to bring that panel forward, if it's not already visible.

**4** Select any light-colored swatch.

● **Note:** When you move the pointer over the swatches, it temporarily changes into an eyedropper. Set the tip of the eyedropper on the swatch you want, and click to select it.

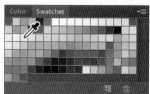

The color you select appears in three places: as the Foreground Color in the Tools panel, in the text color swatch in the options bar, and in the text you selected in the image window.

5 Select another tool in the Tools panel, such as the Move tool ($\vcenter{\hbox{$\blacktriangleright$}}\!\!+$), to deselect the Horizontal Type tool, so you can see the text color.

That's how easy it is to select a color, although there are other methods in Photoshop. However, you'll use a specific color for this project, and it's easier to find it if you change the Swatches panel display.

6 Click the menu button (-≣) on the Swatches panel to open the panel menu, and choose Small List.

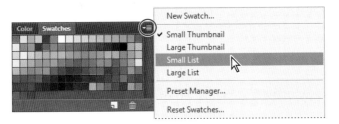

7 Select the Type tool and reselect the text, as you did in steps 1 and 2.

8 In the Swatches panel, scroll about halfway down the list to find the Pure Blue swatch, and then select it.

Now the text appears in the blue color.

9 Select the Move tool and drag the name so it's centered in the brown bar. Then click the Default Foreground And Background Colors button in the Tools panel to make Black the foreground color.

● **Note:** Don't select the Move tool using the V keyboard shortcut, because you're in text-entry mode. Typing V will add the letter to your text in the image window.

Resetting the default colors does not change the color of the text in the image, because that text is no longer selected.

## Undoing actions in Photoshop

In a perfect world, you'd never make a mistake. You'd never click the wrong object. You'd always correctly anticipate how specific actions would bring your design ideas to life exactly as you imagined them. You'd never have to backtrack.

For the real world, Photoshop gives you the power to step back and undo actions so that you can try other options. You can experiment freely, knowing that you can reverse the process.

## Undoing a single action

**Note:** The Undo command isn't available if you've already saved your changes. However, you can still use the Step Backward command and the History panel, as long as you haven't closed the project.

Even beginning computer users quickly come to appreciate the familiar Undo command. You'll use it to move back one step, and then step further backward.

1 Choose Edit > Undo Move, or press Ctrl+Z (Windows) or Command+Z (Mac OS) to undo your last action.

The name moves back to its original position.

2 Choose Edit > Redo Move, or press Ctrl+Z (Windows) or Command+Z (Mac OS) to center the name again.

Undo reverses the last step.   Redo restores the undone step.

The Undo command in Photoshop reverses only one step. This is a practicality, because Photoshop files can be very large, and maintaining multiple Undo steps can tie up a lot of memory, which tends to degrade performance. If you press Ctrl+Z or Command+Z again, Photoshop restores the step you removed initially.

3 Choose Edit > Step Backward, or press Ctrl+Alt+Z (Windows) or Command+Option+Z (Mac OS) to move back one step. The name moves back to its original position.

4 Repeat step 3. The color changes to the first swatch you selected.

## Undoing multiple actions

While you could use the Step Backward command to undo steps one at a time, it's faster and easier to reverse multiple actions using the History panel.

1 Choose Window > History to open the History panel. Then drag the bottom of the History panel to resize it so that you can see more steps.

The History panel records the recent actions you've performed on the image. The current state is selected. Because you've already moved backwards several steps, there are dimmed steps at the end of the list.

**2** Select Move, the last step in the list in the History panel.

The steps you've undone are restored. The name is in its final color, centered on the brown bar. This book cover will look better with the author's name in white at the bottom, though, so you'll remove the brown bar and the current text.

**3** In the History panel, select Modify Hue/Saturation Layer.

► **Tip:** By default, the History panel retains only the last 20 actions. You can change the number of levels in the History panel by choosing Edit > Preferences > Performance (Windows) or Photoshop > Preferences > Performance (Mac OS), and entering a different value for History States.

The brown bar and the author's name disappear from the image window. All the steps beneath the one you selected are dimmed in the History panel. You can click any step to return to that point in the process, but as soon as you perform a new task, Photoshop deletes all dimmed steps.

**4** Double-click the Hue/Saturation adjustment thumbnail (the first thumbnail) in the Hue/Saturation layer in the Layers panel to open the Hue/Saturation options in the Properties panel.

**5** In the Properties panel, enter the following values to change the wallpaper to shades of green:

- Hue: **53**

- Saturation: **44**

- Lightness: **-56**

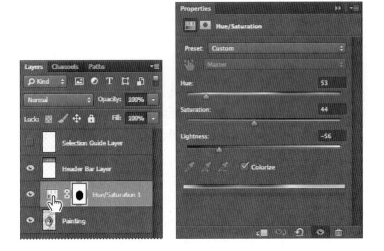

**6** Open the History panel again by choosing Window > History, or by clicking the History panel icon ( ).

Notice that the History panel no longer displays the dimmed actions that were listed after the selected history state and has added a new one.

**7** Select Header Bar Layer in the Layers panel.

This is the layer that contains everything except the painting. You'll add text to it.

**8** Select the Horizontal Type tool (T) from the Tools panel.

**9** Choose Window > Character to open the Character panel. Then select a font (we chose Myriad Pro), and choose **15** pt for the font size. Click the color swatch, select white in the Color Picker, and click OK. Finally, select All Caps (**TT**).

Many type settings are available in the options bar, but there are additional settings in the Character panel.

**10** Click with the type tool toward the bottom of the book cover, and type **Elaine Gruenke**.

**11** Select the Move tool, and position the text so it is centered beneath the painting.

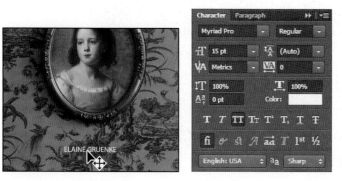

**12** Choose File > Save to save your work.

Congratulations! You've completed your first Photoshop project.

# More about panels and panel locations

Photoshop panels are powerful and varied. Rarely would you need to see all panels simultaneously. That's why they're in panel groups, and why the default configurations leave some panels unopened.

The complete list of panels appears in the Window menu. Check marks appear next to the names of the panels that are open and active in their panel groups. You can open a closed panel or close an open one by selecting the panel name in the Window menu.

You can hide all panels at once—including the options bar and Tools panel— by pressing the Tab key. To reopen them, press Tab again.

● **Note:** When panels are hidden, a thin, semitransparent strip is visible at the edge of the document. Hovering the pointer over the strip displays its contents.

You already used panels in the panel dock when you used the Layers and Swatches panels. You can drag panels to or from the panel dock. This is convenient for bulky panels or ones that you use only occasionally but want to keep handy.

You can arrange panels in other ways, as well:

- To move an entire panel group, drag the title bar to another location in the work area.

- To move a panel to another group, drag the panel tab into that panel group so that a blue highlight appears inside the group, and then release the mouse button.

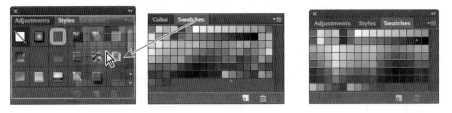

- To dock a panel or panel group, drag the title bar or panel tab onto the top of the dock.

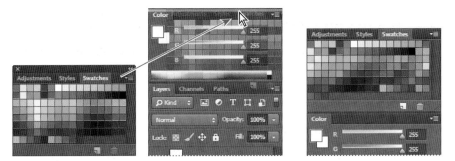

- To undock a panel or panel group so that it becomes a floating panel or panel group, drag its title bar or panel tab away from the dock.

## Expanding and collapsing panels

You can resize panels to use screen space more efficiently and to see fewer or more panel options, either by dragging or clicking to toggle between preset sizes:

- To collapse open panels to icons, click the double arrow in the title bar of the dock or panel group. To expand a panel, click its icon or the double arrow.

- To change the height of a panel, drag its lower right corner.

- To change the width of the dock, position the pointer on the left edge of the dock until it becomes a double-headed arrow, and then drag to the left to widen the dock, or to the right to narrow it.

- To resize a floating panel, move the pointer over the right, left, or bottom edge of the panel until it becomes a double-headed arrow, and then drag the edge in or out. You can also pull the lower right corner in or out.

- To collapse a panel group so that only the dock header bar and tabs are visible, double-click a panel tab or panel title bar. Double-click again to restore it to the expanded view. You can open the panel menu even when the panel is collapsed.

● **Note:** You can collapse, but not resize, the Color, Character, and Paragraph panels.

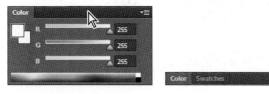

Notice that the tabs for the panels in the panel group and the button for the panel menu remain visible after you collapse a panel.

## Special notes about the Tools panel and options bar

The Tools panel and the options bar share some characteristics with other panels:

- You can drag the Tools panel by its title bar to a different location in the work area. You can move the options bar to another location by dragging the grab bar at the far left end of the panel.

- You can hide the Tools panel and options bar.

However, some panel features are not available or don't apply to the Tools panel or options bar:

- You cannot group the Tools panel or options bar with other panels.

- You cannot resize the Tools panel or options bar.

- You cannot stack the Tools panel or options bar in the panel dock.

- The Tools panel and options bar do not have panel menus.

# Customizing the workspace

**Note:** If you closed 01Working.psd at the end of the previous exercise, open it—or open any other image file—to complete the following exercise.

It's great that Photoshop offers so many ways to control the display and location of the options bar and its many panels, but it can be time-consuming to drag panels around the screen so that you can see some panels for certain projects and other panels for other projects. That's why Photoshop lets you customize your workspace, controlling which panels, tools, and menus are available at any time. In fact, it comes with a few preset workspaces suitable for different types of workflows—typography, painting, and so on. You'll experiment with them.

1   Choose Window > Workspace > Painting. If prompted, click Yes to apply the workspace.

If you've been experimenting with opening, closing, and moving panels, you'll notice that Photoshop closes some panels, opens others, and stacks them neatly in the dock along the right edge of the workspace.

2   Choose Window > Workspace > Photography. If prompted, click Yes to apply the workspace. Different panels appear in the dock.

**3** Click the Workspace Switcher in the options bar, and choose Essentials.

Photoshop returns to the default workspace, which is arranged as you left it. (To return the Essentials workspace to its original configuration, choose Reset Essentials from the Workspace Switcher menu.)

You can choose workspaces from the Window menu or from the pop-up menu in the options bar.

● **Note:** Selecting the Essentials workspace changes the panel configuration, but doesn't restore the menus to their defaults. You can do that now, or leave them altered. You'll reset defaults as you begin work on most lessons that follow.

For times when presets don't suit your purposes, you can customize the workspace to your specific needs. Say, for example, that you do lots of web design, but no digital video work. You can specify which menu items to display in the workspace.

**4** Click the View menu, and choose Pixel Aspect Ratio to see the submenu.

This submenu includes several DV formats that many print and web designers don't need to use.

**5** Choose Window > Workspace > Keyboard Shortcuts & Menus.

The Keyboard Shortcuts And Menus dialog box lets you control which application and panel menu commands are available, as well as create custom keyboard shortcuts for menus, panels, and tools. You can hide commands that you use infrequently, or highlight commonly used commands to make them easier to see.

**6** Click the Menus tab in the Keyboard Shortcuts And Menus dialog box, and then choose Application Menus from the Menu For pop-up menu.

**7** Scroll down to the View menu, and click the triangle to reveal its commands.

Photoshop displays the View menu commands and subcommands.

**8** Scroll down to Pixel Aspect Ratio, and click the eye icon to turn off visibility for all of the DV and video formats—there are seven of them, beginning with D1/DV NTSC (0.91) and ending with DVCPro HD 1080 (1.5).

Photoshop removes them from the menu for this workspace.

**9** Collapse the View menu, and then expand the Image menu commands.

**10** Scroll down to the Image > Mode > RGB Color command, and click None in the Color column. Choose Red from the pop-up menu to highlight this command in red.

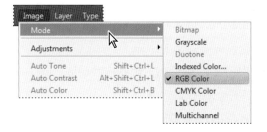

**11** Click OK to close the Keyboard Shortcuts And Menus dialog box.

**12** Choose Image > Mode. RGB Color is now highlighted in red.

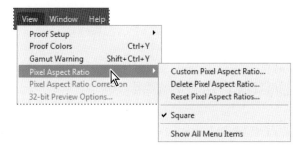

**13** Choose View > Pixel Aspect Ratio. The DV and video formats are no longer included in this submenu.

**14** To save a workspace, choose Window > Workspace > New Workspace. In the New Workspace dialog box, give your workspace a name, select the Keyboard Shortcuts and Menus options, and then click Save.

The custom workspace you save is listed in the Window > Workspace submenu and in the Workspace Switcher on the options bar.

For now, return to the default workspace configuration.

**15** Choose Essentials from the Workspace Switcher on the options bar. Then choose Reset Essentials from the Workspace Switcher to revert to the original workspace definition. Don't save the changes in the current workspace.

**16** Close the file, but leave Photoshop open.

Congratulations again. You've finished Lesson 1!

Now that you're acquainted with the basics of the Photoshop work area, you can begin learning how to create and edit images. Once you know the basics, you can complete the *Adobe Photoshop CC Classroom in a Book* lessons either in sequential order or according to the subjects you find most interesting.

## Finding resources for using Photoshop

For complete and up-to-date information about using Photoshop panels, tools, and other application features, visit the Adobe website. To search for information in Photoshop Help and support documents, as well as other websites relevant to Photoshop users, choose Help > Photoshop Online Help. You can narrow your search results to view only Adobe Help and support documents.

For additional resources, such as tips and techniques and the latest product information, check out the Adobe Community Help page at community.adobe.com/help/main.

# Changing interface settings

By default, the panels, dialog boxes, and background in Photoshop CC are dark. You can lighten the interface or make other changes in the Photoshop Preferences dialog box.

To make changes:

1   Choose Edit > Preferences > Interface (Windows) or Photoshop > Preferences > Interface (Mac OS).

2   Select a different color theme, or make other changes.

When you select a different theme, you can see the changes immediately. You can also select specific colors for different screen modes and change other interface settings in this dialog box.

3   When you're satisfied with the changes, click OK.

## Review questions

1 Describe two types of images you can open in Photoshop.

2 How do you open image files using Adobe Bridge?

3 How do you select tools in Photoshop?

4 Describe two ways to change your view of an image.

5 What are two ways to get more information about Photoshop?

# Review answers

1 You can scan a photograph, transparency, negative, or graphic into the program; capture a digital video image; or import artwork created in a drawing program. You can also import digital photos.

2 Choose File > Browse In Bridge in Photoshop to jump to Bridge. Then, locate the image file you want to open, and double-click its thumbnail to open it in Photoshop.

3 Click a tool in the Tools panel, or press the tool's keyboard shortcut. A selected tool remains active until you select a different tool. To select a hidden tool, either use a keyboard shortcut to toggle through the tools, or hold down the mouse button on the tool in the Tools panel to open a pop-up menu of the hidden tools.

4 Choose commands from the View menu to zoom in on or out from an image, or to fit it onscreen, or use the zoom tools and click or drag over an image to enlarge or reduce the view. You can also use keyboard shortcuts or the Navigator panel to control the display of an image.

5 The Photoshop Help system includes full information about Photoshop features plus keyboard shortcuts, task-based topics, and illustrations. Photoshop also includes a link to the Adobe Systems Photoshop web page for additional information on services, products, and tips pertaining to Photoshop.

# 2 BASIC PHOTO CORRECTIONS

## Lesson overview

In this lesson, you'll learn how to do the following:

- Understand image resolution and size.

- Straighten and crop an image.

- Adjust the tonal range of an image.

- Use the Spot Healing Brush tool to repair part of an image.

- Use content-aware fill to replace an area in an image.

- Use the Clone Stamp tool to touch up areas.

- Use the content-aware Patch tool to remove or replace objects.

- Remove digital artifacts from an image.

- Apply the Smart Sharpen filter to finish retouching photos.

 This lesson will take about an hour to complete. Download the Lesson02 project files from the Lesson & Update Files tab on your Account page at www.peachpit.com, if you haven't already done so. As you work on this lesson, you'll preserve the start files. If you need to restore the start files, download them from your Account page.

PROJECT: VINTAGE PHOTOGRAPH RESTORATION

Adobe Photoshop includes a variety of tools and commands for improving the quality of a photographic image. This lesson steps you through the process of acquiring, resizing, and retouching a vintage photograph.

# Strategy for retouching

**Note:** In this lesson, you retouch an image using only Adobe Photoshop. For other images, it may be more efficient to work in Adobe Camera Raw, which is installed with Photoshop. Or you may wish to start in Camera Raw, and then move on to Photoshop for more advanced retouching. You'll learn about the tools Camera Raw has to offer in Lesson 5, "Correcting and Enhancing Digital Photographs."

How much retouching you do depends on the image you're working on and your goals for it. For many images, you may need only to change the resolution, lighten the image, or repair a minor blemish. For others, you may need to perform several tasks and employ more advanced filters.

## Organizing an efficient sequence of tasks

Most retouching procedures follow these general steps, though not every task may be necessary for all projects:

- Duplicating the original image or scan; working in a copy of the image file makes it easy to recover the original later if necessary

- Ensuring that the resolution is appropriate for the way you'll use the image

- Cropping the image to final size and orientation

- Removing any color casts

- Adjusting the overall contrast or tonal range of the image

- Repairing flaws in scans of damaged photographs (such as rips, dust, or stains)

- Adjusting the color and tone in specific parts of the image to bring out highlights, midtones, shadows, and desaturated colors

- Sharpening the overall focus of the image

The order of the tasks may vary depending on the project, though you should always start by duplicating the image and adjusting its resolution. Likewise, sharpening should usually be your final step. For the other tasks, consider your project and plan accordingly, so that the results of one process do not cause unintended changes to other aspects of the image, making it necessary for you to redo some of your work.

## Adjusting your process for different intended uses

The retouching techniques you apply to an image depend in part on how you'll use the image. Whether an image is intended for black-and-white publication on newsprint or for full-color online distribution affects everything from the resolution of the initial scan to the type of tonal range and color correction that the image requires. Photoshop supports the CMYK color mode for preparing an image to be printed using process colors, as well as RGB and other color modes for web and mobile authoring.

# Resolution and image size

The first step in retouching a photograph in Photoshop is to make sure that the image has an appropriate resolution. The term *resolution* refers to the number of small squares, known as *pixels,* that describe an image and establish its detail. Resolution is determined by *pixel dimensions*, or the number of pixels along the width and height of an image.

**Note:** To determine the image resolution for a photograph you plan to print, follow the computer-graphics rule of thumb for color or grayscale images intended for print on large commercial printers: Scan at a resolution 1.5 to 2 times the screen frequency used by the printer. If the image will be printed using a screen frequency of 133 lpi, scan the image at 200 ppi (133x1.5).

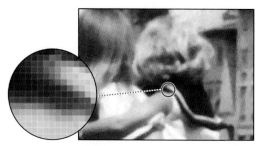

Pixels in a photographic image

In computer graphics, there are different types of resolution:

The number of pixels per unit of length in an image is called the *image resolution*, usually measured in pixels per inch (ppi). An image with a high resolution has more pixels (and therefore a larger file size) than an image of the same dimensions with a low resolution. Images in Photoshop can vary from high resolution (300 ppi or higher) to low resolution (72 ppi or 96 ppi).

The number of pixels per unit of length on a monitor is the *monitor resolution*, also usually measured in pixels per inch (ppi). Image pixels are translated directly into monitor pixels. In Photoshop, if the image resolution is higher than the monitor resolution, the image appears larger onscreen than its specified print dimensions. For example, when you display a 1x1-inch, 144-ppi image on a 72-ppi monitor, the image fills a 2x2-inch area of the screen.

**Note:** It's important to understand what "100% view" means when you work onscreen. At 100%, one image pixel = one monitor pixel. Unless the resolution of your image is exactly the same as the resolution of the monitor, the image size (in inches, for example) onscreen may be larger or smaller than the image size will be when printed.

7x7 inches at 72 ppi; file size 744.2KB
100% onscreen view

7x7 inches at 200 ppi; file size 5.61MB
100% onscreen view

The number of ink dots per inch (dpi) produced by a platesetter or laser printer is the *printer,* or *output, resolution.* Higher resolution images output to higher resolution printers generally produce the best quality. The appropriate resolution for a printed image is determined both by the printer resolution and by the *screen frequency,* or lines per inch (lpi), of the halftone screens used to reproduce images.

Keep in mind that the higher the image resolution, the larger the file size, and the longer the file will take to print or to download from the web.

For more information on resolution and image size, see Photoshop Help.

## Getting started

In this lesson, you'll retouch a scan of a damaged and discolored vintage photograph so it can be shared or printed. The final image size will be 7x7 inches.

You'll start the lesson by comparing the original scan to the finished image.

● **Note:** If Bridge isn't installed, you'll need to install it from Adobe Creative Cloud. For more information, see page 3.

1   Start Adobe Bridge CC by choosing Start > All Programs > Adobe Bridge CC (Windows) or double-clicking Adobe Bridge CC in the Applications folder (Mac OS).

2   In the Favorites panel in the upper left corner of Bridge, click the Lessons folder. Then, in the Content panel, double-click the Lesson02 folder to see its contents.

3   Compare the 02Start.tif and 02End.psd files. To enlarge the thumbnails in the Content panel, drag the Thumbnail slider at the bottom of the Bridge window to the right.

In the 02Start.tif file, notice that the image is crooked, the colors are relatively dull, and the image has a green color cast and a distracting crease. You'll fix all of these problems in this lesson, and a few others. You'll start by cropping and straightening the image.

**4**  Double-click the 02Start.tif thumbnail to open the file in Photoshop.

**5**  In Photoshop, choose File > Save As. Choose Photoshop from the Format menu, and name the file **Working2.psd**. Then click Save.

# Straightening and cropping the image in Photoshop

You'll use the Crop tool to straighten, trim, and scale the photograph. You can use either the Crop tool or the Crop command to crop an image. By default, cropping deletes the cropped pixels.

**1**  In the Tools panel, select the Crop tool (⬚).

**2**  In the options bar, choose W x H x Resolution from the Preset Aspect Ratio menu. (Ratio is its default value.)

**3**  In the options bar, type **7 in** for the width, **7 in** for the height, and **200** px/in for the resolution.

**Tip:** Deselect the Delete Cropped Pixels option if you want to crop nondestructively, so that you can revise the crop later.

A crop grid appears. A *cropping shield* covers the area outside the cropping selection. First, you'll straighten the image.

**4** Click Straighten in the options bar. The pointer changes to the Straighten tool.

**5** Click at the top corner of the photo, and drag a straight line across the top edge of the photo.

Photoshop straightens the image, so that the line you drew is parallel with the top of the image area. You drew a line across the top of the photo, but any line that defines either the vertical or horizontal axis of the image will work.

Now, you'll trim the white border and scale the image.

**6** Drag the corners of the crop grid in to the corners of the photo itself to crop out the white border. If you need to adjust the position of the photo, click and drag it within the crop grid.

▶ **Tip:** You can choose Image > Trim to discard a border area around the edge of the image, based on transparency or edge color.

**7** Press Enter or Return.

The image is now cropped, and the cropped image fills the image window, straightened, sized, and positioned according to your specifications.

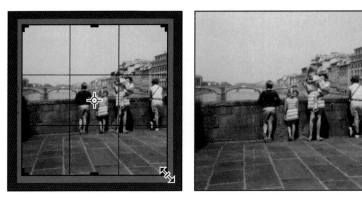

▶ **Tip:** To quickly straighten a photo and crop out the scanned background, choose File > Automate > Crop And Straighten Photos.

**8** To see the image dimensions, choose Document Dimensions from the pop-up menu at the bottom of the application window.

**9** Choose File > Save to save your work. Click OK if you see the Photoshop Format Options dialog box.

## Adjusting the color and tone

You'll use Curves and Levels adjustment layers to remove the color cast and adjust the color and tone in the image.

**1** Click Curves in the Adjustments panel to add a Curves adjustment layer.

**2** Select the White Point tool on the left side of the Properties panel.

Specifying a white point changes all the colors in the image. To set an accurate white point, select a white area in the image.

**3** Click a white stripe on the girl's dress.

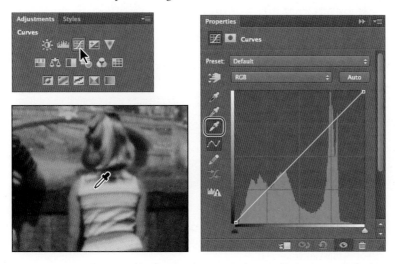

The color tone of the image changes dramatically. You can click different white areas, such as the child's sailor dress, a stripe on the woman's dress, or the girl's sock, to see how each selection changes the color.

In some images, adjusting the white point is enough to remove a color cast and correct the tone of the image. Here, selecting a white point is a good start. You'll use a Levels adjustment layer to fine-tune the tone.

**4** Click Levels in the Adjustments panel to add a Levels adjustment layer.

The Levels histogram in the Properties panel displays the range of dark and light values in the image. You'll learn more about working with levels in Lesson 5. Right now, you just need to know that the left triangle represents the black point, the right triangle represents the white point, and the middle triangle represents the midtones.

**5** Drag the left triangle (blacks) under the histogram to the right, where the blacks are more pronounced. Our value was 15.

**6** Drag the middle triangle a little to the right to adjust the midtones. Our value was .90.

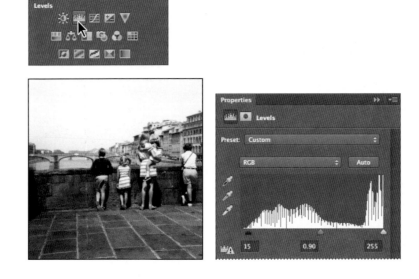

Now that you've adjusted the color, you'll flatten the image so it's easier to work with while you touch it up.

**7** Choose Layer > Flatten Image.

The adjustment layers merge with the Background layer.

## Using the Spot Healing Brush tool

● **Note:** The Healing Brush tool works similarly to the Spot Healing Brush tool, except that it requires you to sample source pixels before retouching an area.

The next task is to remove the crease in the photo. You'll use the Spot Healing Brush to erase the crease. While you're at it, you'll use it to address a few other issues.

The Spot Healing Brush tool quickly removes blemishes and other imperfections. It samples pixels around the retouched area and matches the texture, lighting, transparency, and shading of the sampled pixels to the pixels being healed.

The Spot Healing Brush is excellent for retouching blemishes in portraits, but also works nicely wherever there's a uniform appearance near the areas you want to retouch.

1 Zoom in to see the crease clearly.

2 In the Tools panel, select the Spot Healing Brush tool ( ).

3 In the options bar, open the Brush pop-up panel, and specify a **100%** hard brush that is about **25** px in diameter. Make sure Content-Aware is selected in the options bar.

4 In the image window, drag the Spot Healing Brush down from the top of the crease. You can probably repair the entire crease with four to six neat downward strokes. As you drag, the stroke at first appears black, but when you release the mouse, the painted area is "healed."

5 Zoom in to see the white hair in the upper right area of the image. Then select the Spot Healing Brush again, and paint over the hair.

6 Zoom out, if necessary, to see the full sky. Then click the Spot Healing Brush wherever there are dark areas you want to heal.

7 Save your work so far.

*As owner of Gawain Weaver Art Conservation, Gawain Weaver has conserved and restored original works by artists ranging from Eadward Muybridge to Man Ray, and from Ansel Adams to Cindy Sherman. He teaches workshops internationally as well as online on the care and identification of photographs.*

*Find out more at gawainweaver.com.*

# Real-world photo restoration

The tools in Adobe Photoshop CC make restoration of old or damaged photographs seem like magic, giving virtually anyone the power to scan, retouch, print, and frame their photo collections.

However, when dealing with works by famous artists, museums, galleries, and collectors need to preserve the original object to the greatest degree possible despite deterioration or accidental damage. Professional art conservators are called upon to clean dust and soiling from print surfaces, remove discoloration and staining, repair tears, stabilize prints to prevent future damage, and even paint in missing areas of a work.

*Carleton E. Watkins, Nevada Fall, 700 FT, Yosemite Valley, CA, mammoth albumen print, 155/8"x20¾".*
*This print was removed from its mount to remove the stains and then remounted.*

*"Photograph conservation is both a science and an art," says Weaver. "We must apply what we know about the chemistry of the photograph, its mount, and any varnishes or other coatings in order to safely clean, preserve, and enhance the image. Since we cannot quickly 'undo' a step in a conservation treatment, we must always proceed with great caution and a healthy respect for the fragility of the photographic object whether it's a 160-year-old salt print of Notre Dame or gelatin silver print of Half Dome from the 1970s."*

Many of the manual tools of an art conservator have analogous digital versions in Photoshop:

 An art conservator might wash a photograph to remove the discolored components of the paper, or even use a mild bleaching process known as light-bleaching to oxidize and remove the colored components of a stain or overall discoloration. In Photoshop, you can use a Curves adjustment layer to remove the color cast from an image.

 A conservator working on a fine-art photograph might use special paints and fine brushes to manually "in-paint" damaged areas of a photograph. Likewise, you can use the Spot Healing Brush in Photoshop to spot out specks of dust or dirt on a scanned image.

A conservator might use Japanese papers and wheat-starch paste to carefully repair and rebuild torn paper before finalizing the repair with some skillful in-painting. In Photoshop, you can remove a crease or repair a tear in a scanned image with a few clicks of the Clone tool.

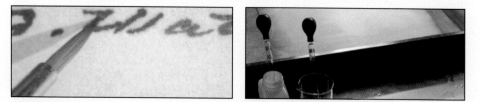

*A fixative was applied to the artist's signature with a small brush to protect it when the mount was washed.*

*"Although our work has always been first and foremost about the preservation and restoration of the original photographic object, there are instances, especially with family photographs, where the use of Photoshop is more appropriate," says Weaver. "More dramatic results can be achieved in far less time. After digitization the original print can be safely stored away, while the digital version can be copied or printed for many family members. Often, we first clean or unfold family photographs to safely reveal as much of the original image as possible, and then we repair the remaining discoloration, stains, and tears on the computer after digitization."*

AFTER

# Using content-aware fill

▶ **Tip:** Many of the techniques in this lesson will work for any blemish. You can experiment with techniques to see which one gives you the best results for the issue you're addressing.

You selected Content-Aware in the options bar when you used the Spot Healing Brush. When Content-Aware is selected, Photoshop matches the replacement pixels with the area around them. You can also use the Content-Aware option when you apply a fill. You'll use content-aware fill to remove a distracting dark shadow from the left side of the image.

1 Select the Rectangular Marquee tool ([]) in the Tools panel.

2 Drag the Rectangular Marquee tool around the shadow on the left side of the image. The selection you make determines the fill. For the best results, select the full shadow, extending above the wall into the water. Keep the selection just to the left of the vertical line in the stone, as in the following image. (You'll use that vertical line in the next exercise.)

3 Choose Edit > Fill.

4 In the Fill dialog box, make sure Content-Aware is chosen in the Use menu, and then click OK.

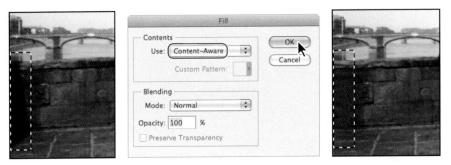

The dark shadow is replaced by a fill that matches the surrounding wall and ground. If you aren't happy with the results, choose Edit > Undo, click somewhere else on the image to deselect, and then repeat steps 2–4 to apply the fill again.

5 When you're happy with the fill, click anywhere else on the image to deselect.

6 Save your work so far.

# Repairing areas with the Clone Stamp tool

The Clone Stamp tool uses pixels from one area of an image to replace the pixels in another part of the image. Using this tool, you can not only remove unwanted objects from your images, but you can also fill in missing areas in photographs you scan from damaged originals.

You'll use the Clone Stamp tool to refine the wall where you applied the content-aware fill, so that there is more definition and variety in the stones.

1  Select the Clone Stamp tool (⬚) in the Tools panel.

2  In the options bar, open the Brush pop-up menu, and set the size to **21** and the hardness to **30%**. Then, make sure that the Aligned option is selected.

3  Move the Clone Stamp tool over the top of the vertical line in the dark area of the stone. That's the line you want to copy elsewhere to better define the filled stone. As you work with this area, you'll have the best results if you select a source that matches the color of the stone you're modifying. (You may want to zoom in to see the stone better.)

4  Alt-click (Windows) or Option-click (Mac OS) to start sampling that part of the image. (When you press Alt or Option, the pointer appears as target cross-hairs.)

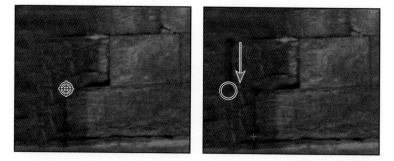

5  Drag the Clone Stamp tool down where you want to define a line between stones (see the image above), and then release the mouse button.

Each time you click the Clone Stamp tool, it begins again with a new source point, in the same relationship to the tool as the first stroke you made. That is, if you begin painting further right, it samples from stone that is further right than the original source point. That's because Aligned is selected in the options bar. Deselect Aligned if you want to start from the same source point each time. For example, you may want to do that to draw multiple vertical lines.

**6** Continue to refine the stones. We cloned lines between the stones and also cloned texture within the stones. You can do as much or as little as you want, resetting the source point as necessary. You can also change the brush size or other settings. Remember that you can undo any cloning you don't like, and if you want to start over completely, choose File > Revert.

**7** When you're satisfied with the appearance of the stones, choose File > Save.

## Applying a content-aware patch

You'll use yet another content-aware tool to remove an unrelated person from the right side of the photo. Using the Patch tool in Content-Aware mode isn't like cloning, because you aren't copying part of the image to another part. Really, it's more like magic.

**1** In the Tools panel, select the Patch tool (⊞), hidden beneath the Spot Healing Brush tool (✐).

**2** In the options bar, choose Content-Aware from the Patch menu. Then choose Very Strict from the Adaptation menu, and make sure that Sample All Layers is selected.

**3** Drag the Patch tool around the boy and his shadow, as closely as possible. You may want to zoom in to see him more clearly.

**4** Click within the area you've just selected, and drag it to the left. Photoshop displays a preview of the content that will replace the boy. Keep dragging to the left until the preview area no longer overlaps the area occupied by the boy, but without overlapping the woman or the girl she's holding. Release the mouse button when the patch is positioned where you want it.

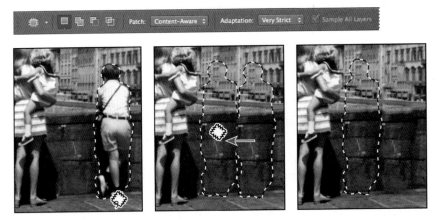

The selection changes to match the area around it. The boy is gone, and where he stood is a section of the bridge wall, and a building.

**5** Choose Select > Deselect.

The effect was pretty impressive, but not quite perfect. You'll use the Clone Stamp tool to smooth out some irregularities in the height of the bridge wall and the windows on the building.

**6** Select the Clone Stamp tool in the Tools panel, and select a **60 px** brush with **30%** hardness.

**7** Select a source point on a stretch where the top of the bridge wall is smooth. Then drag the Clone Stamp tool to even the height of the bridge wall in the patched area.

**8** Select a source point where the bottom of the bridge wall is even, and then drag the Clone Stamp tool across the bottom of the wall where you patched it.

**9** Select a smaller brush size, and deselect Aligned. Then select a source point over the rightmost windows in the lowest row on the building you patched. Click across to create accurate windows there.

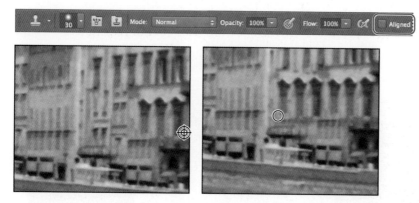

**10** Repeat step 9 to make any adjustments you need to make to the lowest area of the building and the wall that runs in front of it.

**11** If you like, you can use a smaller brush size to touch up the stones in the patched portion of the wall, just as you did on the left side.

**12** Choose Select > Deselect.

**13** Save your work.

## Sharpening the image

The last task you might want to do when retouching a photo is to sharpen the image. There are several ways to sharpen an image in Photoshop, but the Smart Sharpen filter gives you the most control. Because sharpening can emphasize artifacts, you'll remove those first.

**1** Zoom in to about 400% to see the artifacts on the boy's shirt clearly. There are colored dots, created during the scanning process.

**2** Choose Filter > Noise > Dust & Scratches.

**3** In the Dust & Scratches dialog box, leave the default settings with a Radius of 1 pixel and Threshold at 0, and click OK.

The Threshold value determines how dissimilar the pixels should be before they are eliminated. The Radius value determines the size of the area searched for dissimilar pixels. The default values are great for tiny dots of color like the ones in this image.

Now that the artifacts are gone, you can sharpen the image.

4  Choose Filter > Sharpen > Smart Sharpen.

5  In the Smart Sharpen dialog box, make sure that Preview is selected, so you can see the effect of settings you adjust in the image window.

You can drag inside the preview window in the dialog box to see different parts of the image, or use the plus and minus buttons below the thumbnail to zoom in and out.

6  Make sure Lens Blur is chosen in the Remove menu.

You can use the Smart Sharpen filter to remove lens blur, gaussian blur, or motion blur.

7  Drag the Amount slider to about **60%** to sharpen the image.

8  Drag the Radius slider to about **1.5**.

The Radius value determines the number of pixels surrounding the edge pixels that affect the sharpening. The higher the resolution, the higher the Radius setting should usually be.

9  When you're satisfied with the results, click OK to apply the Smart Sharpen filter.

10 Choose File > Save, and then close the project file.

Your image is ready to share or print!

# Extra credit

### Converting a color image to black and white

You can get great results converting a color image to black and white (with or without a tint) in Photoshop.

1  Choose File > Open, and navigate to the bike.jpg file in the Lesson02 folder. Click Open.

2  If the file opens in Camera Raw, click Open Image to open it in Photoshop.

3  In the Adjustments panel, click the Black & White button to add a Black & White adjustment layer.

4  Adjust the color sliders to change the saturation of color channels. You can also experiment with options from the preset menu, such as Darker or Infrared. Or, select the tool in the upper left corner of the Adjustments panel, and then drag it across the image to adjust the colors associated with that area. (We darkened the bike itself and made the background areas lighter.)

5  If you want to add a tint to the photo, select Tint. Then, click the color swatch and select a tint color (we used R=227, G=209, and B=198).

# Review questions

1   What does *resolution* mean?

2   What does the Crop tool do?

3   How can you adjust the tone and color of an image in Photoshop?

4   What tools can you use to remove blemishes in an image?

5   How can you remove digital artifacts such as colored pixels from an image?

# Review answers

1   The term *resolution* refers to the number of pixels that describe an image and establish its detail. *Image resolution* and *monitor resolution* are measured in pixels per inch (ppi). *Printer,* or *output, resolution* is measured in ink dots per inch (dpi).

2   You can use the Crop tool to trim, scale, or straighten an image.

3   To adjust the tone and color of an image in Photoshop, first use the White Point tool in a Curves adjustment layer. Then refine the tone using a Levels adjustment layer.

4   The Healing Brush, Spot Healing Brush, Patch tool, and Clone Stamp tools, as well as content-aware fill, let you replace unwanted portions of an image with other areas of the image. The Clone Stamp tool copies the source area exactly; the Healing Brush and Spot Healing Brush tools blend the area with the surrounding pixels. The Spot Healing Brush tool doesn't require a source area at all; it "heals" areas to match the surrounding pixels. The Patch tool in Content-Aware mode, and content-aware fill replace a selection with content that matches the surrounding area.

5   The Dust & Scratches filter removes digital artifacts from an image.

# 3 WORKING WITH SELECTIONS

## Lesson overview

In this lesson, you'll learn how to do the following:

- Make specific areas of an image active using selection tools.

- Reposition a selection marquee.

- Move and duplicate the contents of a selection.

- Use keyboard-mouse combinations that save time and hand motions.

- Deselect a selection.

- Constrain the movement of a selected area.

- Adjust the position of a selected area using the arrow keys.

- Add to and subtract from a selection.

- Rotate a selection.

- Use multiple selection tools to make a complex selection.

 This lesson will take about an hour to complete. Download the Lesson03 project files from the Lesson & Update Files tab on your Account page at www.peachpit.com, if you haven't already done so. As you work on this lesson, you'll preserve the start files. If you need to restore the start files, download them from your Account page.

PROJECT: SHADOWBOX COLLAGE

Learning how to select areas of an image is of primary importance—you must first select what you want to affect. Once you've made a selection, only the area within the selection can be edited.

# About selecting and selection tools

● **Note:** You'll learn how to select vector areas using the pen tools in Lesson 8, "Vector Drawing Techniques."

Making changes to an area within an image in Photoshop is a two-step process. You first select the part of an image you want to change with one of the selection tools. Then, you use another tool, filter, or other feature to make changes, such as moving the selected pixels to another location or applying a filter to the selected area. You can make selections based on size, shape, and color. The selection process limits changes to within the selected area. Other areas are unaffected.

The best selection tool for a specific area often depends on the characteristics of that area, such as shape or color. There are four types of selections:

**Geometric selections** The Rectangular Marquee tool (▢) selects a rectangular area in an image. The Elliptical Marquee tool (○), which is hidden behind the Rectangular Marquee tool, selects elliptical areas. The Single Row Marquee tool (▭) and Single Column Marquee tool (▯) select either a 1-pixel-high row or a 1-pixel-wide column, respectively.

**Freehand selections** The Lasso tool (⌀) traces a freehand selection around an area. The Polygonal Lasso tool (⌀) sets anchor points in straight-line segments around an area. The Magnetic Lasso tool (⌀) works something like a combination of the other two lasso tools, and gives the best results when good contrast exists between the area you want to select and its surroundings.

**Edge-based selections** The Quick Selection tool (⌀) quickly "paints" a selection by automatically finding and following defined edges in the image.

**Color-based selections** The Magic Wand tool (⌀) selects parts of an image based on the similarity in color of adjacent pixels. It is useful for selecting odd-shaped areas that share a specific range of colors.

# Getting started

First, you'll look at the image you will create as you explore the selection tools in Adobe Photoshop.

1  Start Photoshop, and then immediately hold down Ctrl+Alt+Shift (Windows) or Command+Option+Shift (Mac OS) to restore the default preferences. (See "Restoring default preferences" on page 4.)

2  When prompted, click Yes to confirm that you want to delete the Adobe Photoshop Settings file.

3  Choose File > Browse In Bridge to open Adobe Bridge.

4  In the Favorites panel, click the Lessons folder. Then, double-click the Lesson03 folder in the Content panel to see its contents.

● **Note:** If Bridge isn't installed, you'll be prompted to install it when you choose Browse In Bridge. For more information, see page 3.

5  Study the 03End.psd file. Move the thumbnail slider to the right if you want to see the image in more detail.

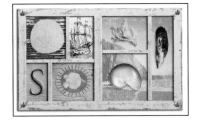

The project is a shadowbox that includes a piece of coral, a sand dollar, a mussel, a nautilus, and a plate of small shells. The challenge in this lesson is to arrange these elements, which were scanned together on the single page you see in the 03Start.psd file.

6  Double-click the 03Start.psd thumbnail to open the image file in Photoshop.

7  Choose File > Save As, rename the file **03Working.psd**, and click Save.

By saving another version of the start file, you don't have to worry about overwriting the original.

# Using the Quick Selection tool

The Quick Selection tool provides one of the easiest ways to make a selection. You simply paint an area of an image, and the tool automatically finds the edges. You can add or subtract areas of the selection until you have exactly the area you want.

The image of the sand dollar in the 03Working.psd file has clearly defined edges, making it an ideal candidate for the Quick Selection tool. You'll select just the sand dollar, not the background behind it.

1  Select the Zoom tool in the Tools panel, and then zoom in so that you can see the sand dollar well.

2  Select the Quick Selection tool (✐) in the Tools panel.

3  Select Auto Enhance in the options bar.

When Auto Enhance is selected, the Quick Selection tool creates better quality selections, with edges that are truer to the object. The selection process is a little slower than using the Quick Selection tool without Auto Enhance, but the results are superior.

4  Click on an off-white area near the outside edge of the sand dollar.

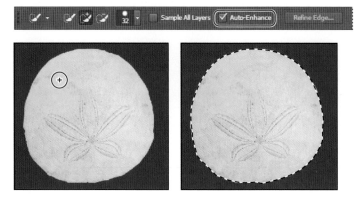

The Quick Selection tool finds the full edge automatically, selecting the entire sand dollar. Leave the selection active so that you can use it in the next exercise.

## Moving a selected area

Once you've made a selection, any changes you make apply exclusively to the pixels within the selection. The rest of the image is not affected by those changes.

To move the selected area to another part of the composition, you use the Move tool. This image has only one layer, so the pixels you move will replace the pixels beneath them. This change is not permanent until you deselect the moved pixels, so you can try different locations for the selection you're moving before you make a commitment.

1  If the sand dollar is not still selected, repeat the previous exercise to select it.

2  Zoom out so you can see both the shadowbox and the sand dollar.

**3** Select the Move tool (). Notice that the sand dollar remains selected.

**4** Drag the selected area (the sand dollar) up to the upper left area of the frame, which is labeled "A." Position it over the silhouette in the frame, leaving the lower left part of the silhouette showing as a shadow.

**5** Choose Select > Deselect, and then choose File > Save.

In Photoshop, it's not easy to lose a selection. Unless a selection tool is active, clicking elsewhere in the image will not deselect the active area. To deliberately deselect a selection, you can choose Select > Deselect, press Ctrl+D (Windows) or Command+D (Mac OS), or click outside the selection with any selection tool to start a different selection.

*Julieanne Kost is an official Adobe Photoshop evangelist.*

## Tool tips from the Photoshop evangelist

### Move tool tip

If you're moving objects in a multilayer file with the Move tool and you suddenly need to select one of the layers, try this: With the Move tool selected, move the pointer over any area of an image and right-click (Windows) or Control-click (Mac OS). The layers that are under the pointer appear in the context menu. Choose the one you'd like to make active.

## Manipulating selections

You can move selections, reposition them as you create them, and even duplicate them. In this section, you'll learn several ways to manipulate selections. Most of these methods work with any selection, but you'll use them here with the Elliptical Marquee tool, which lets you select ovals or perfect circles.

One of the best things about this section is the introduction of keyboard shortcuts that can save you time and arm motions.

## Repositioning a selection marquee while creating it

Selecting ovals and circles can be tricky. It's not always obvious where you should start dragging, so sometimes the selection will be off-center, or the ratio of width to height won't match what you need. In this exercise, you'll learn techniques for managing those problems, including two important keyboard-mouse combinations that can make your Photoshop work much easier.

As you perform this exercise, be very careful to follow the directions about keeping the mouse button or specific keys pressed. If you accidentally release the mouse button at the wrong time, simply start the exercise again from step 1.

1 Select the Zoom tool (🔍), and click the plate of shells at the bottom of the image window to zoom in to at least 100% view (use 200% view if the entire plate of shells will still fit in the image window on your screen).

2 Select the Elliptical Marquee tool (◯), hidden under the Rectangular Marquee tool (▱).

3 Move the pointer over the plate of shells, and drag diagonally across the oval bowl to create a selection, but *do not release the mouse button*. It's OK if your selection does not match the plate shape yet.

If you accidentally release the mouse button, draw the selection again. In most cases—including this one—the new selection replaces the previous one.

4 Still holding down the mouse button, press the spacebar, and continue to drag the selection. Instead of resizing the selection, now you're moving it. Position it so that it more closely aligns with the plate.

● **Note:** You don't have to include every pixel in the bowl of shells, but the selection should be the shape of the bowl, and should contain the shells comfortably.

5 Carefully release the spacebar (but not the mouse button) and continue to drag, trying to make the size and shape of the selection match the oval plate of shells as closely as possible. If necessary, hold down the spacebar again and drag to move the selection marquee into position around the plate of shells.

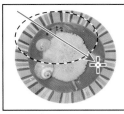 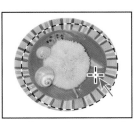 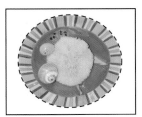

Begin dragging a selection.     Press the spacebar to move it.     Complete the selection.

**6** When the selection border is positioned appropriately, release the mouse button.

**7** Choose View > Fit On Screen or use the slider in the Navigator panel to reduce the zoom view so that you can see all of the objects in the image window.

Leave the Elliptical Marquee tool and the selection active for the next exercise.

## Moving selected pixels with a keyboard shortcut

Now you'll use a keyboard shortcut to move the selected pixels onto the shadowbox. The shortcut temporarily switches the active tool to the Move tool, so you don't need to select it from the Tools panel.

**1** If the plate of shells is not still selected, repeat the previous exercise to select it.

**2** With the Elliptical Marquee tool (○) selected in the Tools panel, press Ctrl (Windows) or Command (Mac OS), and move the pointer within the selection.

The pointer icon now includes a pair of scissors (✂) to indicate that the selection will be cut from its current location.

**3** Drag the plate of shells onto the area of the shadowbox labeled "B." (You'll use another technique to nudge the oval bowl into the exact position in a minute.)

**4** Release the mouse button, but don't deselect the plate of shells.

● **Note:** You can release the Ctrl or Command key after you start dragging, and the Move tool remains active. Photoshop reverts to the previously selected tool when you deselect, whether you click outside the selection or use the Deselect command.

## Moving with the arrow keys

You can make minor adjustments to the position of selected pixels by using the arrow keys. You can nudge the selection in increments of either one pixel or ten pixels.

When a selection tool is active in the Tools panel, the arrow keys nudge the selection border, but not the contents. When the Move tool is active, the arrow keys move the selection border and its contents.

You'll use the arrow keys to nudge the plate of shells. Before you begin, make sure that the plate of shells is still selected in the image window.

**1** Press the Up Arrow key (⬆) on your keyboard a few times to move the oval upward.

Notice that each time you press the arrow key, the plate of shells moves one pixel. Experiment by pressing the other arrow keys to see how they affect the selection.

2  Hold down the Shift key as you press an arrow key.

When you hold down the Shift key, the selection moves ten pixels every time you press an arrow key.

Sometimes the border around a selected area can distract you as you make adjustments. You can hide the edges of a selection temporarily without actually deselecting, and then display the selection border once you've completed the adjustments.

3  Choose View > Show > Selection Edges or View > Extras.

Either command hides the selection border around the plate of shells.

4  Use the arrow keys to nudge the plate of shells until it's positioned over the silhouette, so that there's a shadow on the left and bottom of the plate. Then choose View > Show > Selection Edges to reveal the selection border again.

Hidden selection edges    Visible selection edges

5  Choose Select > Deselect, or press Ctrl+D (Windows) or Command+D (Mac OS).

6  Choose File > Save to save your work so far.

## Using the Magic Wand tool

The Magic Wand tool selects all the pixels of a particular color or color range. It's most useful for selecting an area of similar colors surrounded by areas of very different colors. As with many of the selection tools, after you make the initial selection, you can add or subtract areas of the selection.

The Tolerance option sets the sensitivity of the Magic Wand tool. This value limits or extends the range of pixel similarity. The default tolerance value of 32 selects the color you click plus 32 lighter and 32 darker tones of that color. You may need to adjust the tolerance level up or down depending on the color ranges and variations in the image.

If a multicolored area that you want to select is set against a background of a differ-ent color, it can be much easier to select the background than the area itself. In this procedure, you'll use the Rectangular Marquee tool to select a larger area, and then use the Magic Wand tool to subtract the background from the selection.

1   Select the Rectangular Marquee tool (▢), hidden behind the Elliptical Marquee tool (◯).

2   Drag a selection around the piece of coral. Make sure that your selection is large enough so that a margin of white appears between the coral and the edges of the marquee.

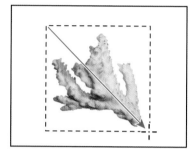

At this point, the coral and the white background area are selected. You'll subtract the white area from the selection so that only the coral remains in the selection.

3   Select the Magic Wand tool (✦), hidden under the Quick Selection tool (✎).

4   In the options bar, confirm that the Tolerance value is **32**. This value determines the range of colors the wand selects.

5   Select the Subtract From Selection button (▣) in the options bar.

A minus sign appears next to the wand in the pointer icon. Anything you select now will be subtracted from the initial selection.

6   Click in the white background area within the selection marquee.

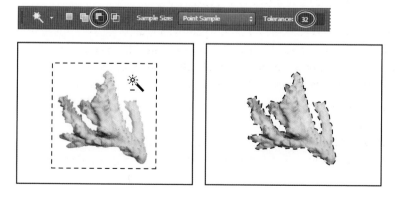

The Magic Wand tool selects the entire background, subtracting it from the selection. Now all the white pixels are deselected, leaving the coral perfectly selected.

**7** Select the Move tool (⮕), and drag the coral to the area of the shadowbox that is labeled "C," positioning it so that a shadow appears to the left and below the coral.

**8** Choose Select > Deselect, and then save your work.

## Softening the edges of a selection

To smooth the hard edges of a selection, you can apply anti-aliasing or feathering, or use the Refine Edge option.

Anti-aliasing smooths the jagged edges of a selection by softening the color transition between edge pixels and background pixels. Since only the edge pixels change, no detail is lost. Anti-aliasing is useful when cutting, copying, and pasting selections to create composite images.

Anti-aliasing is available for the Lasso, Polygonal Lasso, Magnetic Lasso, Elliptical Marquee, and Magic Wand tools. (Select the tool to display its options in the options bar.) To apply anti-aliasing, you must select the option before making the selection. Once a selection is made, you cannot add anti-aliasing to it.

Feathering blurs edges by building a transition boundary between the selection and its surrounding pixels. This blurring can cause some loss of detail at the edge of the selection.

You can define feathering for the marquee and lasso tools as you use them, or you can add feathering to an existing selection. Feathering effects become apparent when you move, cut, or copy the selection.

- To use the Refine Edge option, first make a selection, and then click Refine Edge in the options bar to open its dialog box. You can use the Refine Edge option to smooth the outline, feather it, or contract or expand it.

- To use anti-aliasing, select a lasso tool, or the Elliptical Marquee or Magic Wand tool, and select Anti-alias in the options bar.

- To define a feathered edge for a selection tool, select any of the lasso or marquee tools. Enter a Feather value in the options bar. This value defines the width of the feathered edge and can range from 1 to 250 pixels.

- To define a feathered edge for an existing selection, choose Select > Modify > Feather. Enter a value for the Feather Radius, and click OK.

# Selecting with the lasso tools

As we mentioned earlier, Photoshop includes three lasso tools: the Lasso tool, the Polygonal Lasso tool, and the Magnetic Lasso tool. You can use the Lasso tool to make selections that require both freehand and straight lines, using keyboard shortcuts to move back and forth between the Lasso tool and the Polygonal Lasso tool. You'll use the Lasso tool to select the mussel. It takes a bit of practice to alternate between straight-line and freehand selections—if you make a mistake while you're selecting the mussel, simply deselect and start again.

1   Select the Zoom tool (Q), and click the mussel until the view enlarges to 100%. Make sure you can see the entire mussel in the window.

2   Select the Lasso tool (⌀). Starting at the lower left section of the mussel, drag around the rounded end of the mussel, tracing the shape as accurately as possible. *Do not release the mouse button.*

3   Press the Alt (Windows) or Option (Mac OS) key, and then release the mouse button so that the lasso pointer changes to the polygonal lasso shape (▷). *Do not release the Alt or Option key.*

4   Begin clicking along the end of the mussel to place anchor points, following the contours of the mussel. Be sure to hold down the Alt or Option key throughout this process.

Drag with the Lasso tool.

Click with the Polygonal Lasso tool.

The selection border automatically stretches like a rubber band between anchor points.

5   When you reach the tip of the mussel, hold down the mouse button as you release the Alt or Option key. The pointer again appears as the lasso icon.

6   Carefully drag around the tip of the mussel, holding down the mouse button.

7   When you finish tracing the tip and reach the lower side of the mussel, first press Alt or Option again, and then release the mouse button. Click along the lower side of the mussel with the Polygonal Lasso tool as you did on the top. Continue to trace the mussel until you arrive back at the starting point of your selection near the left end of the image.

**8** Click the starting point of the selection, and then release Alt or Option. The mussel is now entirely selected. Leave the mussel selected for the next exercise.

## Rotating a selection

Now you'll rotate the mussel.

Before you begin, make sure that the mussel is still selected.

**1** Choose View > Fit On Screen to resize the image window to fit on your screen.

**2** Press Ctrl (Windows) or Command (Mac OS) as you drag the selected mussel to the section of the shadowbox labeled "D."

The pointer changes to the Move tool icon when you press Ctrl or Command.

**3** Choose Edit > Transform > Rotate.

The mussel and selection marquee are enclosed in a bounding box.

**4** Move the pointer outside the bounding box so that it becomes a curved, double-headed arrow (↰). Drag to rotate the mussel to a 90-degree angle. You can verify the angle in the Rotate box in the options bar. Press Enter or Return to commit the transformation.

**5** If necessary, select the Move tool (▶✛) and drag to reposition the mussel, leaving a shadow to match the others. When you're satisfied, choose Select > Deselect.

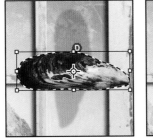  

**6** Choose File > Save.

# Selecting with the Magnetic Lasso tool

You can use the Magnetic Lasso tool to make freehand selections of areas with high-contrast edges. When you draw with the Magnetic Lasso tool, the selection border automatically snaps to the edge between areas of contrast. You can also control the selection path by occasionally clicking the mouse to place anchor points in the selection border.

You'll use the Magnetic Lasso tool to select the nautilus so that you can move it to the shadowbox.

1 Select the Zoom tool (🔍), and click the nautilus to zoom in to at least 100%.

2 Select the Magnetic Lasso tool (🧲), hidden under the Lasso tool (🔾).

3 Click once along the left edge of the nautilus, and then move the Magnetic Lasso tool along the edge to trace its outline.

▶ **Tip:** In low-contrast areas, you may want to click to place your own fastening points. You can add as many as you need. To remove the most recent fastening point, press Delete, and then move the mouse back to the remaining fastening point and continue selecting.

Even though you're not holding down the mouse button, the tool snaps to the edge of the nautilus and automatically adds fastening points.

4 When you reach the left side of the nautilus again, double-click to return the Magnetic Lasso tool to the starting point, closing the selection. Or you can move the Magnetic Lasso tool over the starting point and click once.

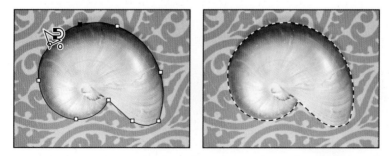

5 Double-click the Hand tool (✋) to fit the image in the image window.

**6** Select the Move tool (✛), and drag the nautilus onto its silhouette in the section of the frame labeled "E," leaving a shadow below it and on the left side.

**7** Choose Select > Deselect, and then choose File > Save.

## Selecting from a center point

In some cases, it's easier to make elliptical or rectangular selections by drawing a selection from an object's center point. You'll use this technique to select the head of the screw for the shadowbox corners.

**1** Select the Zoom tool (🔍), and zoom in on the screw to a magnification of about 300%. Make sure that you can see the entire screw in your image window.

**2** Select the Elliptical Marquee tool (○) in the Tools panel.

**3** Move the pointer to the approximate center of the screw.

**4** Click and begin dragging. Then, without releasing the mouse button, press Alt (Windows) or Option (Mac OS) as you continue dragging the selection to the outer edge of the screw.

The selection is centered over its starting point.

**5** When you have the entire screw selected, release the mouse button first, and then release Alt or Option (and the Shift key if you used it). Do not deselect, because you'll use this selection in the next exercise.

▶ **Tip:** To select a perfect circle, press Shift as you drag. Hold down Shift while dragging the Rectangular Marquee tool to select a perfect square.

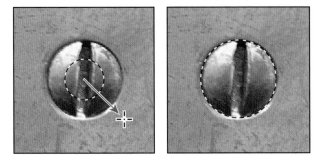

**6** If necessary, reposition the selection border using one of the methods you learned earlier. If you accidentally released the Alt or Option key before you released the mouse button, select the screw again.

# Resizing and copying a selection

Now you'll move the screw to the lower right corner of the wooden shadowbox, and then duplicate it for the other corners.

## Resizing the contents of a selection

You'll start by moving the screw, but it's too large for the space. You'll need to resize it as well.

Before you begin, make sure that the screw is still selected. If it's not, reselect it by completing the previous exercise.

1 Choose View > Fit On Screen so that the entire image fits within the image window.

2 Select the Move tool (▶⊹) in the Tools panel.

3 Position the pointer within the screw selection.

The pointer becomes an arrow with a pair of scissors (▶✂), indicating that dragging the selection will cut it from its current location and move it to the new location.

4 Drag the screw onto the lower right corner of the shadowbox.

5 Choose Edit > Transform > Scale. A bounding box appears around the selection.

6 Press Shift as you drag one of the corner points inward to reduce the screw to about 40% of its original size, or until it is small enough to sit on the shadowbox frame. Then press Enter or Return to commit the change and remove the transformation bounding box.

As you resize the object, the selection marquee resizes, too. Pressing the Shift key as you resize the selection constrains the proportions so that the reduced object isn't distorted.

7 Use the Move tool to reposition the screw after resizing it, so that it is centered in the corner of the shadowbox frame.

 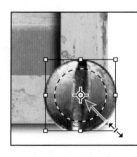 

8 Leaving the screw selected, choose File > Save to save your work.

## Moving and duplicating a selection simultaneously

You can move and duplicate a selection at the same time. You'll copy the screw for the other three corners of the frame. If the screw is no longer selected, reselect it now, using the techniques you learned earlier.

**1** With the Move tool (▸₊) selected, press Alt (Windows) or Option (Mac OS) as you position the pointer inside the screw selection.

The pointer changes, displaying the usual black arrow and an additional white arrow, which indicates that a duplicate will be made when you move the selection.

**2** Continue holding down the Alt or Option key as you drag a duplicate of the screw straight up to the top right corner of the frame. Release the mouse button and the Alt or Option key, but don't deselect the duplicate image.

**3** Hold down Alt+Shift (Windows) or Option+Shift (Mac OS), and drag a new copy of the screw straight left to the upper left corner of the frame.

Pressing the Shift key as you move a selection constrains the movement horizontally or vertically in 45-degree increments.

**4** Repeat step 3 to drag a fourth screw to the lower left corner of the frame.

**5** When you're satisfied with the position of the fourth screw, choose Select > Deselect, and then choose File > Save.

## Copying selections

You can use the Move tool to copy selections as you drag them within or between images, or you can copy and move selections using the Copy, Copy Merged, Paste and Paste Into commands. Dragging with the Move tool saves memory, because the clipboard is not used as it is with the commands.

Photoshop has several copy and paste commands:

- Copy copies the selected area on the active layer.
- Copy Merged creates a merged copy of all the visible layers in the selected area.
- Paste pastes a cut or copied selection into another part of the image or into another image as a new layer.
- Paste Into pastes a cut or copied selection inside another selection in the same or a different image. The source selection is pasted onto a new layer, and the destination selection border is converted into a layer mask.

Keep in mind that when a selection is pasted between images with different resolutions, the pasted data retains its pixel dimensions. This can make the pasted portion appear out of proportion to the new image. Use the Image Size command to make the source and destination images the same resolution before copying and pasting.

# Cropping an image

Now that your composition is in place, you'll crop the image to a final size. You can use either the Crop tool or the Crop command to crop an image.

1  Select the Crop tool (⊞), or press C to switch from the current tool to the Crop tool. Photoshop displays a crop boundary around the entire image.

2  In the options bar, make sure Ratio is selected in the Preset pop-up menu and that there are no ratio values specified. Then confirm that Delete Cropped Pixels is selected.

When Ratio is selected but no ratio values are specified, you can crop the image with any proportions.

**▶ Tip:** To crop an image with its original proportions intact, choose Original Ratio from the Preset pop-up menu in the options bar.

**3** Drag the crop handles so that the shadowbox is in the highlighted area, omitting the backgrounds from the original objects at the bottom of the image. Crop the frame so that there's an even area of white around it.

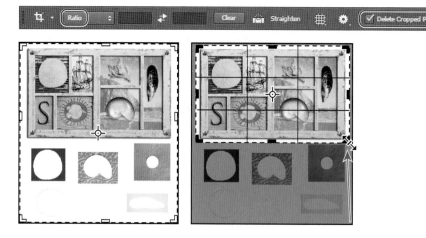

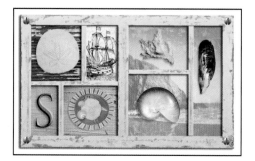

**4** When you're satisfied with the position of the crop area, click the Commit Current Crop Operation button (✔) in the options bar.

**5** Choose File > Save to save your work.

You've used several different selection tools to move all the seashells into place. The shadowbox is complete!

## Review questions

1 Once you've made a selection, what area of the image can be edited?

2 How do you add to and subtract from a selection?

3 How can you move a selection while you're drawing it?

4 When drawing a selection with the Lasso tool, how should you finish drawing the selection to ensure it's the shape you want?

5 What does the Quick Selection tool do?

6 How does the Magic Wand tool determine which areas of an image to select? What is tolerance, and how does it affect a selection?

## Review answers

1 Only the area within an active selection can be edited.

2 To add to a selection, click the Add To Selection button in the options bar, and then click the area you want to add. To subtract from a selection, click the Subtract From Selection button in the options bar, and then click the area you want to subtract. You can also add to a selection by pressing Shift as you drag or click; to subtract, press Alt (Windows) or Option (Mac OS) as you drag or click.

3 To reposition a selection, without releasing the mouse button, hold down the spacebar and drag.

4 To make sure that the selection is the shape you want when you use the Lasso tool, end the selection by dragging across the starting point of the selection. If you start and stop the selection at different points, Photoshop draws a straight line between the start point of the selection and the end point of the selection.

5 The Quick Selection tool expands outward from where you click to automatically find and follow defined edges in the image.

6 The Magic Wand tool selects adjacent pixels based on their similarity in color. The Tolerance value determines how many color tones the Magic Wand tool will select. The higher the tolerance setting, the more tones are selected.

# 4  LAYER BASICS

## Lesson overview

In this lesson, you'll learn how to do the following:

- Organize artwork on layers.

- Create, view, hide, and select layers.

- Rearrange layers to change the stacking order of artwork.

- Apply blending modes to layers.

- Resize and rotate layers.

- Apply a gradient to a layer.

- Apply a filter to a layer.

- Add text and layer effects to a layer.

- Add an adjustment layer.

- Save a copy of the file with the layers flattened.

 This lesson will take less than an hour to complete. Download the Lesson04 project files from the Lesson & Update Files tab on your Account page at www.peachpit.com, if you haven't already done so. As you work on this lesson, you'll preserve the start files. If you need to restore the start files, download them from your Account page.

PROJECT: TRAVEL POSTCARD

Adobe Photoshop lets you isolate different parts of an image on layers. Each layer can then be edited as discrete artwork, allowing tremendous flexibility in composing and revising an image.

# About layers

Every Photoshop file contains one or more *layers*. New files are generally created with a *background layer*, which contains a color or an image that shows through the transparent areas of subsequent layers. All new layers in an image are transparent until you add text or artwork (pixel values).

Working with layers is analogous to placing portions of a drawing on clear sheets of film, such as those viewed with an overhead projector: Individual sheets may be edited, repositioned, and deleted without affecting the other sheets. When the sheets are stacked, the entire composition is visible.

# Getting started

You'll start the lesson by viewing an image of the final composition.

1   Start Photoshop, and then immediately hold down Ctrl+Alt+Shift (Windows) or Command+Option+Shift (Mac OS) to restore the default preferences. (See "Restoring default preferences" on page 4.)

2   When prompted, click Yes to delete the Adobe Photoshop Settings file.

● **Note:** If Mini Bridge and Bridge aren't installed, you'll be prompted to install them. For more information, see page 3.

3   Choose File > Browse In Mini Bridge to open the Mini Bridge panel. If Bridge isn't running in the background, click Launch Bridge.

You can access many of the features of Adobe Bridge without leaving Photoshop. The Mini Bridge panel lets you browse, select, open, and import files while you're working with your image in Photoshop.

4   In the Mini Bridge panel, choose Favorites from the pop-up menu on the left.

5   In the Favorites panel, double-click the Lessons folder, and then double-click the Lesson04 folder.

6   In the Content panel, select the 04End.psd file. Press the spacebar for a full-screen view.

This layered composite represents a postcard. You will create it now, and, in doing so, learn how to create, edit, and manage layers.

7   Press the spacebar again to return to the Mini Bridge panel, and then double-click the 04Start.psd file to open it in Photoshop.

8   Choose File > Save As, rename the file **04Working.psd**, and click Save. Click OK if you see the Photoshop Format Options dialog box.

Saving another version of the start file frees you to make changes without worrying about overwriting the original.

# Using the Layers panel

The Layers panel lists all the layers in an image, displaying the layer names and thumbnails of the content on each layer. You can use the Layers panel to hide, view, reposition, delete, rename, and merge layers. The layer thumbnails are automatically updated as you edit the layers.

1   If the Layers panel is not visible in the work area, choose Window > Layers.

The Layers panel lists five layers for the 04Working.psd file (from top to bottom): Postage, HAWAII, Flower, Pineapple, and Background.

2   Select the Background layer to make it active (if it's not already selected). Notice the layer thumbnail and the icons on the Background layer listing:

- The lock icon (🔒) indicates that the layer is protected.

- The eye icon (👁) indicates that the layer is visible in the image window. If you click the eye, the image window no longer displays that layer.

**Tip:** Use the context menu to hide or resize the layer thumbnail. Right-click (Windows) or Control-click (Mac OS) a thumbnail in the Layers panel to open the context menu, and then choose a thumbnail size.

The first task for this project is to add a photo of the beach to the postcard. First, you'll open the beach image in Photoshop.

**3** In the Mini Bridge panel, double-click the Beach.psd file in the Lesson04 folder to open it in Photoshop.

The Layers panel changes to display the layer information for the active Beach.psd file. Notice that only one layer appears in the Beach.psd image: Layer 1, not Background. (For more information, see the sidebar "About the background layer.")

## About the background layer

When you create a new image with a white or colored background, the bottom layer in the Layers panel is named Background. An image can have only one background layer. You cannot change the stacking order of a background layer, its blending mode, or its opacity. You can, however, convert a background layer to a regular layer.

When you create a new image with transparent content, the image doesn't have a background layer. The bottom layer isn't constrained like the background layer; you can move it anywhere in the Layers panel, and change its opacity and blending mode.

### To convert a background layer into a regular layer:

1   Double-click the name Background in the Layers panel, or choose Layer > New > Layer From Background.

2   Rename the layer, and set any other layer options.

3   Click OK.

### To convert a regular layer into a background layer:

1   Select a layer in the Layers panel.

2   Choose Layer > New > Background From Layer.

# Renaming and copying a layer

To add content to an image and simultaneously create a new layer for it, drag an object or layer from one file into the image window of another file. Whether you drag from the image window of the original file or from its Layers panel, only the active layer is reproduced in the destination file.

You'll drag the Beach.psd image onto the 04Working.psd file. Before you begin, make sure that both the 04Working.psd and Beach.psd files are open, and that the Beach.psd file is selected.

First, you'll give Layer 1 a more descriptive name.

1   In the Layers panel, double-click the name Layer 1, type **Beach**, and then press Enter or Return. Keep the layer selected.

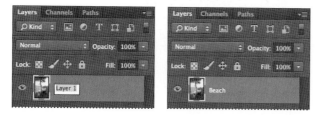

2   Choose Window > Arrange > 2-Up Vertical. Photoshop displays both of the open image files. Select the Beach.psd image so that it is the active file.

3   Select the Move tool (⊹), and use it to drag the Beach.psd image onto the 04Working.psd image window.

▶ **Tip:** If you hold down Shift as you drag an image from one file into another, the dragged image automatically centers itself in the target image window.

The Beach layer now appears in the 04Working.psd file image window and its Layers panel, between the Background and Pineapple layers. Photoshop always adds new layers directly above the selected layer; you selected the Background layer earlier.

4 Close the Beach.psd file without saving changes to it.

5 Double-click the Mini Bridge tab to close the panel.

## Viewing individual layers

The 04Working.psd file now contains six layers. Some of the layers are visible and some are hidden. The eye icon (👁) next to a layer thumbnail in the Layers panel indicates that the layer is visible.

1 Click the eye icon (👁) next to the Pineapple layer to hide the image of the pineapple.

You can hide or show a layer by clicking this icon or clicking in its column—also called the Show/Hide Visibility column.

**2**  Click again in the Show/Hide Visibility column to display the pineapple.

## Adding a border to a layer

Now you'll add a white border around the Beach layer to create the impression that it's a photograph.

**1**  Select the Beach layer. (To select the layer, click the layer name in the Layers panel.)

The layer is highlighted, indicating that it is active. Changes you make in the image window affect the active layer.

**2**  To make the opaque areas on this layer more obvious, hide all layers except the Beach layer: Press Alt (Windows) or Option (Mac OS) as you click the eye icon (◉) next to the Beach layer.

The white background and other objects in the image disappear, leaving only the beach image against a checkerboard background. The checkerboard indicates transparent areas of the active layer.

**3**  Choose Layer > Layer Style > Stroke.

The Layer Style dialog box opens. Now you'll select the options for the white stroke around the beach image.

**4** Specify the following settings:

- Size: **5 px**

- Position: Inside

- Blend Mode: Normal

- Opacity: **100**%

- Color: White (Click the Color box, and select white in the Color Picker.)

**5** Click OK. A white border appears around the beach photo.

# Rearranging layers

The order in which the layers of an image are organized is called the *stacking order*. The stacking order determines how the image is viewed—you can change the order to make certain parts of the image appear in front of or behind other layers.

You'll rearrange the layers so that the beach image is in front of another image that is currently hidden in the file.

1  Make the Postage, HAWAII, Flower, Pineapple, and Background layers visible by clicking the Show/Hide Visibility column next to their layer names.

The beach image is almost entirely blocked by images on other layers.

2  In the Layers panel, drag the Beach layer up so that it is positioned between the Pineapple and Flower layers—when you've positioned it correctly, you'll see a thick line between the layers in the panel—and then release the mouse button.

▶ **Tip:** You can also control the stacking order of layered images by selecting them in the Layers panel and choosing Layer > Arrange, and then choosing Bring To Front, Bring Forward, Send To Back, or Send Backward.

The Beach layer moves up one level in the stacking order, and the beach image appears on top of the pineapple and background images, but under the postage, flower, and the word "HAWAII."

## Changing the opacity of a layer

You can reduce the opacity of any layer to let other layers show through it. In this case, the postmark is too dark on the flower. You'll edit the opacity of the Postage layer to let the flower and other images show through.

1   Select the Postage layer, and then click the arrow next to the Opacity field to display the Opacity slider. Drag the slider to **25**%. You can also type the value in the Opacity box or scrub the Opacity label.

The Postage layer becomes partially transparent, so you can see the other layers underneath. Notice that the change in opacity affects only the image area of the Postage layer. The Pineapple, Beach, Flower, and HAWAII layers remain opaque.

2   Choose File > Save to save your work.

## Duplicating a layer and changing the blending mode

You can apply different blending modes to a layer. *Blending modes* affect how the color pixels on one layer blend with pixels on the layers underneath. First you'll use blending modes to increase the intensity of the image on the Pineapple layer so that it doesn't look so dull. Then you'll change the blending mode on the Postage layer. (Currently, the blending mode for both layers is Normal.)

1   Click the eye icons next to the HAWAII, Flower, and Beach layers to hide them.

2   Right-click or Control-click the Pineapple layer, and choose Duplicate Layer from the context menu. (Make sure you click the layer name, not its thumbnail, or you'll see the wrong context menu.) Click OK in the Duplicate Layer dialog box.

A layer called "Pineapple copy" appears above the Pineapple layer in the Layers panel.

*Julieanne Kost is an official Adobe Photoshop evangelist.*

# Tool tips from the Photoshop evangelist

## Blending effects

Blending layers in a different order or on different groups changes the effect. You can apply a blending mode to an entire layer group and get a very different result than if you apply the same blending mode to each of the layers individually. When a blending mode is applied to a group, Photoshop treats the group as a single merged object and then applies the blending mode. Experiment with blending modes to get the effect you want.

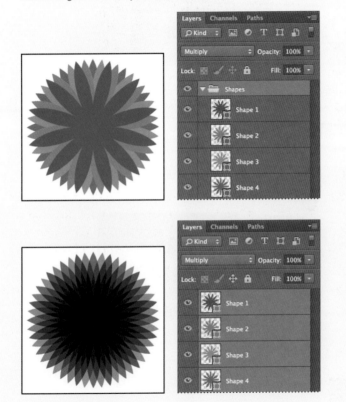

**3** With the Pineapple copy layer selected, choose Overlay from the Blending Modes menu in the Layers panel.

The Overlay blending mode blends the Pineapple copy layer with the Pineapple layer beneath it to create a vibrant, more colorful pineapple with deeper shadows and brighter highlights.

▶ **Tip:** For more about blending modes, including definitions and visual examples, see Photoshop Help.

**4** Select the Postage layer, and choose Multiply from the Blending Modes menu.

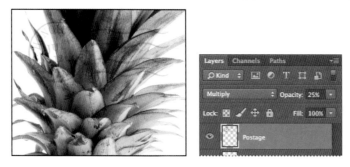

The Multiply blending mode multiplies the colors in the underlying layers with the color in the top layer. In this case, the postmark becomes a little stronger.

**5** Choose File > Save to save your work.

## Resizing and rotating layers

You can resize and transform layers.

**1** Click the Visibility column on the Beach layer to make it visible.

**2** Select the Beach layer in the Layers panel, and choose Edit > Free Transform.

A Transform bounding box appears around the beach image. The bounding box has handles on each corner and each side.

First, you'll resize and angle the layer.

**3** Press Shift as you drag a corner handle inward to scale the beach photo down by about 50%. (Watch the Width and Height percentages in the options bar.)

**4** With the bounding box still active, position the pointer just outside one of the corner handles until it becomes a curved double arrow. Drag clockwise to rotate the beach image approximately 15 degrees. You can also enter **15** in the Set Rotation box in the options bar.

**5** Click the Commit Transform button (✔) in the options bar.

**6** Make the Flower layer visible. Then, select the Move tool (▶✛), and drag the beach photo so that its corner is tucked neatly beneath the flower, as in the illustration.

**7** Choose File > Save.

## Using a filter to create artwork

Next, you'll create a new layer with no artwork on it. (Adding empty layers to a file is comparable to adding blank sheets of acetate to a stack of images.) You'll use this layer to add realistic-looking clouds to the sky with a Photoshop filter.

1   In the Layers panel, select the Background layer to make it active, and then click the Create A New Layer button (⬜) at the bottom of the Layers panel.

A new layer, named Layer 1, appears between the Background and Pineapple layers. The layer has no content, so it has no effect on the image.

● **Note:** You can also create a new layer by choosing Layer > New > Layer, or by choosing New Layer from the Layers panel menu.

2   Double-click the name Layer 1, type **Clouds**, and press Enter or Return to rename the layer.

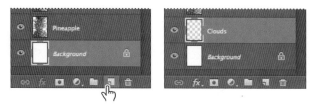

3   In the Tools panel, click the Foreground Color swatch, select a sky blue color from the Color Picker, and click OK. We selected a color with the following values: R=48, G=138, and B=174. The Background Color remains white.

4   With the Clouds layer still active, choose Filter > Render > Clouds.

Realistic-looking clouds appear behind the image.

5   Choose File > Save.

## Dragging to add a new layer

You can add a layer to an image by dragging an image file from the desktop, Bridge, or Explorer (Windows) or the Finder (Mac OS). You'll add another flower to the postcard now.

1 If Photoshop fills your monitor, reduce the size of the Photoshop window:

- In Windows, click the Maximize/Restore button (▣) in the upper right corner, and then drag the lower right corner of the Photoshop window to make it smaller.

- In Mac OS, click the green Maximize/Restore button (◉) in the upper left corner of the image window.

2 In Photoshop, select the Pineapple copy layer in the Layers panel to make it the active layer.

3 In Explorer (Windows) or the Finder (Mac OS), navigate to the Lessons folder you downloaded from the peachpit.com website. Then navigate to the Lesson04 folder.

4 Select Flower2.psd, and drag it from Explorer or the Finder onto your image.

The Flower2 layer appears in the Layers panel, directly above the Pineapple copy layer. Photoshop places the image as a Smart Object, which is a layer you can edit without making permanent changes. You'll work with Smart Objects in Lessons 5 and 8.

**5** Position the Flower2 layer in the lower left corner of the postcard, so that about half of the flower is visible.

**6** Click the Commit Transform button (✔) in the options bar to accept the layer.

## Adding text

Now you're ready to create some type using the Horizontal Type tool, which places the text on its own type layer. You'll then edit the text and apply a special effect.

**1** Make the HAWAII layer visible. You'll add text just below this layer, and apply special effects to both layers.

**2** Choose Select > Deselect Layers, so that no layers are selected.

**3** Click the Foreground Color swatch in the Tools panel, and then select a shade of grassy green in the Color Picker. Click OK to close the Color Picker.

**4** In the Tools panel, select the Horizontal Type tool (T). Then, choose Window > Character to open the Character panel. Do the following in the Character panel:

- Select a serif font (we used Birch Std; if you use a different font, adjust other settings accordingly).

- Select a font style (we used Regular).

- Select a large font size (we used 36 points).

- Select a large tracking value (🔠) (we used 250).

- Click the Faux Bold button (T).

- Click the All Caps button (TT).

- Select Crisp from the Anti-aliasing menu (ᵃₐ).

**5** Click just below the "H" in the word "HAWAII," and type **Island Paradise**. Then click the Commit Any Current Edits button (✔) in the options bar.

● **Note:** If you make a mistake when you click to set the type, simply click away from the type and repeat step 5.

The Layers panel now includes a layer named Island Paradise with a "T" thumbnail, indicating that it is a type layer. This layer is at the top of the layer stack.

The text appears where you clicked, which probably isn't exactly where you want it to be positioned.

**6** Select the Move tool (▸✛), and drag the "Island Paradise" text so that it is centered below "HAWAII."

# Applying a gradient to a layer

You can apply a color gradient to all or part of a layer. In this example, you'll apply a gradient to the HAWAII type to make it more colorful. First you'll select the letters, and then you'll apply the gradient.

1  Select the HAWAII layer in the Layers panel to make it active.

2  Right-click or Control-click the thumbnail in the HAWAII layer, and choose Select Pixels.

Everything on the HAWAII layer (the white lettering) is selected. Now that you've selected the area to fill, you'll apply a gradient.

3  In the Tools panel, select the Gradient tool (⬛).

4  Click the Foreground Color swatch in the Tools panel, select a bright shade of orange in the Color Picker, and click OK. The Background Color should still be white.

5  In the options bar, make sure that Linear Gradient (⬛) is selected.

▶ **Tip:** To list the gradient options by name rather than by sample, click the menu button in the gradient picker, and choose either Small List or Large List. Or, hover the pointer over a thumbnail until a tool tip appears, showing the gradient name.

6  In the options bar, click the arrow next to the Gradient Editor box to open the Gradient Picker. Select the Foreground To Background swatch (it's the first one), and then click anywhere outside the gradient picker to close it.

7  With the selection still active, drag the Gradient tool from the bottom to the top of the letters. If you want to be sure you drag straight up, press the Shift key as you drag.

The gradient extends across the type, starting with orange at the bottom and gradually blending to white at the top.

**8** Choose Select > Deselect to deselect the HAWAII type.

**9** Save the work you've done so far.

## Applying a layer style

You can enhance a layer by adding a shadow, stroke, satin sheen, or other special effect from a collection of automated and editable layer styles. These styles are easy to apply, and they link directly to the layer you specify.

Like layers, layer styles can be hidden by clicking eye icons (👁) in the Layers panel. Layer styles are nondestructive, so you can edit or remove them at any time. You can apply a copy of a layer style to a different layer by dragging the effect onto the destination layer.

Earlier, you used a layer style to add a stroke to the beach photo. Now, you'll add drop shadows to the text to make it stand out.

**1** Select the Island Paradise layer, and then choose Layer > Layer Style > Drop Shadow.

**2** In the Layer Style dialog box, make sure that the Preview option is selected, and then, if necessary, move the dialog box so that you can see the Island Paradise text in the image window.

▶ **Tip:** You can also open the Layer Style dialog box by clicking the Add A Layer Style button at the bottom of the Layers panel and then choosing a layer style, such as Bevel And Emboss, from the pop-up menu.

3   In the Structure area, select Use Global Light, and then specify the following settings:

- Blend Mode: Multiply

- Opacity: **75**%

- Angle: **78** degrees

- Distance: **5** px

- Spread: **30**%

- Size: **10** px

Photoshop adds a drop shadow to the "Island Paradise" text in the image.

4   Click OK to accept the settings and close the Layer Style dialog box.

Photoshop nests the layer style in the Island Paradise layer. First it lists Effects, and then the layer styles applied to the layer. An eye icon (●) appears next to the effect category and next to each effect. To turn off an effect, click its eye icon. Click the visibility column again to restore the effect. To hide all layer styles, click the eye icon next to Effects. To collapse the list of effects, click the arrow next to the layer.

**5** Make sure that eye icons appear for both items nested in the Island Paradise layer.

**6** Press Alt (Windows) or Option (Mac OS) and drag the Effects line or the fx symbol (*fx*) onto the HAWAII layer.

The Drop Shadow layer style is applied to the HAWAII layer, using the same settings you applied to the Island Paradise layer. Now you'll add a green stroke around the word HAWAII.

**7** Select the HAWAII layer in the Layers panel, click the Add A Layer Style button (*fx*) at the bottom of the panel, and then choose Stroke from the pop-up menu.

**8** In the Structure area of the Layer Styles dialog box, specify the following settings:

- Size: **4** px

- Position: Outside

- Blend Mode: Normal

- Opacity: **100**%

- Color: Green (Select a shade that goes well with the one you used for the "Island Paradise" text.)

**9** Click OK to apply the stroke.

Now you'll add a drop shadow and a satin sheen to the flower.

**10** Select the Flower layer, and choose Layer > Layer Style > Drop Shadow. Then change the following settings in the Structure area:

- Opacity: **60**%

- Distance: **13** px

- Spread: **9**%.

- Make sure Use Global Light is selected, and that the Blend Mode is Multiply. Do not click OK.

| Layer Style | | |
| --- | --- | --- |
| Styles | Drop Shadow — Structure | OK |
| Blending Options: Default | Blend Mode: Multiply | Cancel |
| ☐ Bevel & Emboss | Opacity: 60 % | New Style... |
| ☐ Contour | | ☑ Preview |
| ☐ Texture | Angle: 78 ° ☑ Use Global Light | |
| ☐ Stroke | Distance: 13 px | |
| ☐ Inner Shadow | Spread: 9 % | |
| ☐ Inner Glow | Size: 5 px | |
| ☐ Satin | | |

**11** With the Layer Style dialog box still open, select Satin on the left. Then make sure Invert is selected, and apply the following settings:

- Color (next to Blend Mode): Fuchsia (choose a color that complements the flower color)

- Opacity: **20**%

- Distance: **22** px

**12** Click OK to apply both layer styles.

# Adding an adjustment layer

Adjustment layers can be added to an image to apply color and tonal adjustments without permanently changing the pixel values in the image. For example, if you add a Color Balance adjustment layer to an image, you can experiment with different colors repeatedly, because the change occurs only on the adjustment layer. If you decide to return to the original pixel values, you can hide or delete the adjustment layer.

You've used adjustment layers in other lessons. Here, you'll add a Hue/Saturation adjustment layer to change the color of the purple flower. An adjustment layer affects all layers below it in the image's stacking order unless a selection is active when you create it or you create a clipping mask.

1  Select the Flower2 layer in the Layers panel.

2  Click the Hue/Saturation icon in the Adjustments panel to add a Hue/Saturation adjustment layer.

3  In the Properties panel, apply the following settings

- Hue: **43**

- Saturation: **19**

- Lightness: **0**

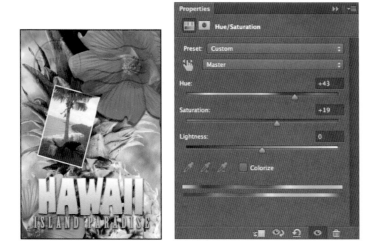

The changes affect the Flower2, Pineapple Copy, Pineapple, Clouds, and Background layers. The effect is interesting, but you only want to change the Flower2 layer.

**4** Right-click (Windows) or Ctrl-click (Mac OS) the Hue/Saturation adjustment layer, and choose Create Clipping Mask.

An arrow appears in the Layers panel, indicating that the adjustment layer applies only to the Flower2 layer. You'll learn more about clipping masks in Lessons 6 and 7.

## Updating layer effects

Layer effects are automatically updated when you make changes to a layer. You can edit the text and watch how the layer effect tracks the change. First, you'll use the new search feature in the Layers panel to isolate the text layer.

**1** In the Layers panel, choose Kind from the Pick A Filter Type menu.

The filter type determines the search options available to you.

**2** Select the Filter For Type Layers button from the filter options at the top of the Layers panel.

Only the Island Paradise layer is listed in the Layers panel. The search feature lets you find specific layers quickly, but has no effect on which layers are visible or their stacking order.

**Tip:** You can search for layers in the Layers panel by layer type, layer name, effect, mode, attribute, and color. When you work in a complex file with numerous layers, searching for the layer you need can save you time.

**3** Select the Island Paradise layer in the Layers panel.

**4** In the Tools panel, select the Horizontal Type tool (T).

**5** In the options bar, set the font size to **32** points, and press Enter or Return.

Although you didn't select the text by dragging the Type tool (as you would have to do in a word processing program), "Island Paradise" now appears in 32-point type.

**6** Using the Horizontal Type tool, click between "Island" and "Paradise," and type **of**.

As you edit the text, the layer styles are applied to the new text.

**7** You don't actually need the word "of," so delete it.

● **Note:** You don't have to click the Commit Any Current Edits button after making the text edits, because selecting the Move tool has the same effect.

**8** Select the Move tool (⊕), and drag "Island Paradise" to center it beneath the word "HAWAII."

**9** Click the red Filtering On/Off button at the top of the Layers panel to toggle filtering off and see all the layers in the file.

**10** Choose File > Save.

# Adding a border

The Hawaii postcard is nearly done. The elements are almost all arranged correctly in the composition. You'll finish up by positioning the postmark and then adding a white postcard border.

1  Select the Postage layer, and then use the Move tool (⊹) to drag it to the middle right of the image, as in the illustration.

2  Select the Island Paradise layer in the Layers panel, and then click the Create A New Layer button (◻) at the bottom of the panel.

3  Choose Select > All.

4  Choose Select > Modify > Border. In the Border Selection dialog box, type **10** pixels for the Width, and click OK.

A 10-pixel border is selected around the entire image. Now, you'll fill it with white.

5  Select white for the Foreground Color, and then choose Edit > Fill.

6  In the Fill dialog box, choose Foreground Color from the Use menu, and click OK.

7  Choose Select > Deselect.

8  Double-click the Layer 1 name in the Layers panel, and rename the layer **Border.**

# Flattening and saving files

When you finish editing all the layers in your image, you can merge or *flatten* layers to reduce the file size. Flattening combines all the layers into a single background layer. However, you cannot edit layers once you've flattened them, so you shouldn't flatten an image until you are certain that you're satisfied with all your design decisions. Rather than flattening your original PSD files, it's a good idea to save a copy of the file with its layers intact, in case you need to edit a layer later.

**Note:** If the sizes do not appear in the status bar, click the status bar pop-up menu arrow, and choose Show > Document Sizes.

To appreciate what flattening does, notice the two numbers for the file size in the status bar at the bottom of the image window. The first number represents what the file size would be if you flattened the image. The second number represents the file size without flattening. This lesson file, if flattened, would be 2–3MB, but the current file is much larger. So flattening is well worth it in this case.

1   Select any tool but the Type tool (T), to be sure that you're not in text-editing mode. Then choose File > Save (if it is available) to be sure that all your changes have been saved in the file.

2   Choose Image > Duplicate.

3   In the Duplicate Image dialog box, name the file **04Flat.psd**, and click OK.

4   Leave the 04Flat.psd file open, but close the 04Working.psd file.

5   Choose Flatten Image from the Layers panel menu.

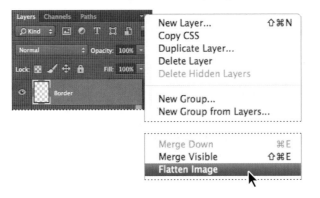

Only one layer, named Background, remains in the Layers panel.

6  Choose File > Save. Even though you chose Save rather than Save As, the Save As dialog box appears.

7  Make sure the location is the Lessons/Lesson04 folder, and then click Save to accept the default settings and save the flattened file.

You have saved two versions of the file: a one-layer, flattened copy as well as the original file, in which all the layers remain intact.

You've created a colorful, attractive postcard. This lesson only begins to explore the vast possibilities and the flexibility you gain when you master the art of using Photoshop layers. You'll get more experience and try out different techniques for layers in almost every chapter as you move forward in this book.

▶ **Tip:** If you want to flatten only some of the layers in a file, click the eye icons to hide the layers you don't want to flatten, and then choose Merge Visible from the Layers panel menu.

## About layer comps

Layer comps provide one-click flexibility in switching between different views of a multilayered image file. A layer comp is simply a definition of the settings in the Layers panel. Once you've defined a layer comp, you can change as many settings as you please in the Layers panel and then create another layer comp to preserve that configuration of layer properties. Then, by switching from one layer comp to another, you can quickly review the two designs. The beauty of layer comps becomes apparent when you want to demonstrate a number of possible design arrangements. When you've created a few layer comps, you can review the design variations without having to tediously select and deselect eye icons or change settings in the Layers panel.

Say, for example, that you are designing a brochure, and you're producing a version in English as well as in French. You might have the French text on one layer, and the English text on another in the same image file. To create two different layer comps, you would simply turn on visibility for the French layer and turn off visibility for the English layer, and then click the Create New Layer Comp button on the Layer Comps panel. Then you'd do the inverse—turn on visibility for the English layer and turn off visibility for the French layer, and click the Create New Layer Comp button— to create an English layer comp.

To view the different layer comps, click the Apply Layer Comp box for each comp in the Layer Comps panel in turn. With a little imagination, you can appreciate how much time this saves for more complex variations. Layer comps can be an especially valuable feature when the design is in flux or when you need to create multiple versions of the same image file.

# Extra credit

## Merging photos

Take the blinking and bad poses out of an otherwise great family portrait with the Auto-Align Layers feature.

1   Open FamilyPhoto.psd in your Lesson04 folder.

2   In the Layers panel, turn Layer 2 on and off to see the two similar photos. When both layers are visible, Layer 2 shows the tall man in the center blinking, and the two girls in the front looking away.

You'll align the two photos, and then use the Eraser tool to brush out the parts of the photo on Layer 2 that you want to improve.

3   Make both layers visible, and Shift-click to select them. Choose Edit > Auto-Align Layers; click OK to accept the default Auto position. Toggle the eye icon next to Layer 2 off and on to see that the layers are perfectly aligned.

Now for the fun part! You'll brush out the photo where you want to improve it.

4   Select the Eraser tool in the Tools panel, and pick a soft, 45-pixel brush in the options bar. Select Layer 2, and start brushing in the center of the blinking man's head to reveal the smiling face below.

5   Use the Eraser tool on the two girls looking away, revealing the image below, where they look into the camera.

You've created a natural family snapshot.

# Review questions

1 What is the advantage of using layers?

2 When you create a new layer, where does it appear in the Layers panel stack?

3 How can you make artwork on one layer appear in front of artwork on another layer?

4 How can you apply a layer style?

5 When you've completed your artwork, what can you do to minimize the file size without changing the quality or dimensions?


# Review answers

1 Layers let you move and edit different parts of an image as discrete objects. You can also hide individual layers as you work on other layers.

2 A new layer always appears immediately above the active layer.

3 You can make artwork on one layer appear in front of artwork on another layer by dragging layers up or down the stacking order in the Layers panel, or by using the Layer > Arrange subcommands—Bring To Front, Bring Forward, Send To Back, and Send Backward. However, you can't change the layer position of a background layer.

4 To apply a layer style, select the layer, and then click the Add A Layer Style button in the Layers panel, or choose Layer > Layer Style > [style].

5 To minimize file size, you can flatten the image, which merges all the layers onto a single background. It's a good idea to duplicate image files with layers intact before you flatten them, in case you have to make changes to a layer later.

# 5 CORRECTING AND ENHANCING DIGITAL PHOTOGRAPHS

## Lesson overview

In this lesson, you'll learn how to do the following:

- Process a proprietary camera raw image and save your adjustments.

- Make typical corrections to a digital photograph, including removing red eye and noise and bringing out shadow and highlights detail.

- Apply optical lens correction to an image.

- Align and blend two images to extend the depth of field.

- Adopt best practices for organizing, managing, and saving your images.

- Merge images of different exposures to create a high dynamic range (HDR) image.

 This lesson will take about 1½ hours to complete. Download the Lesson05 project files from the Lesson & Update Files tab on your Account page at www.peachpit.com, if you haven't already done so. As you work on this lesson, you'll preserve the start files. If you need to restore the start files, download them from your Account page.

PROJECT: ADVANCED PHOTO RETOUCHING

Whether you have a collection of digital images amassed for clients or projects, or a personal collection that you want to refine, archive, and preserve for posterity, Photoshop has an array of tools for importing, editing, and archiving digital photographs.

# Getting started

In this lesson, you'll edit several digital images using Photoshop and Adobe Camera Raw, which comes with Photoshop. You'll use a variety of techniques to touch up and improve the appearance of digital photographs. You'll start by viewing the before and after images in Adobe Bridge.

1 Start Photoshop, and then immediately hold down Ctrl+Alt+Shift (Windows) or Command+Option+Shift (Mac OS) to restore the default preferences. (See "Restoring default preferences" on page 4.)

2 When prompted, click Yes to delete the Adobe Photoshop Settings file.

● **Note:** If you haven't installed Bridge, you'll be prompted to do so when you choose Browse In Bridge. For more information, see page 3.

3 Choose File > Browse In Bridge to open Adobe Bridge.

4 In the Favorites panel in Bridge, click the Lessons folder. Then, in the Content panel, double-click the Lesson05 folder to open it.

5 Adjust the thumbnail slider, if necessary, so that you can see the thumbnail previews clearly. Then look at the 05A_Start.crw and 05A_End.psd files.

05A_Start.crw                    05A_End.psd

The original photograph of a Spanish-style church is a camera raw file, so it doesn't have the usual .psd file extension you've worked with so far in this book. It was shot with a Canon Digital Rebel camera and has the Canon proprietary .crw file extension. You'll process this proprietary camera raw image to make it brighter, sharper, and clearer, and then save it as a JPEG file for the web and as a PSD file so that you could work on it further in Photoshop.

**6** Compare the 05B_Start.nef and 05B_End.psd thumbnail previews.

05B_Start.nef        05B_End.psd

This time, the start file was taken with a Nikon camera, and the raw image has an .nef extension. You'll perform color corrections and image enhancements in Camera Raw and Photoshop to achieve the end result.

**7** Look at the 05C_Start.psd and 05C_End.psd thumbnail previews.

05C_Start.psd        05C_End.psd

You'll make several corrections to this portrait of a girl on the beach, including bringing out shadow and highlight detail, removing red eye, and sharpening the image.

**8** Look at the 05D_Start.psd and 05D_End.psd thumbnail previews.

05D_Start.psd                    05D_End.psd

The original image is distorted, with the columns appearing to be bowed. You'll correct the lens barrel distortion.

**9** Look at the 05E_Start.psd and 05E_End.psd thumbnail previews.

05E_Start.psd                    05E_End.psd

The first image has two layers. Depending on which layer is visible, either the glass in the foreground or the beach in the background is in focus. You'll extend the depth of field to make both clear. Then you'll add posts and apply an iris blur to the glass.

# About camera raw files

A *camera raw* file contains unprocessed picture data from a digital camera's image sensor. Many digital cameras can save images in camera raw format. The advantage of camera raw files is that they let the photographer—rather than the camera—interpret the image data and make adjustments and conversions. (In contrast, shooting JPEG images with your camera locks the camera's processing into the image.) Because the camera doesn't do any image processing when you shoot a camera raw photo, you can use Adobe Camera Raw to set the white balance, tonal range, contrast, color saturation, and sharpening. Think of camera raw files as photo negatives. You can go back and reprocess the file any time you like to achieve the results you want.

To create camera raw files, set your digital camera to save files in its own, possibly proprietary, raw file format. When you download the file from your camera, it has a file extension such as .nef (from Nikon) or .crw (from Canon). In Bridge or Photoshop, you can process camera raw files from a myriad of supported digital cameras from Canon, Kodak, Leica, Nikon, and other makers—and even process multiple images simultaneously. You can then export the proprietary camera raw files to DNG, JPEG, TIFF, or PSD file format.

**Note:** The Photoshop Raw format (.raw extension) is a file format for transferring images between applications and computer platforms. Don't confuse Photoshop Raw with camera raw file formats.

You can process camera raw files obtained from supported cameras, but you can also open TIFF and JPEG images in Camera Raw, which includes some editing features that aren't in Photoshop. However, you won't have the same flexibility with white balance and other settings if you're using a TIFF or JPEG image. Although Camera Raw can open and edit a camera raw image file, it cannot save an image in camera raw format.

# Processing files in Camera Raw

When you make adjustments to an image in Camera Raw, such as straightening or cropping the image, Photoshop and Bridge preserve the original file data. This way, you can edit the image as you desire, export the edited image, and keep the original intact for future use or other adjustments.

## Opening images in Camera Raw

You can open Camera Raw from either Bridge or Photoshop, and you can apply the same edits to multiple files simultaneously. This is especially useful if you're working with images that were all shot in the same environment, and which therefore need the same lighting and other adjustments.

Camera Raw provides extensive controls for adjusting white balance, exposure, contrast, sharpness, tone curves, and much more. In this exercise, you'll edit one image and then apply the settings to similar images.

1   In Bridge, open the Lessons/Lesson05/Mission folder, which contains three shots of the Spanish church you previewed earlier.

2   Shift-click to select all of the images—Mission01.crw, Mission02.crw, and Mission03.crw—and then choose File > Open In Camera Raw.

A. Filmstrip
B. Toggle Filmstrip
C. Toolbar
D. Toggle Preview
E. RGB values
F. Image adjustment tabs
G. Histogram
H. Camera Raw Settings menu
I. Zoom levels
J. Click to display workflow options
K. Multi-image navigation controls
L. Adjustment sliders

The Camera Raw dialog box displays a large preview of the first image, and a filmstrip down the left side displays all open images. The histogram in the upper right corner shows the tonal range of the selected image; the workflow options link below the preview window displays the selected image's color space, bit depth, size, and resolution. Tools along the top of the dialog box let you zoom, pan, straighten, and make other adjustments to the image. Tabbed panels on the right side of the dialog box give you more nuanced options for adjusting the image: You can correct the white balance, adjust the tone, sharpen the image, remove noise, adjust color, and make other changes. You can also save settings as a preset, and then apply them later.

For the best results using Camera Raw, plan your workflow to move from left to right and top to bottom. That is, you'll often want to use the tools across the top first, and then move through the panels in order, making changes as necessary.

You will explore these controls now as you edit the first image file.

3   Click each thumbnail in the filmstrip to preview all the images before you begin. Or, you can click the Forward button under the main preview window to cycle through them. When you've seen all three, select the Mission01.crw image again.

4   Make sure that Preview is selected at the top of the dialog box, so that you can see the effect of the adjustments you're about to make.

## Adjusting white balance

An image's white balance reflects the lighting conditions under which it was captured. A digital camera records the white balance at the time of exposure; this is the value that initially appears in the Camera Raw dialog box image preview.

White balance comprises two components. The first is *temperature*, which is measured in kelvins and determines the level of "coolness" or "warmness" of the image—that is, its cool blue-green tones or warm yellow-red tones. The second component is *tint*, which compensates for magenta or green color casts in the image.

Depending on the settings you're using on your camera and the environment in which you're shooting (for example, if there's glare or uneven lighting), you may want to adjust the white balance for the image. If you plan to modify the white balance, make that the first thing you do, as it will affect all other changes in the image.

1   If the Basic panel isn't already displayed on the right side of the dialog box, click the Basic button (◉) to open it.

By default, As Shot is selected in the White Balance menu. Camera Raw applies the white balance settings that were in your camera at the time of exposure. Camera Raw includes several White Balance presets, which you can use as a starting point to see different lighting effects.

**2**  Choose Cloudy from the White Balance menu.

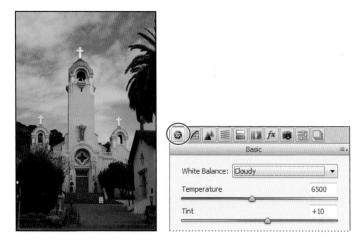

Camera Raw adjusts the temperature and tint for a cloudy day. Sometimes a preset does the trick. In this case, though, there's still a blue cast to the image. You'll adjust the white balance manually.

**3**  Select the White Balance tool (🖊) at the top of the Camera Raw dialog box.

To set an accurate white balance, select an object that should be white or gray. Camera Raw uses that information to determine the color of the light in which the scene was shot, and then adjusts for scene lighting automatically.

**4**  Click the white clouds in the image. The lighting of the image changes.

**5**  Click a different area of the clouds. The lighting shifts.

You can use the White Balance tool to find the best lighting for the scene quickly and easily. Clicking different areas changes the lighting without making any permanent changes to the file, so you can experiment freely.

**6**  Click the clouds directly to the left of the steeple. This selection removes most of the color casts and results in realistic lighting.

**7**  Move the Tint slider to **-22** to intensify the greens.

▶ **Tip:** To undo the settings, press Ctrl+Z (Windows) or Command+Z (Mac OS). To compare the changes you've made in the current panel with the original image, deselect Preview. Select Preview again to see the modified image.

## Making tonal adjustments in Camera Raw

Other sliders in the Basic panel affect exposure, brightness, contrast, and saturation in the image. Except for Contrast, moving a slider to the right lightens the affected areas of the image, and moving it to the left darkens those areas. Exposure essentially defines the *white point*, or the lightest point of the image, so that Camera Raw adjusts everything else accordingly. Conversely, the Blacks slider sets the *black point*, or the darkest point in the image. The Highlights and Shadows sliders increase detail in the highlights and the shadows, respectively.

The Contrast slider adjusts the contrast. For more nuanced contrast adjustments, you can use the Clarity slider, which adds depth to an image by increasing local contrast, especially on the midtones.

▶ **Tip:** For the best effect, increase the Clarity slider until you see halos near the edge details, and then reduce the setting slightly.

The Saturation slider adjusts the saturation of all colors in the image equally. The Vibrance slider, on the other hand, has a greater effect on undersaturated colors. You can use it to bring life to a background without oversaturating any skin tones in the image, for example.

You can use the Auto option to let Camera Raw attempt to correct the image tone, or you can select your own settings.

1   Click Auto in the Basic panel.

Camera Raw increases the exposure and changes several other settings. You could use this as a starting point. However, in this exercise, you'll return to the default settings and adjust them yourself.

2   Click Default in the Basic panel.

3   Change the sliders as follows:

- Exposure: **+0.20**
- Contrast: **+18**
- Highlights: **+8**
- Shadows: **+63**
- Whites: **+12**
- Blacks: **-14**
- Clarity: **+3**
- Vibrance: **+4**
- Saturation: **+1**

These settings help pump up the midtones of the image, so that it looks bolder and more dimensional without being oversaturated.

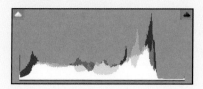

## About the Camera Raw histogram

The histogram in the upper right corner of the Camera Raw dialog box simultaneously shows the red, green, and blue channels of the selected image, and updates interactively as you adjust any settings. Also, as you move any tool over the preview image, the RGB values for the area under the cursor appear below the histogram.

## Applying sharpening

▶ **Tip:** If you want to make an adjustment to only a specific part of an image, use the Adjustment Brush tool or the Graduated Filter tool. With the Adjustment Brush tool, you can apply Exposure, Highlights, Clarity, and other adjustments by "painting" them onto the photo. With the Graduated Filter tool, you can apply the same types of adjustments gradually across a region of a photo.

Photoshop offers several sharpening filters, but when you need to sharpen an entire image, Camera Raw provides the best control. The sharpening controls are in the Detail panel. To see the effect of sharpening in the preview panel, you must view the image at 100% or greater.

1   Double-click the Zoom tool (🔍) on the left side of the toolbar to zoom in to 100%. Then select the Hand tool (✋), and pan the image to see the cross at the top of the mission tower.

2   Click the Detail tab (◢) to open the Detail panel.

The Amount slider determines how much sharpening Camera Raw applies. Typically, you'll want to exaggerate the amount of sharpening first, and then adjust it after you've set the other sliders.

3   Move the Amount slider to **100**.

The Radius slider determines the pixel area Camera Raw analyzes as it sharpens the image. For most images, you'll get the best results if you keep the radius low, even below one pixel. A larger radius can begin to cause an unnatural look, almost like a watercolor.

4   Move the Radius slider to **0.9**.

The Detail slider determines how much detail you'll see. Even when this slider is set to 0, Camera Raw performs some sharpening. Typically, you'll want to keep the Detail setting relatively low.

**5** Move the Detail slider to **25**, if it isn't already there.

The Masking slider determines which parts of the image Camera Raw sharpens. When the Masking value is high, Camera Raw sharpens only those parts of the image that have strong edges.

**6** Move the Masking slider to **61**.

After you've adjusted the Radius, Detail, and Masking sliders, you can lower the Amount slider to finalize the sharpening.

**7** Decrease the Amount slider to **70**.

▶ **Tip:** Press Alt (Windows) or Option (Mac OS) as you move the Masking slider to see what Camera Raw will sharpen.

Sharpening the image gives stronger definition to the details and edges. The Masking slider lets you target the sharpening effect to the lines in the image, so that artifacts don't appear in unfocused or background areas.

When you make adjustments in Camera Raw, the original file data is preserved. Your adjustment settings for the image are stored either in the Camera Raw database file or in "sidecar" XMP files that accompany the original image file in the same folder. These XMP files retain the adjustments you made in Camera Raw when you move the image file to a storage medium or another computer.

**Note:** If you zoom out, the image won't appear to be sharpened. You can preview sharpening effects only at zoom levels of 100% or greater.

## Synchronizing settings across images

All three of the mission images were shot at the same time under the same lighting conditions. Now that you've made the first one look stunning, you can automatically apply the same settings to the other two images. You do this using the Synchronize command.

1  In the upper left corner of the Camera Raw dialog box, click Select All to select all of the images in the filmstrip.

2  Click the Synchronize button.

The Synchronize dialog box appears, listing all the settings you can apply to the images. By default, all options except Crop, Spot Removal, and Local Adjustments are selected. You can accept the default for this project, even though you didn't change all the settings.

3  Click OK in the Synchronize dialog box.

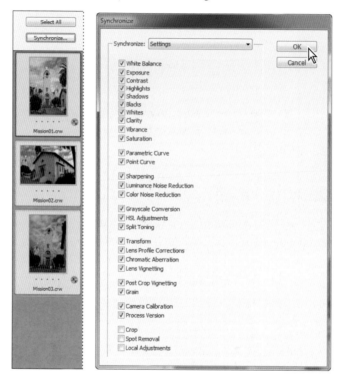

When you synchronize the settings across all of the selected images, the thumbnails update to reflect the changes you made. To preview the images, click each thumbnail in the filmstrip.

## Saving Camera Raw changes

You can save your changes in different ways for different purposes. First, you'll save the images with adjustments as low-resolution JPEG files that you can share on the web. Then, you'll save one image, Mission01, as a Photoshop file that you can open as a Smart Object in Photoshop. When you open an image as a Smart Object in Photoshop, you can return to Camera Raw at any time to make further adjustments.

1   Click Select All in the Camera Raw dialog box to select all three images.

2   Click Save Images in the lower left corner.

3   In the Save Options dialog box, do the following:

   • Choose Save In Same Location from the Destination menu.

   • In the File Naming area, leave "Document Name" in the first box.

   • Choose JPEG from the Format menu.

These settings will save your corrected images as smaller, downsampled JPEG files, which you can share with colleagues on the web. Your files will be named Mission01.jpg, Mission02.jpg, and Mission03.jpg.

4   Click Save.

**Note:** Before sharing these images on the web, you would probably want to open them in Photoshop and resize them to 640x480 pixels. They are currently much larger, and most viewers would need to scroll to see the full-size images.

Bridge returns you to the Camera Raw dialog box, and indicates how many images have been processed until all the images have been saved. The CRW thumbnails still appear in the Camera Raw dialog box. In Bridge, however, you now also have JPEG versions as well as the original CRW image files, which you can continue to edit or leave for another time.

Now, you'll open a copy of the Mission01 image in Photoshop.

5   Select the Mission01.crw image thumbnail in the filmstrip in the Camera Raw dialog box. Then press the Shift key, and click Open Object at the bottom of the dialog box.

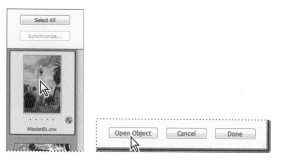

▶ **Tip:** To make the Open Object button the default, click the workflow options link (in blue) below the preview window, select Open In Photoshop As Smart Objects, and click OK.

The Open Object button opens the image as a Smart Object in Photoshop; you can double-click the Smart Object thumbnail in the Layers panel to return to Camera Raw to continue making adjustments at any time. If you click Open Image, the image opens as a standard Photoshop image. Pressing the Shift key changes the Open Image button to the Open Object button.

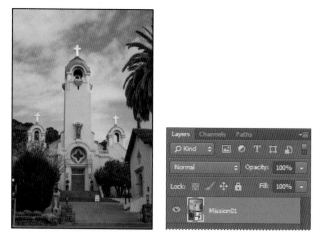

6   In Photoshop, choose File > Save As. In the Save As dialog box, choose Photoshop for the Format, rename the file **Mission_Final.psd**, navigate to the Lesson05 folder, and click Save. Click OK if the Photoshop Format Options dialog box appears. Then close the file.

# About saving files in Camera Raw

Every camera model saves raw images in a unique format, but Adobe Camera Raw can process many raw file formats. Camera Raw processes the raw files with default image settings based on built-in camera profiles for supported cameras and the EXIF data.

You can save the proprietary files in DNG format (the format saved by Adobe Camera Raw), JPEG, TIFF, and PSD. All of these formats can be used to save RGB and CMYK continuous-tone, bitmapped images, and all of them except DNG are also available in the Photoshop Save and Save As dialog boxes.

- The **DNG (Adobe Digital Negative)** format contains raw image data from a digital camera and metadata that defines what the image data means. DNG is meant to be an industry-wide standard format for raw image data, helping photographers manage the variety of proprietary raw formats and providing a compatible archival format. (You can save this format only from the Camera Raw dialog box.)

- The **JPEG (Joint Photographic Experts Group)** file format is commonly used to display photographs and other continuous-tone RGB images on the web. Higher-resolution JPEG files may be used for other purposes, including high-quality printing. JPEG format retains all color information in an image, but compresses file size by selectively discarding data. The greater the compression, the lower the image quality.

- **TIFF (Tagged Image File Format)** is used to exchange files between applications and computer platforms. TIFF is a flexible format supported by virtually all paint, image-editing, and page layout applications. Also, virtually all desktop scanners can produce TIFF images.

- **PSD format** is the Photoshop native file format. Because of the tight integration between Adobe products, other Adobe applications such as Adobe Illustrator and Adobe InDesign can directly import PSD files and preserve many Photoshop features.

Once you open a file in Photoshop, you can save it in many different formats, including Large Document Format (PSB), Cineon, Photoshop Raw, or PNG. Not to be confused with camera raw file formats, the Photoshop Raw format (RAW) is a file format for transferring images between applications and computer platforms.

For more information about file formats in Camera Raw and Photoshop, see Photoshop Help.

# Applying advanced color correction

You'll use Levels, the Healing Brush tool, and other Photoshop features to enhance the image of this model.

## Adjust the white balance in Camera Raw

▶ **Tip:** In addition to opening files in Camera Raw when you start the editing process, you can apply Camera Raw settings as a filter to any file in Photoshop. Choose Filter > Camera Raw Filter, adjust the settings, and click OK.

The original image of the bride has a slight color cast. You'll start your color corrections in Camera Raw, setting the white balance and adjusting the overall tone of the image.

1  In Bridge, navigate to the Lesson05 folder. Select the 05B_Start.nef file, and choose File > Open In Camera Raw.

2  In Camera Raw, select the White Balance tool (🖉), and then click a white area in the model's dress to adjust the temperature and remove a green color cast.

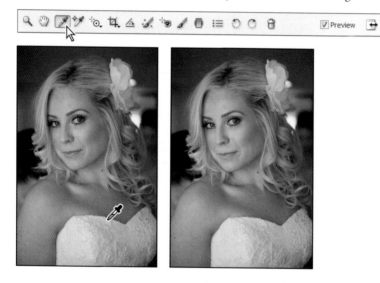

3  Adjust other sliders in the Basic panel to brighten and intensify the image:

   • Increase Exposure at **0.30**.

   • Increase Contrast to **15**.

   • Increase Clarity to **+8**.

**4** Press the Shift key, and click Open Object.

The image opens in Photoshop as a Smart Object.

## Adjusting levels

The tonal range of an image represents the amount of contrast, or detail, in the image and is determined by the image's distribution of pixels, ranging from the darkest pixels (black) to the lightest pixels (white). You'll use a Levels adjustment layer to fine-tune the tonal range in this image.

**1** In Photoshop, choose File > Save As. Name the file **Model_final.psd**, and click Save. Click OK if you see the Photoshop Format Options dialog box.

**2** Click the Levels button in the Adjustments panel.

Photoshop adds a Levels adjustment layer to the Layers panel. The Levels controls and a histogram appear in the Properties panel. The histogram displays the range of dark and light values in the image. The left (black) triangle represents the shadows; the right (white) triangle represents the highlights; and the middle (gray) triangle represents the midtones, or gamma. Unless you're aiming for a special effect, the ideal histogram has its black point at the beginning of the data and its white point at the end of the data, and the middle portion has fairly uniform peaks and valleys, representing adequate pixel data in the midtones.

**3** Click the Calculate A More Accurate Histogram button (![icon]) on the left side of the histogram. Photoshop replaces the histogram.

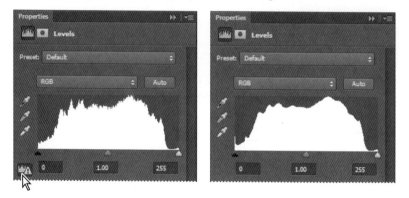

There is a small bump on the far right side of the histogram, representing the current white point, but the bulk of the data ends further to the left. You want to set the white point to match the end of that data.

**4** Drag the right (white) triangle toward the left to the point where the histogram indicates the lightest colors begin.

As you drag, the third Input Levels value (beneath the histogram graph) changes, and so does the image itself.

**5** Pull the middle (gray) triangle a little bit to the right to slightly darken the midtones. We moved it to a value of .90.

## Editing the saturation in Camera Raw

The Levels adjustments helped significantly, but our bride looks a little sunburned. You'll adjust the saturation in Camera Raw to even out her skin tone.

1  Double-click the 05B_Start layer thumbnail to open the Smart Object in Camera Raw.

2  Click the HSL/Grayscale button (≣) to display that panel.

3  Click the Saturation tab.

4  Move the following sliders to reduce the amount of red in the skin:

  • Reduce Reds to -**2**.

  • Reduce Oranges to -**10**.

  • Reduce Magentas to  -**3**.

5  Click OK to return to Photoshop.

## Using the Healing Brush tools to remove blemishes

Now you're ready to give the model's face some focused attention. You'll use the Healing Brush and Spot Healing Brush tools to heal blemishes, smooth the skin, remove red veins from the eyes, and even hide the nose jewelry.

1  In the Layers panel, select the 05B_Start layer. Then, choose Duplicate Layer from the Layers panel menu. Name the new layer **Corrections**, and click OK.

Working on a duplicate layer preserves the original pixels so you can make changes later. You can't make changes using the Healing Brush tools on a Smart Object, so first you'll rasterize the layer.

2  Choose Layer > Smart Objects > Rasterize.

3  Zoom in on the model's face so that you can see it clearly.

4  Select the Spot Healing Brush tool (✐).

5  In the options bar, select the following settings:

•  Brush size: **35** px

•  Mode: Normal

•  Type: Content-Aware

6  With the Spot Healing Brush tool, brush out the nose jewelry. A single click may be enough.

Because you've selected Content-Aware in the options bar, the Spot Healing Brush tool replaces the nose stud with skin that is similar to that around it.

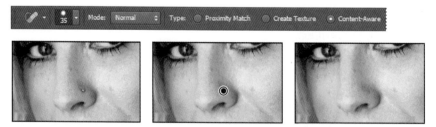

7  Paint over fine lines around the eyes and mouth. You can also brush away freckles and moles on her face, neck, arms, and chest. Experiment with simply clicking, using very short strokes, and creating longer brush strokes. You can also experiment with different settings. For example, to soften the lines around the mouth, we selected Proximity Match in the options bar and the Lighten blending mode. Remove obtrusive or distracting lines and blemishes, but leave enough that the face retains its character.

The Healing Brush tool may be a better option for larger blemishes. With the Healing Brush tool, you have more control over the pixels Photoshop samples.

8 Select the Healing Brush tool (✐), hidden under the Spot Healing Brush tool (✐). Select a brush with a size of **45** pixels and a hardness of **100**%.

9 Alt-click (Windows) or Option-click (Mac OS) an area on her cheek to create the sampling source.

10 Brush over the large mole on her cheek to replace it with the color you sampled. You'll smooth out the texture later.

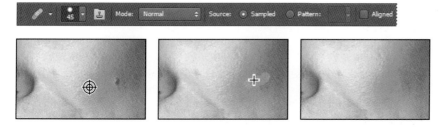

11 Use the Healing Brush tool to heal any larger blemishes that remain.

12 Choose File > Save to save your work so far.

## Enhancing an image using the Dodge and Sponge tools

You'll use the Sponge and Dodge tools to brighten the eyes and lips.

1 Select the Sponge tool (◉), hidden under the Dodge tool (🔍). In the options bar, make sure Vibrance is selected, and then select the following settings:

• Brush size: **35** px

• Brush hardness: **0**%

• Mode: Saturate

• Flow: **50**%

2 Move the Sponge tool over the irises in the eyes to increase their saturation.

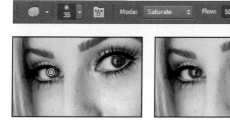

*Steps continue on page 138*

*A photographer for more than 25 years, Jay Graham began his career designing and building custom homes. Today, Graham has clients in the advertising, architectural, editorial, and travel industries.*

*See Jay Graham's portfolio on the web at jaygraham.com.*

# Pro photo workflow

## Good habits make all the difference

A sensible workflow and good work habits will keep you enthused about digital photography, help your images shine—and save you from the night terrors of losing work you never backed up. Here's an outline of the basic workflow for digital images from a professional photographer with more than 25 years' experience. To help you get the most from the images you shoot, Jay Graham offers guidelines for setting up your camera, creating a basic color workflow, selecting file formats, organizing images, and showing off your work.

*Graham uses Adobe Photoshop Lightroom® to organize thousands of images.*

*"The biggest complaint from people is they've lost their image. Where is it? What does it look like?" says Graham. "So naming is important."*

### Start out right by setting up your camera preferences

If your camera has the option, it's generally best to shoot in its camera raw file format, which captures all the image information you need. With one camera raw photo, says Graham, "You can go from daylight to an indoor tungsten image without degradation" when it's reproduced. If it makes more sense to shoot in JPEG for your project, use fine compression and high resolution.

### Start with the best material

Get all the data when you capture—at fine compression and high resolution. You can't go back later.

### Organize your files

Name and catalogue your images as soon after downloading them as possible. "If the camera names files, eventually it resets and produces multiple files with the same name," says Graham. Use Adobe Photoshop Lightroom to rename, rank, and add metadata to the photos you plan to keep; cull those you don't.

Graham names his files by date (and possibly subject). He would store a series of photos taken Dec. 12, 2011 at Stinson Beach in a folder named "20111212_Stinson_01"; within the folder, he names each image incrementally, and each image has a unique filename. "That way, it lines up on the hard drive real easily," he says. Follow Windows naming conventions to keep filenames usable on non-Macintosh platforms (32 characters maximum; only numbers, letters, underscores, and hyphens).

### Convert raw images to Adobe Camera Raw

It may be best to convert all your camera raw images to the DNG format. Unlike many cameras' proprietary raw formats, this open-source format can be read by any device.

### Keep a master image

Save your master in PSD, TIFF, or DNG format, not JPEG. Each time a JPEG is re-edited and saved, compression is reapplied, and the image quality degrades.

### Show off to clients and friends

When you prepare your work for delivery, choose the appropriate color file for the destination. Convert the image to that profile, rather than assigning the profile. sRGB is generally best for viewing electronically or for printing from most online printing services. Adobe 1998 or Colormatch are the best profiles to use for RGB images destined for traditionally printed material such as brochures. Adobe 1998 or ProPhoto RGB are best for printing with inkjet printers. Use 72 dpi for electronic viewing and 180 dpi or higher for printing.

### Back up your images

You've devoted a lot of time and effort to your images: don't lose them. Because the lifespan of CDs and DVDs is uncertain, it's best to back up to an external hard drive (or drives!), ideally set to back up automatically. "The question is not if your [internal] hard drive is going to crash," says Graham, reciting a common adage. "It's when."

**3** Change the brush size to **70** px, and the flow to **10%**. Then brush the Sponge tool over the lips to saturate them.

You can use the Sponge tool to desaturate color, too. You'll reduce the red in the corner of the eye.

**4** Change the brush size to **45** px, and the flow to **50%**. Then choose Desaturate from the Mode menu in the options bar.

**5** Brush over the corner of the eye to reduce the red.

**6** Select the Dodge tool (🔍), hidden beneath the Sponge tool.

**7** In the options bar, change the brush size to **60** px and the Exposure to **10%**. Choose Highlights in the Range menu.

**8** Brush the Dodge tool over the eyes—the whites and the irises—to brighten them.

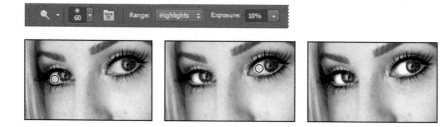

**9** With the Dodge tool still selected, select Shadows from the Range menu in the options bar.

**10** Use the Dodge tool to lighten the shadow area above the eyes and the areas around the irises to bring out the color.

## Adjusting skin tones

In Photoshop, you can select a color range that targets skin tones so that it's easier to adjust the levels and color tone of skin without affecting the entire image. The skin tone color range selects other areas of the image with a similar color, but if you're making slight adjustments, this is usually acceptable.

**1** Choose Select > Color Range.

**2** In the Color Range dialog box, choose Skin Tones from the Select menu.

The preview shows that much of the image has been selected.

**3** Select Detect Faces.

The preview in the selection changes. Now, the face, hair highlights, and lighter areas of the dress are selected.

**4** Decrease the Fuzziness slider to **10** to refine the selection. Then click OK.

The selection appears on the image itself as animaged dotted lines (sometimes called *marching ants.* You'll apply a Curves adjustment layer to the selection to reduce the overall red in the skin tone of the image.

**5** Click the Curves icon in the Adjustments panel.

Photoshop adds a Curves adjustment layer above the Corrections layer.

6   Choose Red from the color channel menu in the Properties panel. Then click in the middle of the graph, and pull the curve down very slightly. The selected areas become less red. Be careful not to pull the curve down too far, or a green cast will appear. You can see the difference you've made by clicking the Toggle Layer Visibility button.

Because you selected the skin tones before applying the Curves adjustment layer, the skin color shifts but the background is unchanged. The adjustment affects slightly more of the image than the skin itself, but the effect blends well and is subtle.

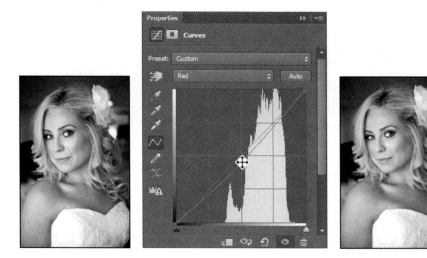

## Applying surface blur

You're almost done with the model. As a finishing touch, you'll apply the Surface Blur filter to give her a smooth appearance.

1   Select the Corrections layer, and choose Layer > Duplicate Layer. Name the layer **Surface Blur**, and click OK in the Duplicate Layer dialog box.

2   With the Surface Blur layer selected, choose Filter > Blur > Surface Blur.

3   In the Surface Blur dialog box, leave the Radius at 5 pixels, and move the Threshold to **10** levels. Then click OK.

The Surface Blur filter has left the model looking a little glassy. You'll reduce its effect by reducing its opacity.

**4** With the Surface Blur layer selected, change the Opacity to **40%** in the Layers panel.

She looks more realistic now, but you can target the surface blur more precisely using the Eraser tool.

**5** Select the Eraser tool (![eraser icon]). In the options bar, select a brush between **10** and **50** pixels, with **10%** hardness. Set the opacity to **90%**.

**6** Brush over the eyes, eyebrows, the defining lines of the nose, and the detail in the dress. You're erasing part of the blurred layer to let the sharper layer below show through in these areas.

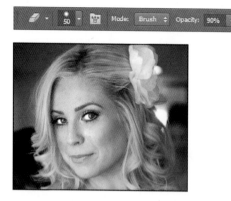

**7** Zoom out so you can see the entire image.

**8** Save your work.

**9** Choose Layer > Flatten Image to flatten the layers and reduce the image size.

**10** Save the image again, and then close it.

# Correcting digital photographs in Photoshop

As you've seen, Photoshop provides many features to help you easily improve the quality of digital photographs. These include the ability to bring out details in the shadow and highlight areas of an image, gracefully remove red eye, reduce unwanted noise, and sharpen targeted areas of an image. To explore these capabilities, you will edit a different digital image now: a portrait of a girl on the beach.

## Adjusting shadows and highlights

To bring out the detail in dark or light areas of an image, you can use the Shadows/Highlights command. Shadows/Highlights adjustments work best when the subject of the image is silhouetted against strong backlighting or is washed out because the camera flash was too close. You can also use the adjustments to pull details from the shadows in an image that is otherwise well-lit.

**1** Choose File > Open, and navigate to the Lesson05 folder. Then double-click the 05C_Start.psd image to open it in Photoshop.

**2** Choose File > Save As. Name the file **05C_Working.psd**, and click Save.

**3** Choose Image > Adjustments > Shadows/Highlights.

Photoshop automatically applies default settings to the image, lightening the background. You'll customize the settings to bring out more detail in both the shadows and the highlights, and to enhance the sunset.

**4** In the Shadows/Highlights dialog box, select Show More Options to expand the dialog box. Then do the following:

- In the Shadows area, set Amount to **50**%, Tonal Width to **50**%, and Radius to **38** px.

- In the Highlights area, set Amount to **14**%, Tonal Width to **46**%, and Radius to **43** px.

- In the Adjustments area, drag the Color Correction slider to **+5**, set the Midtone Contrast slider to **+22**, and leave the Black Clip and White Clip settings at their defaults.

**5** Click OK to accept your changes.

**6** Choose File > Save to save your work so far.

# Camera Shake Reduction

Even with a steady hand, unintended camera motion can occur with slow shutter speeds or long focal lengths. The Camera Shake Reduction filter reduces the resulting camera shake, giving you a sharper image.

*Before applying the Camera Shake Reduction filter*

You'll get the best results if you apply the filter to a particular part of an image, rather than the entire image. It can be especially useful if text has become illegible due to camera shake.

To use the Camera Shake Reduction filter, open the image, and choose Filter > Sharpen > Shake Reduction. The filter automatically analyzes the image, selects a region of interest, and corrects the blur. Use the Detail loupe to examine the preview. That may be all you need to do. If so, click OK to close the Shake Reduction dialog box and apply the filter.

*After applying the Camera Shake Reduction filter*

If you want to make further adjustments, expand the Advanced area of the dialog box. You can change the region of interest, or adjust its size; view and resize the blur trace, which is the shape and size of the camera shake that Photoshop identified; and adjust the Smoothing and Artifact Suppression values to correct noise and artifacts. You can even save the blur trace to use the settings on another image. For full information about the Camera Shake Reduction filter, see Photoshop Help.

## Correcting red eye

*Red eye* occurs when the retina of a subject's eye is reflected by the camera flash. It commonly occurs in photographs of a subject in a darkened room, because the subject's irises are wide open. Red eye is easy to fix in Photoshop. In this exercise, you will remove the red eye from the girl's eyes in the portrait.

1   Select the Zoom tool (🔍), and then drag a marquee around the girl's eyes to zoom in to them. You may need to deselect Scrubby Zoom in the options bar to drag a marquee.

2   Select the Red Eye tool (✚⊙), hidden under the Healing Brush tool (✐).

3   In the options bar, leave Pupil Size set to 50%, but change Darken Amount to **75%**.

The Darken Amount specifies how dark the pupil should be.

4   Click on the red area in the girl's left eye. The red reflection disappears.

5   Click on the red area in the girl's right eye to remove that reflection, as well.

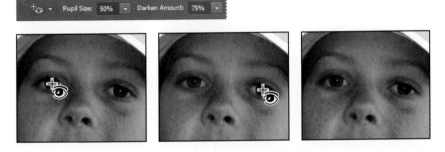

6   Double-click the Zoom tool to zoom out to 100%.

7   Choose File > Save to save your work so far.

## Reducing noise

Random, extraneous pixels that aren't part of the image detail are called *noise*. Noise can result from using a high ISO setting on a digital camera, from underexposure, or from shooting in darkness with a long shutter speed. Scanned images may contain noise that results from the scanning sensor, or from a grain pattern from the scanned film.

There are two types of image noise: *luminance noise*, which is grayscale data that makes an image look grainy or patchy; and *color noise*, which appears as colored artifacts in the image. The Reduce Noise filter can address both types of noise in individual color channels while preserving edge detail, and can also correct JPEG compression artifacts.

First, zoom in to the girl's face to get a good look at the noise in this image.

1  Using the Zoom tool (🔍), click in the center of the face and zoom in to about 300%.

The noise in this image is speckled and rough, with uneven graininess in the skin. Using the Reduce Noise filter, you can smooth out this area.

2  Choose Filter > Noise > Reduce Noise, and then zoom in to see the noise clearly in the preview window.

3  In the Reduce Noise dialog box, do the following:

- Increase Strength to **8**. (Strength controls the amount of luminance noise.)

- Decrease Preserve Details to **30**%.

- Increase Reduce Color Noise to **80**%.

- Move Sharpen Details to **30**%.

● **Note:** To correct noise in individual channels of the image, select Advanced, and click the Per Channel tab to adjust the settings in each channel.

You don't need to select Remove JPEG Artifact, because this image is not a JPEG and has no JPEG artifacts.

4 Drag to position the face in the preview area. Click and hold the mouse button down in the preview area to see the "before" image, and release the mouse button to see the corrected result.

5 Click OK to apply your changes and to close the Reduce Noise dialog box, and then double-click the Zoom tool to return to 100%.

6 Choose File > Save to save your work, and then close the file.

## Correcting image distortion

The Lens Correction filter fixes common camera lens flaws, such as barrel and pincushion distortion, chromatic aberration, and vignetting. *Barrel distortion* is a lens defect that causes straight lines to bow out toward the edges of the image. *Pincushion distortion* is the opposite effect, causing straight lines to bend inward. *Chromatic aberration* appears as a color fringe along the edges of image objects. *Vignetting* occurs when the edges of an image, especially the corners, are darker than the center.

Some lenses exhibit these defects depending on the focal length or the f-stop used. The Lens Correction filter can apply settings based on the camera, lens, and focal length that were used to make the image. The filter can also rotate an image or fix image perspective caused by tilting a camera vertically or horizontally. The filter's image grid makes it easier and more accurate to make these adjustments than using the Transform command.

In this exercise, you will adjust the lens distortion in an image of a Greek temple.

1 Choose File > Open. Navigate to the Lesson05 folder, and then double-click the 05D_Start.psd image to open it in Photoshop.

The columns in this image bend toward the camera and appear to be warped. This photo was shot at a range that was too close with a wide-angle lens.

2 Choose File > Save As. In the Save As dialog box, name the file **Columns_Final.psd**, and save it in the Lesson05 folder. Click OK if the Photoshop Format Options dialog box appears.

3 Choose Filter > Lens Correction. The Lens Correction dialog box opens.

**4**   Select Show Grid at the bottom of the dialog box, if it's not already selected.

An alignment grid overlays the image, next to options for removing distortion, correcting chromatic aberration, removing vignettes, and transforming perspective.

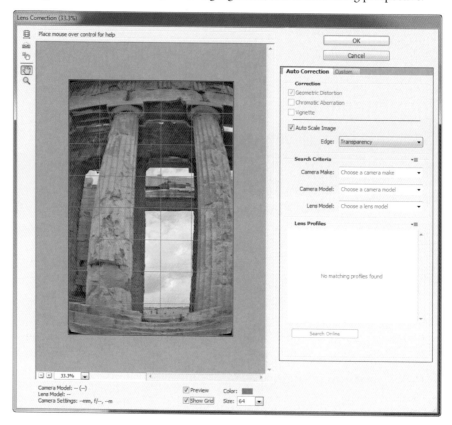

The Lens Correction dialog box includes auto-correction options. You'll adjust one setting in the Auto Correction tab and then customize the settings.

**5**   In the Correction area of the Auto Correction tab, make sure Auto Scale Image is selected, and that Transparency is selected from the Edge menu.

**6**   Select the Custom tab.

**7**   In the Custom tab, drag the Remove Distortion slider to about **+52.00** to remove the barrel distortion in the image. Alternatively, you could select the Remove Distortion tool (⊞) and drag in the image preview area until the columns are straight.

The adjustment causes the image borders to bow inward. However, because you selected Auto Scale Image, the Lens Correction filter automatically scales the image to adjust the borders.

**Tip:** Watch the alignment grid as you make these changes so that you can see when the vertical columns are straightened in the image.

8  Click OK to apply your changes and close the Lens Correction dialog box.

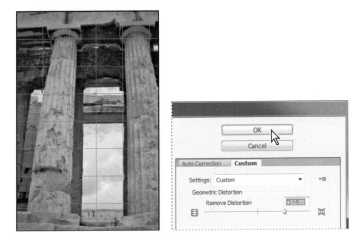

The curving distortion caused by the wide-angle lens and low shooting angle are eliminated.

9  (Optional) To see the effect of your change in the main image window, press Ctrl+Z (Windows) or Command+Z (Mac OS) twice to undo and redo the filter.

10 Choose File > Save to save your changes, click OK if the Photoshop Format Options dialog box appears, and then close the image.

# Adding depth of field

When you're shooting a photo, you often have to choose to focus either the background or the foreground. If you want the entire image to be in focus, take two photos—one with the background in focus and one with the foreground in focus—and then merge the two in Photoshop.

Because you'll need to align the images exactly, it's helpful to use a tripod to keep the camera steady. Even with a handheld camera, though, you can get some amazing results. You'll add depth of field to an image of a wine glass in front of a beach.

1  In Photoshop, choose File > Open. Navigate to the Lessons/Lesson05 folder, and double-click the 05E_Start.psd file to open it.

2  Choose File > Save As. Name the file **Glass_Final.psd**, and save it in the Lesson05 folder. Click OK if the Photoshop Format Options dialog box appears.

3  In the Layers panel, hide the Beach layer, so that only the Glass layer is visible. The glass is in focus, but the background is blurred. Then, show the Beach layer and hide the Glass layer. Now the beach is in focus, but the glass is blurred.

You'll merge the layers, using the part of each layer that is in focus. First, you need to align the layers.

**4** Show both layers again, and then Shift-click to select both of them.

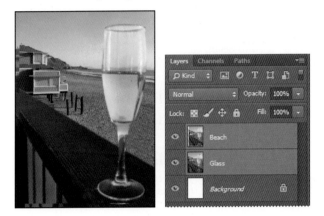

**5** Choose Edit > Auto-Align Layers.

Because these images were shot from the same angle, Auto will work just fine.

**6** Select Auto, if it isn't already selected. Make sure neither Vignette Removal nor Geometric Distortion is selected. Then click OK to align the layers.

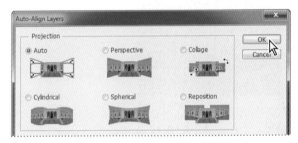

Now that the layers are perfectly aligned, you're ready to blend them.

**7** Make sure both layers are still selected in the Layers panel. Then choose Edit > Auto-Blend Layers.

**8**   Select Stack Images and Seamless Tones And Colors, and then click OK.

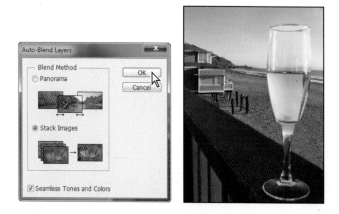

Both the wine glass and the beach behind it are in focus. Now, you'll merge the layers to make it easier to make other adjustments.

**9**   Choose Layer > Merge Visible.

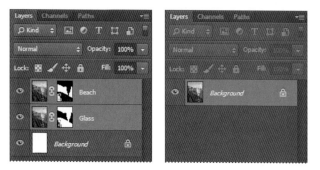

## Extending objects with the Content-Aware Move tool

You'll use the Content-Aware Move tool to add a few more posts to the beach, so that they echo the deck rails, creating a smoother rhythm for the composition.

**1**   Select the Content-Aware Move tool (✖), which is hidden beneath the Red Eye Removal tool (⁺◦).

2   In the options bar, choose Extend from the Mode menu and Strict from the Adaptation menu.

3   Draw a marquee around the two pier posts on the end of the row, including some of the sand where their shadows fall.

4   Drag the selection slightly down and to the right of the original posts to continue the row.

When you release the mouse, Photoshop adds two new posts and blends them in with the scene neatly.

5   Choose Select > Deselect.

## Adding interactive blur

Interactive blurs let you customize the blur as you preview it on your image. You'll apply an iris blur to add a vignette around the glass. You'll apply the blur as a Smart Filter so that you can modify it later if you want to.

1   Choose Layer > Smart Objects > Convert To Smart Object.

2   Choose Filter > Blur > Iris Blur.

A blur ellipse is centered on your image. You can adjust the location and scope of the blur by moving the center pin, feather handles, and ellipse handles. Photoshop also opens the Blur Tools and Blur Effects panels.

3   Drag the center pin so that it's on the right side of the wine glass.

4   Click the ellipse and drag to enlarge the scope of the blur.

**5** Press Alt (Windows) or Option (Mac OS) as you click and drag the feather handles to match those in the second image below. Pressing Alt or Option lets you drag each handle separately.

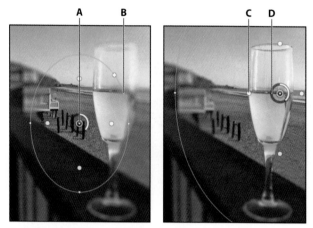

**A.** Center Pin **B.** Ellipse **C.** Feather handle **D.** Focus Ring

**6** Click and drag next to the focus ring to reduce the amount of blur to **6** px, creating a gradual but noticeable blur. You can also change the amount of blur by moving the Blur slider in the Iris Blur area of the Blur Tools panel.

**7** Click OK in the options bar to apply the blur.

The image looks great. You're almost done. You'll just add a Vibrance adjustment layer to give the image a little extra punch.

**8**  Click the Vibrance button in the Adjustments panel.

**9**  Move the Vibrance slider to **+33**, and then move the Saturation slider to **-5**.

The Vibrance adjustment layer affects all the layers beneath it.

**10**  Choose File > Save to save your work. Then close the file.

You've enhanced five images, using different techniques to adjust lighting and tone, remove red eye, correct lens distortion, add depth of field, and more. You can use these techniques separately or together on your own images.

# Extra credit

### High dynamic range (HDR) images

When you look at the world, your eyes adapt to different brightness levels so that you can see the detail in shadows or highlights. Cameras and computer monitors, however, are more limited in the dynamic range (the ratio between dark and bright regions) they can reproduce. The ability to create high dynamic range (HDR) images in Photoshop lets you bring the brightness you can see in the real world into your images. HDR images are used mostly in movies, special effects, and other high-end photography. However, you can create an HDR image using multiple photographs, each captured at a different exposure, to bring the detail revealed in each shot into a single image.

You'll use the Merge To HDR Pro filter to combine three photos of a streetscape.

1   In Bridge, open the Lesson05/HDR_ExtraCredit folder, and view the StreetA.jpg, StreetB.jpg, and StreetC.jpg files. These images are of the same scene, shot at different exposures. Though we're using JPEG images, you could use raw images, too.

2   In Photoshop, choose File > Automate > Merge To HDR Pro.

3   In the Merge To HDR Pro dialog box, click Browse. Then navigate to the Lesson05/HDR_ExtraCredit folder, and Shift-select the StreetA.jpg, StreetB.jpg, and StreetC.jpg files. Click OK or Open.

4   Make sure Attempt To Automatically Align Source Images is selected, and then click OK.

Photoshop opens each of the files briefly and merges them into a single image. That image appears in the Merge To HDR Pro dialog box, with default settings applied. The three images you merged are shown in the lower left corner of the dialog box.

5    Adjust the following settings in the Merge To HDR Pro dialog box:

- In the Edge Glow area, move the Radius slider to **403** px and the Strength to **0.75**. These settings determine how a glow effect is applied.

- In the Tone And Detail area, change the Gamma to **1.15**, Exposure to **0.30**, and Detail to **300**%. Each of these settings affects the overall tone of the image.

- In the Advanced area, change the Shadow to **2**% and Highlight to **11**% to specify how much detail is revealed in shadows and highlights. Change the Vibrance to **65**% and the Saturation to **55**% to adjust the color intensity.

6    Click OK to accept the changes and close the Merge To HDR Pro dialog box. Photoshop merges the layers into a single layer as it applies the settings you chose.

7    Choose File > Save. Save the file as **ExtraCredit_final.psd.**

8    Close the file.

# Review questions

**1** What happens to camera raw images when you edit them in Camera Raw?

**2** What is the advantage of the Adobe Digital Negative (DNG) file format?

**3** How do you correct red eye in Photoshop?

**4** Describe how to fix common camera lens flaws in Photoshop. What causes these defects?

# Review answers

1   A camera raw file contains unprocessed picture data from a digital camera's image sensor. Camera raw files give photographers control over interpreting the image data, rather than letting the camera make the adjustments and conversions. When you edit the image in Camera Raw, it preserves the original raw file data. This way, you can edit the image as you desire, export it, and keep the original intact for future use or other adjustments.

2   The Adobe Digital Negative (DNG) file format contains the raw image data from a digital camera as well as metadata that defines what the image data means. DNG is an industry-wide standard for camera raw image data that helps photographers manage proprietary camera raw file formats and provides a compatible archival format.

3   Red eye occurs when the retinas of a subject's eyes are reflected by the camera flash. To correct red eye in Adobe Photoshop, zoom in to the subject's eyes, select the Red Eye tool, and then click the red eyes.

4   The Lens Correction filter fixes common camera lens flaws, such as barrel and pincushion distortion, in which straight lines bow out towards the edges of the image (barrel) or bend inward (pincushion); chromatic aberration, where a color fringe appears along the edges of image objects; and vignetting at the edges of an image, especially corners, that are darker than the center. Defects can occur from incorrectly setting the lens's focal length or f-stop, or by tilting the camera vertically or horizontally.

# 6 MASKS AND CHANNELS

## Lesson overview

In this lesson, you'll learn how to do the following:

- Create a mask to remove a subject from a background.

- Refine a mask to include complex edges.

- Create a quick mask to make changes to a selected area.

- Edit a mask using the Properties panel.

- Manipulate an image using Puppet Warp.

- Save a selection as an alpha channel.

- View a mask using the Channels panel.

- Load a channel as a selection.

- Isolate a channel to make specific image changes.

 This lesson will take about an hour to complete. Download the Lesson06 project files from the Lesson & Update Files tab on your Account page at www.peachpit.com, if you haven't already done so. As you work on this lesson, you'll preserve the start files. If you need to restore the start files, download them from your Account page.

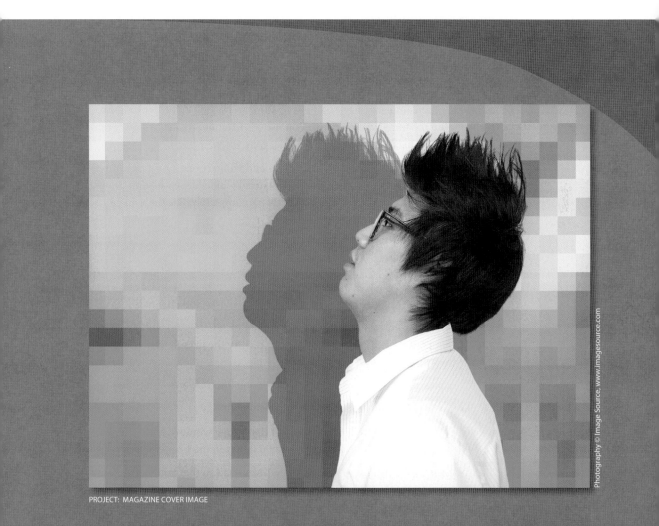

PROJECT: MAGAZINE COVER IMAGE

Use masks to isolate and manipulate specific parts of an image. The cutout portion of a mask can be altered, but the area surrounding the cutout is protected from change. You can create a temporary mask to use once, or you can save masks for repeated use.

# Working with masks and channels

Photoshop masks isolate and protect parts of an image, just as masking tape protects window panes or trim from paint when a house is painted. When you create a mask based on a selection, the area you haven't selected is *masked,* or protected from editing. With masks, you can create and save time-consuming selections and then use them again. In addition, you can use masks for other complex editing tasks—for example, to apply color changes or filter effects to an image.

In Photoshop, you can make temporary masks, called *quick masks,* or you can create permanent masks and store them as special grayscale channels called *alpha channels.* Photoshop also uses channels to store an image's color information. Unlike layers, channels do not print. You use the Channels panel to view and work with alpha channels.

A key concept in masking is that black hides and white reveals. As in life, rarely is anything black and white. Shades of gray partially hide, depending on the gray levels (255 is the value for black, hiding artwork completely; 0 is the value for white, revealing artwork completely).

# Getting started

First, you'll view the image that you'll create using masks and channels.

1   Start Photoshop, and then immediately hold down Ctrl+Alt+Shift (Windows) or Command+Option+Shift (Mac OS) to restore the default preferences. (See "Restoring default preferences" on page 4.)

2   When prompted, click Yes to delete the Adobe Photoshop Settings file.

3   Choose File > Browse In Bridge to open Adobe Bridge.

4   Click the Favorites tab on the left side of the Bridge window. Select the Lessons folder, and then double-click the Lesson06 folder in the Content panel.

5   Study the 06End.psd file. To enlarge the thumbnail so that you can see it more clearly, move the thumbnail slider at the bottom of the Bridge window to the right.

In this lesson, you'll create a magazine cover. The model for the cover was photographed in front of a different background. You'll use masking and the Refine Mask feature to place the model on the appropriate background.

6   Double-click the 06Start.psd thumbnail to open it in Photoshop. Click OK if you see an Embedded Profile Mismatch dialog box.

● **Note:** If Bridge isn't installed, you'll be prompted to install it when you choose Browse In Bridge. For more information, see page 3.

# Creating a mask

You'll use the Quick Selection tool to create the initial mask in order to separate the model from the background.

1 Choose File > Save As, rename the file **06Working.psd**, and click Save. Click OK if the Photoshop Format Options dialog box appears.

Saving a working version of the file lets you return to the original if you need it.

2 Select the Quick Selection tool (✐). In the options bar, set up a brush with a size of **15** px and hardness of **100%**.

3 Drag to select the man. It's fairly easy to select his shirt and face, but the hair is trickier. Don't worry if the selection isn't perfect. You'll refine the mask in the next exercise.

▶ **Tip:** For help making selections, refer to Lesson 3, "Working with Selections."

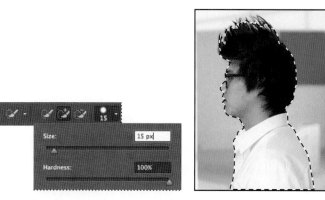

4 At the bottom of the Layers panel, click the Add Layer Mask button (▣) to create a layer mask.

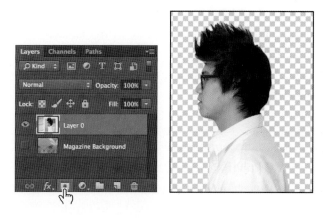

The selection becomes a pixel mask, and it appears as part of Layer 0 in the Layers panel. Everything outside the selection is transparent, represented by a checkerboard pattern.

# About masks and masking

Alpha channels, channel masks, clipping masks, layer masks, vector masks—what's the difference? In some cases, they're interchangeable: A channel mask can be converted to a layer mask, a layer mask can be converted to a vector mask, and vice versa.

Here's a brief description to help you keep them all straight. What they have in common is that they all store selections, and they all let you edit an image nondestructively, so you can return at any time to your original.

- An **alpha channel**—also called a *mask* or *selection*—is an extra channel added to an image; it stores selections as grayscale images. You can add alpha channels to create and store masks.

- A **layer mask** is like an alpha channel, but it's attached to a specific layer. A layer mask controls which part of a layer is revealed or hidden. It appears as a blank thumbnail next to the layer thumbnail in the Layers panel until you add content to it; a black outline indicates that it's selected.

- A **vector mask** is essentially a layer mask made up of vectors, not pixels. Resolution-independent, vector masks have crisp edges and are created with the pen or shape tools. They don't support transparency, so their edges can't be feathered. Their thumbnails appear the same as layer mask thumbnails.

- A **clipping mask** applies to a layer. It confines the influence of an effect to specific layers, rather than to everything below the layer in the layer stack. Using a clipping mask clips layers to a base layer; only that base layer is affected. Thumbnails of a clipped layer are indented with a right-angle arrow pointing to the layer below. The name of the clipped base layer is underlined.

- A **channel mask** restricts editing to a specific channel (for example, a Cyan channel in a CMYK image). Channel masks are useful for making intricate, fringed, or wispy-edged selections. You can create a channel mask based on a dominant color in an image or a pronounced contrast in an isolated channel, for example, between the subject and the background.

# Refining a mask

The mask is pretty good, but the Quick Selection tool couldn't quite capture all of the model's hair. The mask is also a little choppy around the contours of the shirt and face. You'll smooth the mask, and then fine-tune the area around the hair.

1  Choose Window > Properties to open the Properties panel.

2  If it isn't already selected, click the mask on Layer 0 in the Layers panel.

**3** In the Properties panel, click Mask Edge. The Refine Mask dialog box opens.

**4** In the View Mode area of the dialog box, click the arrow next to the preview window. Choose On Black from the pop-up menu.

The mask appears against a black background, which makes it easier to see the edge of the white shirt and the face.

**5** In the Adjust Edge area of the dialog box, move the sliders to create a smooth, unfeathered edge along the shirt and face. The optimal settings depend on the selection you created, but they'll probably be similar to ours. We moved the Smooth slider to 15, Contrast to 40%, and Shift Edge to -8%.

6  In the Output area of the dialog box, select Decontaminate Colors. Choose New Layer With Layer Mask from the Output To menu.

7  Select the Zoom tool in the Refine Mask dialog box, and then click the face to zoom in so you can see its edges more clearly.

8  Select the Refine Radius tool (⟍) in the Refine Mask dialog box. Use it to paint out any white background that remains around the lips and the nose. Press the left bracket ([) to decrease the brush size and the right bracket (]) to increase it.

9  When you're satisfied with the mask around the face, click OK.

A new layer, named Layer 0 copy, appears in the Layers panel. You'll use this layer to add the spikes to the mask of the hair.

10  With Layer 0 copy active, click Mask Edge in the Properties panel to open the Refine Mask dialog box again.

11  From the View pop-up menu, choose On White. The black hair shows up well against the white matte. If necessary, zoom out or use the Hand tool to reposition the image so that you can see all of the hair.

12  Select the Refine Radius tool in the Refine Mask dialog box. Press the ] key to increase the size of the brush. (The options bar displays the brush size; we used 300 px at first.) Then, begin brushing along the top of the hair, high enough to include the spikes. Press the [ key a few times to decrease the brush size by about half. Then, paint along the right side of the head, where the hair is a solid color, to pick up any small, fine hairs that protrude.

As you paint, Photoshop refines the mask edge, including the hair, but eliminating most of the background. If you were painting on a layer mask, the background would be included. The Refine Mask feature is good, but it's not perfect. You'll clean up any areas of background that are included with the hair.

13 Select the Erase Refinements tool (✐), hidden behind the Refine Radius tool in the Refine Mask dialog box. Click once or twice in each area where background color shows. When you erase an area, the Refine Mask feature erases similar colors, cleaning up more of the mask for you. Be careful not to erase the refinements you made to the hair edge. You can undo a step or use the Refine Radius tool to restore the edge if necessary.

14 Select Decontaminate Colors, and move the Amount slider to **85**%. Choose New Layer With Layer Mask from the Output To menu. Then click OK.

15 In the Layers panel, make the Magazine Background layer visible. The model appears in front of an orange patterned background.

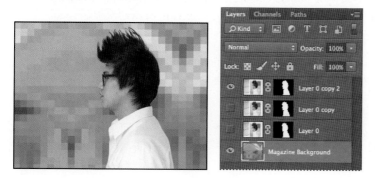

## Tool tips from the Photoshop evangelist

### Zoom tool shortcuts

Often when you are editing an image, you'll need to zoom in to work on a detail and then zoom out again to see the changes in context. Here are several keyboard shortcuts that make zooming even faster and easier.

- With any tool selected, press Ctrl (Windows) or Command (Mac OS) with the plus sign (+) to zoom in, or with the minus sign (-) to zoom out.

- Double-click the Zoom tool in the Tools panel to return the image to 100% view.

- When Scrubby Zoom is selected in the options bar, just drag the Zoom tool to the left to zoom in or drag it to the right to zoom out.

- Press Alt (Windows) or Option (Mac OS) to change the Zoom In tool to the Zoom Out tool, and click the area of the image you want to reduce. Each Alt/Option-click reduces the image by the next preset increment.

## Creating a quick mask

You'll create a quick mask to change the color of the glasses frames. First, you'll clean up the Layers panel.

1  Hide the Magazine Background layer so you can focus on the model. Then delete the Layer 0 and Layer 0 copy layers. Click Yes or Delete to confirm deletion of the layers or their masks, if prompted; you do not need to apply the mask to the current layer because Layer 0 copy 2 already has the mask applied.

2  Double-click the Layer 0 copy 2 layer name, and rename it **Model**.

3  Click the Edit In Quick Mask Mode button in the Tools panel. (By default, you have been working in Standard mode.)

In Quick Mask mode, a red overlay appears as you make a selection, masking the area outside the selection the way a rubylith, or red acetate, was used to mask images in traditional print shops. You can apply changes only to the unprotected area that is visible and selected. Notice that the highlight for the selected layer in the Layers panel appears gray instead of blue, indicating you're in Quick Mask mode.

4   In the Tools panel, select the Brush tool (✐).

5   In the options bar, make sure that the mode is Normal. Open the Brush pop-up panel, and select a small brush with a diameter of **13** px. Click outside the panel to close it.

6   Paint the earpiece of the glasses frames. The area you paint will appear red, creating a mask.

7   Continue painting with the Brush tool to mask the earpiece of the frames and the frame around the lenses. Reduce the brush size to paint around the lenses. Don't worry about the hair overlapping the earpiece; go ahead and paint over it.

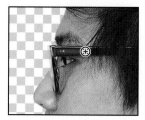 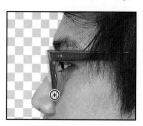 

In Quick Mask mode, Photoshop automatically defaults to Grayscale mode, with a foreground color of black, and a background color of white. When using a painting or editing tool in Quick Mask mode, keep these principles in mind:

- Painting with black adds to the mask (the red overlay) and decreases the selected area.

- Painting with white erases the mask (the red overlay) and increases the selected area.

- Painting with gray partially adds to the mask.

8   Click the Edit In Standard Mode button to exit Quick Mask Mode.

The unmasked area is selected. Unless you save a quick mask as a more permanent alpha-channel mask, Photoshop discards the temporary mask once it is converted to a selection.

9   Choose Select > Inverse to select the area you originally masked.

10  Choose Image > Adjustments > Hue/Saturation.

11  In the Hue/Saturation dialog box, change the Hue to **70**. The new green color fills the glasses frame. Click OK.

12  Choose Select > Deselect.

13  Save your work so far.

## Manipulating an image with Puppet Warp

The Puppet Warp feature gives you flexibility in manipulating an image. You can reposition areas, such as hair or an arm, just as you might pull the strings on a puppet. You place pins where you want to control movement. You'll use Puppet Warp to tilt the model's head back, so he appears to be looking up.

1   Zoom out so you can see the entire model.

2   With the Model layer selected in the Layers panel, choose Edit > Puppet Warp.

A mesh appears over the visible areas in the layer—in this case, the mesh appears over the model. You'll use the mesh to place pins where you want to control movement (or to ensure there is no movement).

3   Click around the edges of the shirt. Each time you click, Puppet Warp adds a pin. Approximately 10 pins should work.

The pins you've added around the shirt will keep it in place as you tilt the head.

4   Select the pin at the nape of the neck. A white dot appears in the center of the pin to indicate that it's selected.

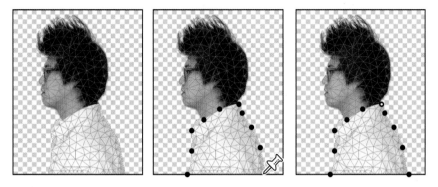

5   Press Alt (Windows) or Option (Mac OS). A larger circle appears around the pin and a curved double arrow appears next to it. Continue pressing Alt or Option as you drag the pointer to rotate the head backwards. You can see the angle of rotation in the options bar; you can enter **135** there to rotate the head back.

**Note:** Be careful not to Alt-click or Option-click the dot itself, or you'll delete the pin.

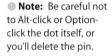

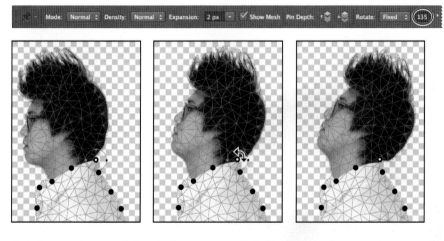

6   When you're satisfied with the rotation, click the Commit Puppet Warp button (✔) in the options bar, or press Enter or Return.

7   Save your work so far.

# Working with channels

Just as different information in an image is stored on different layers, channels also let you access specific kinds of information. Alpha channels store selections as gray-scale images. Color information channels store information about each color in an image; for example, an RGB image automatically has red, green, blue, and composite channels.

To avoid confusing channels and layers, think of channels as containing an image's color and selection information; think of layers as containing painting and effects.

You'll use an alpha channel to create a shadow for the model. Then, you'll convert the image to CMYK mode and use the Black channel to add color highlights to the hair.

## Using an alpha channel to create a shadow

You've already created a mask of the model. To create a shadow, you want to essentially duplicate that mask and then shift it. You'll use an alpha channel to make that possible.

1   In the Layers panel, Ctrl-click (Windows) or Command-click (Mac OS) the layer icon in the Model layer. The masked area is selected.

2   Choose Select > Save Selection. In the Save Selection dialog box, make sure New is chosen in the Channel menu. Then name the channel **Model Outline,** and click OK.

Nothing changes in the Layers panel or in the image window. However, a new channel named Model Outline has been added to the Channels panel.

3   Click the Create A New Layer icon (🖺) at the bottom of the Layers panel. Drag the new layer below the Model layer. Then double-click its name, and rename it **Shadow**.

4   With the Shadow layer selected, choose Select > Refine Edge. In the Refine Edge dialog box, move the Shift Edge slider to +**36**%. Then click OK.

5   Choose Edit > Fill. In the Fill dialog box, choose Black from the Use menu, and then click OK.

The Shadow layer displays a filled-in black outline of the model. Shadows aren't usually as dark as the person that casts them. You'll reduce the layer opacity.

6   In the Layers panel, change the layer opacity to **30**%.

The shadow is in exactly the same position as the model, where it can't be seen. You'll shift it.

7   Choose Select > Deselect to remove the selection.

8   Choose Edit > Transform > Skew. Rotate the shadow by hand, or enter **-15**° in the Rotate field in the options bar. Then drag the shadow to the left, or enter **845** in the X field in the options bar. Click the Commit Transform button (✔) in the options bar, or press Enter or Return, to accept the transformation.

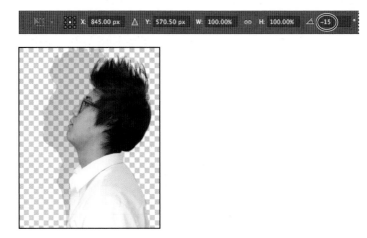

9   Choose File > Save to save your work so far.

## About alpha channels

If you work in Photoshop very long, you're bound to work with alpha channels. It's a good idea to know a few things about them.

*   An image can contain up to 56 channels, including all color and alpha channels.

*   All channels are 8-bit grayscale images, capable of displaying 256 levels of gray.

*   You can specify a name, color, mask option, and opacity for each channel. (The opacity affects the preview of the channel, not the image.)

*   All new channels have the same dimensions and number of pixels as the original image.

*   You can edit the mask in an alpha channel using the painting tools, editing tools, and filters.

*   You can convert alpha channels to spot-color channels.

## Adjusting an individual channel

You're almost done with the magazine cover image. All that remains is to add color highlights to the model's hair. You'll convert the image to CMYK mode so you can take advantage of the Black channel to do just that.

1   Select the Model layer in the Layers panel.

2   Choose Image > Mode > CMYK Color. Click Don't Merge in the dialog box that appears, because you want to keep your layers intact. Click OK if you're prompted about color profiles.

3   Alt-click (Windows) or Option-click (Mac OS) the visibility icon for the Model layer to hide the other layers.

4   Select the Channels tab. In the Channels panel, select the Black channel. Then choose Duplicate Channel from the Channels panel menu. Name the channel **Hair**, and click OK.

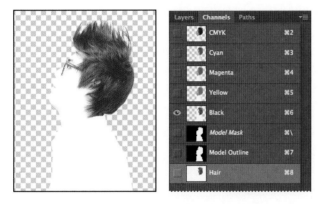

Individual channels appear in grayscale. If more than one channel is visible in the Channels panel, the channels appear in color.

5   Make the Hair channel visible, and hide the Black channel. Then select the Hair channel, and choose Image > Adjustments > Levels.

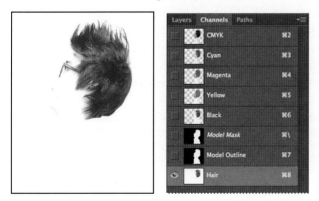

**6** In the Levels dialog box, adjust the levels to move Black to **85**, Midtones to **1**, and White to **165**. Click OK.

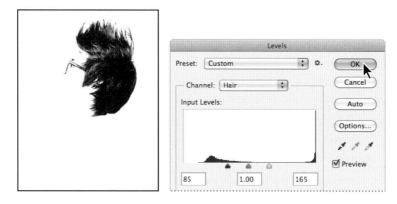

**7** With the Hair channel still selected, choose Image > Adjustments > Invert. The channel appears white against a black background.

**8** Select the Brush tool, and click the Switch Foreground And Background Colors icon in the Tools panel to make the Foreground color black. Then paint over the glasses, eyes, and anything in the channel that isn't hair.

**9** Click the Load Channel As Selection icon at the bottom of the Channels panel.

**10** Select the Layers tab. In the Layers panel, select the Model layer.

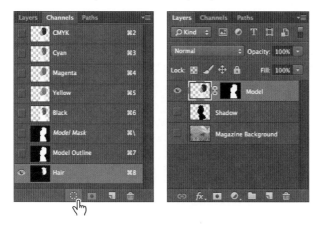

**11** Choose Select > Refine Edge. In the Refine Edge dialog box, move the Feather slider to **1.2** px, and then click OK.

**12** Choose Image > Adjustments > Hue/Saturation. Select Colorize, and then move the sliders as follows, and click OK:

- Hue: **230**

- Saturation: **56**

- Lightness: **11**

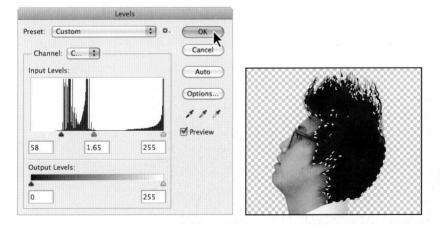

**13** Choose Image > Adjustments > Levels. In the Levels dialog box, move the sliders so that the Black slider is positioned where the blacks peak, the White slider where the whites peak, and the Midtones in between. Then click OK. We used the values 58, 1.65, 255, but your values may vary.

**14** In the Layers panel, make the Shadow and Magazine Background layers visible.

**15** Choose Select > Deselect.

**16** Choose File > Save.

Your magazine cover is ready to go!

## Masking tips and shortcuts

Mastering masks can help you work more efficiently in Photoshop. These tips will help get you started.

- Masks are nondestructive, which means that you can edit the masks later without losing the pixels that they hide.

- When editing a mask, be aware of the color selected in the Tools panel. Black hides, white reveals, and shades of gray partially hide or reveal. The darker the gray, the more is hidden by the mask.

- To reveal a layer's content without masking effects, turn off the mask by Shift-clicking the layer mask thumbnail, or choose Layer > Layer Mask > Disable. A red X appears over the mask thumbnail in the Layers panel when the mask is disabled.

- To turn a layer mask back on, Shift-click the layer mask thumbnail with the red X in the Layers panel, or choose Layer > Layer Mask > Enable. If the mask doesn't show up in the Layers panel, choose Layer > Layer Mask > Reveal All to display it.

- Unlink a layer from its mask to move the two independently and shift the mask's boundaries separately from the layer. To unlink a layer or group from its layer mask or vector mask, click the link icon between the thumbnails in the Layers panel. To relink them, click the blank space between the two thumbnails.

- To convert a vector mask to a layer mask, select the layer containing the vector mask you want to convert, and choose Layer > Rasterize > Vector Mask. Note, however, that once you rasterize a vector mask, you can't change it back into a vector object.

- To modify a mask, use the Density and Feather sliders in the Properties panel. The Density slider determines the opacity of the mask: At 100%, the mask is fully in effect; at lower opacities, the contrast lessens; and at 0%, the mask has no effect. The Feather slider softens the edge of the mask.

# Review questions

1  What is the benefit of using a quick mask?

2  What happens to a quick mask when you deselect it?

3  When you save a selection as a mask, where is the mask stored?

4  How can you edit a mask in a channel once you've saved it?

5  How do channels differ from layers?

# Review answers

1  Quick masks are helpful for creating quick, one-time selections. In addition, using a quick mask is an easy way to edit a selection using the painting tools.

2  The quick mask disappears when you deselect it.

3  Masks are saved in channels, which can be thought of as storage areas for color and selection information in an image.

4  You can paint on a mask in a channel using black, white, and shades of gray.

5  Channels are used as storage areas for saved selections. Unless you explicitly display a channel, it does not appear in the image or print. Layers can be used to isolate various parts of an image so that they can be edited as discrete objects with the painting or editing tools or other effects.

# 7 TYPOGRAPHIC DESIGN

## Lesson overview

In this lesson, you'll learn how to do the following:

- Use guides to position text in a composition.

- Make a clipping mask from type.

- Merge type with other layers.

- Format text.

- Distribute text along a path.

- Create and apply type styles.

- Control type and positioning using advanced features.

 This lesson will take less than an hour to complete. Download the Lesson07 project files from the Lesson & Update Files tab on your Account page at www.peachpit.com, if you haven't already done so. As you work on this lesson, you'll preserve the start files. If you need to restore the start files, download them from your Account page.

PROJECT: MAGAZINE COVER LAYOUT

Photography © Image Source, www.imagesource.com

Photoshop provides powerful, flexible text tools so you can add type to your images with great control and creativity.

# About type

Type in Photoshop consists of mathematically defined shapes that describe the letters, numbers, and symbols of a typeface. Many typefaces are available in more than one format, the most common formats being Type 1 or PostScript fonts, TrueType, and OpenType (see "OpenType in Photoshop" later in this lesson).

When you add type to an image in Photoshop, the characters are composed of pixels and have the same resolution as the image file—zooming in on characters shows jagged edges. However, Photoshop preserves the vector-based type outlines and uses them when you scale or resize type, save a PDF or EPS file, or print the image to a PostScript printer. As a result, you can produce type with crisp, resolution-independent edges, apply effects and styles to type, and transform its shape and size.

# Getting started

In this lesson, you'll work on the layout for the cover of a technology magazine. You'll start with the artwork you created in Lesson 6: The cover has a model, his shadow, and the orange background. You'll add and stylize type for the cover, including warping the text.

You'll start the lesson by viewing an image of the final composition.

1   Start Photoshop, and then immediately hold down Ctrl+Alt+Shift (Windows) or Command+Option+Shift (Mac OS) to restore the default preferences. (See "Restoring default preferences" on page 4.)

2   When prompted, click Yes to delete the Adobe Photoshop Settings file.

3   Choose File > Browse In Bridge to open Adobe Bridge.

● **Note:** If Bridge is not installed, you'll be prompted to download and install it. See page 3 for more information.

4   In the Favorites panel on the left side of Bridge, click the Lessons folder, and then double-click the Lesson07 folder in the Content panel.

5   Select the 07End.psd file. Increase the thumbnail size to see the image clearly by dragging the thumbnail slider to the right.

You'll apply the type treatment in Photoshop to finish the magazine cover. All of the type controls you need are available in Photoshop, so you don't have to switch to another application to complete the project.

● **Note:** Though this lesson starts where Lesson 6 left off, use the 07Start.psd file. We've included a path and a sticky note in the start file that won't be in the 06Working.psd file you saved.

6   Double-click the 07Start.psd file to open it in Photoshop.

7   Choose File > Save As, rename the file **07Working.psd**, and click Save.

8   Click OK if the Photoshop Format Options dialog box appears.

**9** Choose Typography from the Workspace Switcher in the options bar.

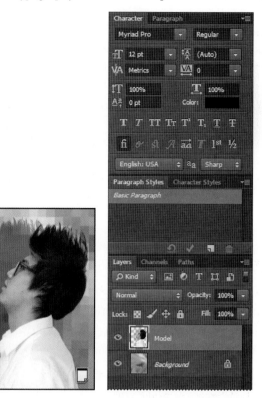

The Typography workspace displays the Character, Paragraph, Paragraph Styles, Character Styles, Layers, and Paths panels that you'll use in this lesson.

# Creating a clipping mask from type

A *clipping mask* is an object or a group of objects whose shape masks other artwork so that only areas that lie within the clipping mask are visible. In effect, you are clipping the artwork to conform to the shape of the object (or mask). In Photoshop, you can create a clipping mask from shapes or letters. In this exercise, you'll use letters as a clipping mask to allow an image in another layer to show through the letters.

## Adding guides to position type

The 07Working.psd file includes a background layer, which will be the foundation for your typography. You'll start by zooming in on the work area and using ruler guides to help position the type.

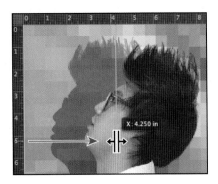

1  Choose View > Fit On Screen to see the whole cover clearly.

2  Choose View > Rulers to display rulers along the left and top borders of the image window.

3  Drag a vertical guide from the left ruler to the center of the cover (4.25").

## Adding point type

Now you're ready to add type to the composition. You can create horizontal or vertical type anywhere in an image. You can enter *point type* (a single letter, word, or line) or *paragraph type*. You will do both in this lesson. First, you'll create point type.

1  In the Layers panel, select the Background layer.

2  Select the Horizontal Type tool (T), and, in the options bar, do the following:

  • Choose a sans serif typeface, such as Myriad Pro, from the Font Family pop-up menu, and choose Semibold from the Font Style pop-up menu.

  • Type **144 pt** for the Size, and press Enter or Return.

  • Click the Center Text button.

3  In the Character panel, change the Tracking value to **100**.

**Note:** After you type, you must commit your editing in the layer by clicking the Commit Any Current Edits button or switching to another tool or layer. You cannot commit to current edits by pressing Enter or Return; doing so merely creates a new line of type.

4  Click on the center guide you added to set an insertion point, and type **DIGITAL** in all capital letters. Then click the Commit Any Current Edits button (✔) in the options bar.

The word "DIGITAL" is added to the cover, and it appears in the Layers panel as a new type layer, DIGITAL. You can edit and manage the type layer as you would any other layer. You can add or change the text, change the orientation of the type, apply anti-aliasing, apply layer styles and transformations, and create masks. You can move, restack, and copy a type layer, or edit its layer options, just as you would for any other layer.

5    Press Ctrl (Windows) or Command (Mac OS), and drag the "DIGITAL" text to move it to the top of the cover, if it's not there already.

6    Choose File > Save to save your work so far.

## Making a clipping mask and applying a shadow

You added the letters in black, the default text color. However, you want the letters to appear to be filled with an image of a circuit board, so you'll use the letters to make a clipping mask that will allow another image layer to show through.

1    Choose File > Open, and open the circuit_board.tif file, which is in the Lesson07 folder.

2    Choose Window > Arrange > 2-Up Vertical. The circuit_board.tif and 07Working.psd files appear onscreen together. Click the circuit_board.tif file to ensure that it's the active window.

3    Select the Move tool. Then, hold down the Shift key as you drag the Background layer from the Layers panel in the circuit_board.tif file onto the center of the 07Working.psd file.

Pressing Shift as you drag centers the circuit_board.tif image in the composition.

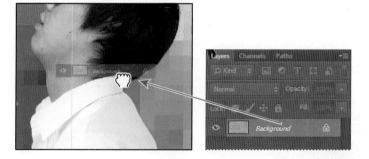

A new layer—Layer 1— appears in the Layers panel for the 07Working.psd file. This new layer contains the image of the circuit board, which will show through the type. But before you make the clipping mask, you'll resize the circuit board image, as it's currently too large for the composition.

4    Close the circuit_board.tif file without saving any changes to it.

5    In the 07Working.psd file, select Layer 1, and then choose Edit > Transform > Scale.

**6** Grab a corner handle on the bounding box for the circuit board. Press Alt+Shift (Windows) or Option+Shift (Mac OS) as you resize it to approximately the same width as the area of text.

Pressing Shift retains the proportions; Alt or Option keeps it centered.

**7** Reposition the circuit board so that the image covers the text, and press Enter or Return to confirm the transformation.

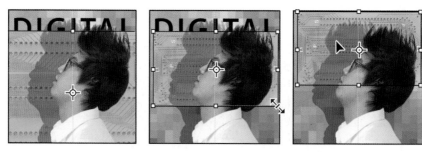

**8** Double-click the Layer 1 name, and change it to **Circuit Board**. Then press Enter or Return, or click away from the name in the Layers panel, to apply the change.

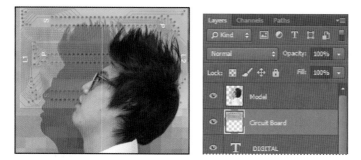

▶ **Tip:** You can also make a clipping mask by holding down the Alt (Windows) or Option (Mac OS) key and clicking between the Circuit Board and DIGITAL type layers.

**9** Select the Circuit Board layer, if it isn't already selected, and choose Create Clipping Mask from the Layers panel menu (⬝≡).

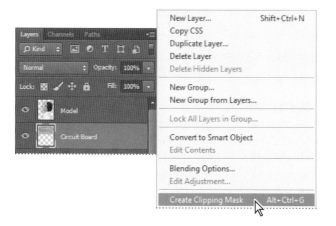

The circuit board now shows through the DIGITAL letters. A small arrow in the Circuit Board layer and the underlined type layer name indicate the clipping mask is applied. Next, you'll add an inner shadow to give the letters depth.

10 Select the DIGITAL layer to make it active, click the Add A Layer Style button (*fx*) at the bottom of the Layers panel, and then choose Inner Shadow from the pop-up menu.

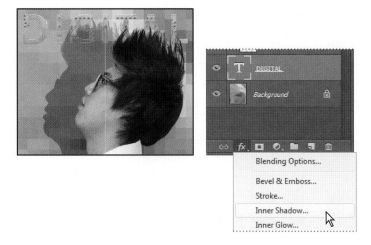

11 In the Layer Style dialog box, change the Blend Mode to Multiply, Opacity to **48**%, Distance to **18**, Choke to **0**, and Size to **16**. Then click OK.

12 Choose File > Save to save your work so far.

# Creating type on a path

In Photoshop, you can create type that follows along a path you create with a pen or shape tool. The direction the type flows depends on the order in which anchor points were added to the path. When you use the Horizontal Type tool to add text to a path, the letters are perpendicular to the baseline of the path. If you change the location or shape of the path, the type moves with it.

You'll create type on a path to make it look as if questions are coming from the model's mouth. We've already created the path for you.

1 In the Layers panel, select the Background layer.

2 Select the Paths tab in the Layers panel group.

3 In the Paths panel, select the path named Speech Path.

The path appears to be coming out of the model's mouth.

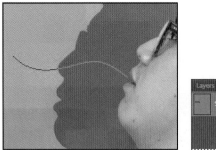

4 Select the Horizontal Type tool.

5 In the options bar, click the Right Align Text button.

*Julieanne Kost is an official Adobe Photoshop evangelist.*

# Tool tips from the Photoshop evangelist

### Type tool tricks

- Shift-click in the image window with the Horizontal Type tool (T) to create a new type layer—in case you're close to another block of type and Photoshop tries to autoselect it.

- Double-click the thumbnail icon on any type layer in the Layers panel to select all of the type on that layer.

- With any text selected, right-click (Windows) or Control-click (Mac OS) on the text to access the context menu. Choose Check Spelling to run a spell check.

**6** In the Character panel, select the following settings:

- Font Family: Myriad Pro
- Font Style: Regular
- Font Size (⊤̣): **16** pt
- Tracking (⧖): **-10**
- Color: White
- All Caps (TT)

**7** Move the Type tool over the path. When a small slanted line appears across the I-bar, click the end of the path closest to the model's mouth, and type **What's new with games?**

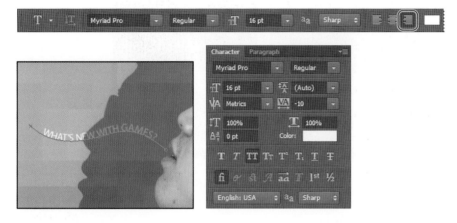

**8** Select the word "GAMES," and change its font style to Bold. Click the Commit Any Current Edits button (✔) in the options bar.

**9** Click the Layers tab to bring it forward. In the Layers panel, select the What's new with games? layer, and then choose Duplicate Layer from the Layers panel menu. Name the new layer **What's new with music?**, and click OK.

**10** With the Type tool, select "GAMES," and replace it with **music**. Click the Commit Any Current Edits button in the options bar.

**11** Choose Edit > Free Transform Path. Rotate the left side of the path approximately 30 degrees, and then shift the path up above the first path, and a little to the right, as in the image below. Click the Commit Transform button in the options bar.

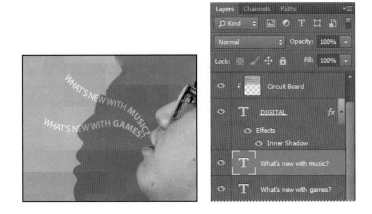

**12** Repeat steps 9–11, replacing the word "GAMES" with **phones**. Rotate the left side of the path approximately -30 degrees, and move it below the original path.

**13** Choose File > Save to save your work so far.

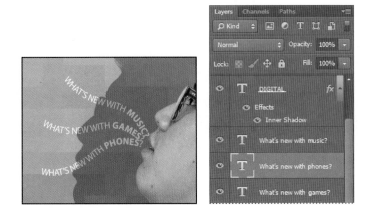

# Warping point type

The text on a path is more interesting than straight lines would be, but you'll warp the text to make it more playful. *Warping* lets you distort type to conform to a variety of shapes, such as an arc or a wave. The warp style you select is an attribute of the type layer—you can change a layer's warp style at any time to change the overall shape of the warp. Warping options give you precise control over the orientation and perspective of the warp effect.

1   Scroll or use the Hand tool (👋) to move the visible area of the image window so that the sentences to the left of the model are in the center of the screen.

2   Right-click (Windows) or Control-click (Mac OS) the What's new with games? layer in the Layers panel, and choose Warp Text from the context menu.

3   In the Warp Text dialog box, choose Wave from the Style menu, and select the Horizontal option. Specify the following values: Bend, +**33**%; Horizontal Distortion, -**23**%; and Vertical Distortion, +**5**%. Then click OK.

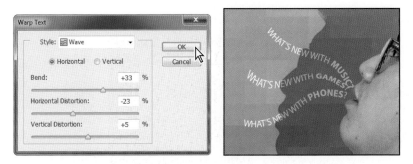

The words "What's new with games?" appear to float like a wave on the cover.

**4** Repeat steps 2 and 3 to warp the other two text layers you typed on a path.

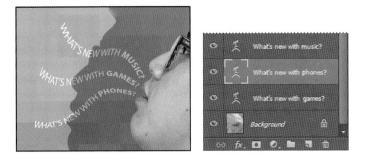

**5** Save your work.

# Designing paragraphs of type

All of the text you've written on this cover so far has been a few discrete words or lines—point type. However, many designs call for full paragraphs of text. You can design complete paragraphs of type in Photoshop; you can even apply paragraph styles. You don't have to switch to a dedicated page layout program for sophisticated paragraph type controls.

## Using guides for positioning

You will add paragraphs to the cover in Photoshop. First, you'll add some guides to the work area to help you position the paragraph, and create a new paragraph style.

**1** Drag a guide from the left vertical ruler, placing it approximately ¼" from the right side of the cover.

**2** Drag a guide down from the top horizontal ruler, placing it approximately 2" from the top of the cover.

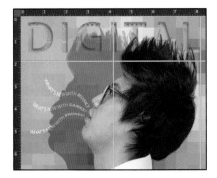

## Adding paragraph type from a sticky note

You're ready to add the text. In a real design environment, the text might be provided to you in a word-processing document or the body of an email message, which you could copy and paste into Photoshop. Or you might have to type it in. Another easy way to add a bit of text is for the copywriter to attach it to the image file in a sticky note, as we've done for you here.

1 Select the Move tool, and then double-click the yellow sticky note in the lower right corner of the image window to open the Notes panel. Expand the Notes panel, if necessary, to see all the text.

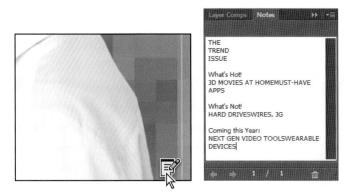

2 In the Notes panel, select all the text. Press Ctrl+C (Windows) or Command+C (Mac OS) to copy the text to the clipboard. Close the Notes panel.

3 Select the Model layer. Then, select the Horizontal Type tool (T).

4 Press Shift as you click where the guidelines intersect, about ¼" from the right edge and 2" from the top of the cover. Continue to hold the Shift key as you start to drag a text box down and to the left. Then release the Shift key and continue dragging until the box is about 4 inches wide by 8 inches high, the top and right edges aligned with the guides you just added.

5 Press Ctrl+V (Windows) or Command+V (Mac OS) to paste the text. The new text layer is at the top of the Layers panel, so the text appears in front of the model.

The pasted text is 16 pts, and it's right-aligned, because those were the latest text settings you'd used.

▶ **Tip:** Press Shift as you start to drag a text box to ensure that Photoshop creates a new text layer, instead of selecting an existing text layer.

● **Note:** If the text isn't visible, make sure the new type layer is above the Model layer in the Layers panel.

**6** Select the first three lines ("The Trend Issue"), and then apply the following settings in the Character panel:

- Font Family: Myriad Pro (or another sans serif font)
- Font Style: Regular
- Font Size (T̲): **70** pt
- Leading (Å): **55** pt
- Tracking (VA): **50**
- Color: White

**7** Select just the word "Trend," and change the Font Style to Bold.

**8** Click the Commit Any Current Edits button (✔) in the options bar.

**9** Choose Select > Deselect Layers to ensure that no layers are selected.

You've formatted the title.

## Working with type styles

You'll create paragraph styles and character styles to format additional text. A paragraph style is a collection of type attributes that you can apply to an entire paragraph with a single click. A character style is a collection of attributes that you can apply to individual characters. Type styles in Photoshop are similar to styles in page layout applications such as Adobe InDesign and popular word-processing applications, but you'll probably notice some differences in the way they work. By default, all text you create in Photoshop has the Basic Paragraph style applied.

# Creating paragraph styles

You'll create paragraph styles for the remaining pasted text.

1 Click the Create New Paragraph Style button (⬛) at the bottom of the Paragraph Styles panel.

2 Double-click Paragraph Style 1 to change its attributes.

3 In the Paragraph Style Options dialog box, specify the following settings:

- Style Name: **Cover Teasers**
- Font Family: Myriad Pro
- Font Style: Regular
- Font Size: **28** pt
- Leading (🔠): **28** pt
- Color: White

▶ **Tip:** You can use the same paragraph and character styles across multiple files. To save the current styles as defaults for all new documents, choose Type > Save Default Type Styles. If you want to use your default styles in an existing document, choose Type > Load Default Type Styles.

4 Select Indents And Spacing from the list on the left in the Paragraph Style Options dialog box.

5 Choose Right from the Alignment menu, and then click OK.

You've created a style that you can apply to quickly format the teaser titles on the cover. You'll create another style for the subheadings, which should be smaller.

6 Click the Create New Paragraph Style button at the bottom of the Paragraph Styles panel again.

**7** Double-click Paragraph Style 1, and then specify the following:

- Style Name: **Teaser Subheads**
- Font Family: Myriad Pro
- Font Style: Regular
- Font Size: **22** pt
- Leading: **28** pt
- Color: White

**8** Select Indents And Spacing from the list on the left in the Paragraph Style Options dialog box.

**9** Choose Right from the Alignment menu, and then click OK.

## Applying paragraph styles

Applying a paragraph style is easy. With the text selected, simply click the style name. If the text has been changed from the Basic Paragraph style, Photoshop retains those overrides and applies only the attributes of the style that do not conflict with the overrides. In that case, clear any overrides to apply all the style's attributes.

**1** Select the "What's Hot!" text, and then select Cover Teasers in the Paragraph Styles panel.

Photoshop applies some of the Cover Teasers attributes to the paragraph, but not all of them, because there were style overrides in effect when you applied the style.

**2** Click the Clear Override button (🗘) at the bottom of the Paragraph Styles panel.

**3** Select the text beneath "What's Hot," and then select Teaser Subheads in the Paragraph Styles panel. Click the Clear Override button again.

**4** Repeat steps 1–3 for the "What's Not" and "Coming this year" sections.

You'll make one more change to this text frame, this time without a style.

5  Select "Coming this year" and all the text that follows it. Then, in the Character panel, change the text color to Black.

6  Finally, click the Commit Any Current Edits button to accept the type changes.

## Editing paragraph styles

Paragraph styles make it easy to apply attributes to text, and also to change attributes across multiple paragraphs quickly. Editing paragraph styles, rather than individual paragraphs, ensures consistency. You'll edit the Cover Teasers style to make the headings bold.

1  Choose Select > Deselect Layers so that nothing is selected in the Layers panel.

2  Double-click the Cover Teasers style in the Paragraph Styles panel.

3  Choose Bold from the Font Style menu.

4  Click OK.

Photoshop applies the change everywhere the Cover Teasers paragraph style is applied in the document.

## Creating character styles

You used paragraph styles to apply attributes to entire paragraphs of text. Character styles let you apply character-level attributes (such as font size, font style, or color) to individual characters, overriding paragraph styles or other formatting. You'll create a character style to emphasize some of the words on the cover.

1  Make sure no layers are selected in the Layers panel. (Choose Select > Deselect Layers if necessary.)

2  Click the Character Styles tab to bring the panel to the front.

3  Click the Create New Character Style button.

4  Double-click Character Style 1 to edit it.

▶ **Tip:** Use the Adobe Illustrator Glyphs panel to preview OpenType options: Copy your text in Photoshop and paste it into an Illustrator document. Then, choose Window > Type > Glyphs. Select the text you want to change, and choose Show > Alternates For Current Selection. Double-click a glyph to apply it, and when you've finished, copy and paste the new type into your Photoshop file.

**5** In the Character Style Options dialog box, specify the following settings, and then click OK:

- Style Name: **Emphasis**
- Font Family: Myriad Pro
- Font Style: Bold Italic

**6** With the Horizontal Type tool, select "must-have" in the "What's Hot!" section.

**7** Click the new Emphasis style in the Character Styles panel.

**8** Repeat steps 6–7 to apply the Emphasis style to "hard drives" and "next gen."

**9** Click the Commit Any Current Edits button in the options bar.

You applied the same character style each time, and in each instance, Photoshop applied the Bold Italic font style. Notice that the character style didn't affect any other attributes. Where the type was white, it remained white; where it was black, it remained black.

# OpenType in Photoshop

OpenType is a cross-platform font file format developed jointly by Adobe and Microsoft. The format uses a single font file for both Mac OS and Windows, so you can move files from one platform to another without font substitution or reflowed text. OpenType offers widely expanded character sets and layout features, such as swashes and discretionary ligatures, that aren't available in traditional PostScript and TrueType fonts. This, in turn, provides richer linguistic support and advanced typography control. Here are some highlights of OpenType.

**The OpenType menu** The Character panel menu includes an OpenType submenu that displays all available features for a selected OpenType font, including ligatures, alternates, and fractions. Dimmed features are unavailable for that typeface; a check mark appears next to features that have been applied.

**Discretionary ligatures** To add a discretionary ligature to two OpenType letters, such as to "th" in the Bickham Script Standard typeface, select them in the image, and choose OpenType > Discretionary Ligatures from the Character panel menu.

**Swashes** Adding swashes or alternate characters works the same way. Select the letter, such as a capital "T" in Bickham Script, and choose OpenType > Swash to change the ordinary capital into a dramatically ornate swash T.

**True fractions** To create true fractions, type the fractions characters—for example, 1/2. Then, select the characters, and from the Character panel menu, choose OpenType > Fractions. Photoshop applies the true fraction (½).

# Adding a rounded rectangle

You're almost done with the text for the magazine cover. All that remains to do is to add the volume number in the upper right corner. First, you'll create a rectangle with rounded corners to serve as a background for the volume number.

1   Select the Rounded Rectangle tool (◉), hidden beneath the Rectangle tool (▣), in the Tools panel.

**2**  Draw a rectangle in the space above the letter "L" in the upper right corner of the cover, placing its right edge along the guide.

**3**  In the Properties panel, type **67** px for the width, and then make sure the stroke width is 3 pt.

**4**  Click the fill color swatch in the Properties panel, and select the Pastel Yellow Orange swatch in the third row.

By default, all the corners in the rectangle have the same radius. In Photoshop CC, you can adjust the radius for each corner separately. You can even return to edit the corners later if you want to. You'll change the rectangle so that only the lower left corner is rounded.

**5**  Unlink the corner radius values in the Properties panel. Then change the bottom left corner to **16 px**, and set all the others to **0 px**.

**6**  With the Move tool, drag the rectangle to the top of the image so it hangs down like a ribbon.

**7**  Select Show Transform Controls in the options bar. Drag the bottom of the rectangle down so that it's close to the letter "L." You want the rectangle to be long enough to contain the text. Then click the Commit Transform button (✔).

# Adding vertical text

You're ready to add the volume number on top of the ribbon.

**1**  Choose Select > Deselect Layers. Then select the Vertical Type tool (↓T), which is hidden under the Horizontal Type tool.

**2**  Press the Shift key, and click inside the rectangle you just created.

Pressing the Shift key as you click ensures that you create a new text box instead of selecting the title.

**3**  Type **VOL 9**.

The letters are too large to view. You'll need to change their size to see them.

4  Choose Select > All, and then, in the Character panel, select the following:

- Font Family: a serif typeface, such as Myriad Pro
- Font Style: a light or narrow style, such as Light Condensed
- Font size: **15** pt
- Tracking: **10**
- Color: Black

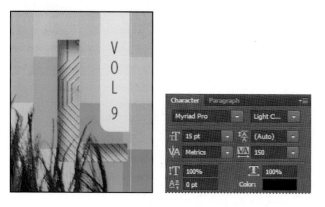

5  Click the Commit Any Current Edits button (✔) in the options bar. Your vertical text now appears as the layer named VOL 9. Use the Move tool (▶⊹) to center it in the ribbon, if necessary.

Now, you'll clean up a bit.

6  Click the note to select it. Then right-click (Windows) or Control-click (Mac OS) and choose Delete Note from the context menu; click Yes to confirm that you want to delete the note.

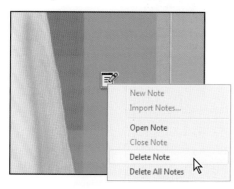

7  Hide the guides: Choose the Hand tool (✋), and then press Ctrl+; (Windows) or Command+; (Mac OS). Then zoom out to get a nice look at your work.

**8** Choose File > Save to save your work.

Congratulations! You've added and stylized all of the type on the Digital magazine cover. Now that the magazine cover is ready to go, you'll flatten it and prepare it for printing.

**9** Choose File > Save As, rename the file **07Working_flattened**, and click Save. Click OK if you see the Photoshop Format Options dialog box.

Keeping a layered version lets you return to the 07Working.psd file in the future to edit it.

**10** Choose Layer > Flatten Image.

**11** Choose File > Save, and then close the image window.

## Saving as Photoshop PDF

The type you've added consists of vector-based outlines, which remain crisp and clear as you zoom in or resize them. However, if you save the file as a JPEG or TIFF image, Photoshop rasterizes the type, so you lose that flexibility. When you save a Photoshop PDF file, vector type is included.

You can preserve other Photoshop editing capabilities in a Photoshop PDF file, too. For example, you can retain layers, color information, and even notes.

To ensure you can edit the file later, select Preserve Photoshop Editing Capabilities in the Save Adobe PDF dialog box.

To preserve any notes in the file and convert them to Acrobat comments when you save to PDF, select Notes in the Save area of the Save As dialog box.

You can open a Photoshop PDF file in Acrobat or Photoshop, place it in another application, or print it. For more information about saving as Photoshop PDF, see Photoshop Help.

## Review questions

1 How does Photoshop treat type?

2 How is a text layer the same as or different from other layers in Photoshop?

3 What is a clipping mask, and how do you make one from type?

4 What is a paragraph style?

## Review answers

1 Type in Photoshop consists of mathematically defined shapes that describe the letters, numbers, and symbols of a typeface. When you add type to an image in Photoshop, the characters are composed of pixels and have the same resolution as the image file. However, Photoshop preserves the vector-based type outlines and uses them when you scale or resize type, save a PDF or EPS file, or print the image to a PostScript printer.

2 Type that is added to an image appears in the Layers panel as a text layer that can be edited and managed in the same way as any other kind of layer. You can add and edit the text, change the orientation of the type, and apply anti-aliasing as well as move, restack, copy, and change the options for layers.

3 A clipping mask is an object or group whose shape masks other artwork so that only areas that lie within the shape are visible. To convert the letters on any text layer to a clipping mask, select both the text layer and the layer you want to show through the letters, and then choose Create Clipping Mask from the Layers panel menu.

4 A paragraph style is a collection of type attributes that you can quickly apply to an entire paragraph.

# 8 VECTOR DRAWING TECHNIQUES

## Lesson overview

In this lesson, you'll learn how to do the following:

- Differentiate between bitmap and vector graphics.

- Draw straight and curved paths using the Pen tool.

- Convert a path to a selection, and convert a selection to a path.

- Save paths.

- Draw and edit shape layers.

- Draw custom shapes.

- Import and edit a Smart Object from Adobe Illustrator.

 This lesson will take about 90 minutes to complete. Download the Lesson08 project files from the Lesson & Update Files tab on your Account page at www.peachpit.com, if you haven't already done so. As you work on this lesson, you'll preserve the start files. If you need to restore the start files, download them from your Account page.

RETRO TOYZ

PROJECT: TOY PACKAGE DESIGN

Unlike bitmap images, vector images retain their crisp edges when you enlarge them to any size. You can draw vector shapes and paths in your Photoshop images and add vector masks to control what is shown in an image.

# About bitmap images and vector graphics

Before working with vector shapes and vector paths, it's important to understand the basic differences between the two main categories of computer graphics: *bitmap images* and *vector graphics*. You can use Photoshop to work with either type of graphic; in fact, you can combine both bitmap and vector data in an individual Photoshop image file.

Bitmap images, technically called *raster images*, are based on a grid of dots known as *pixels*. Each pixel is assigned a specific location and color value. In working with bitmap images, you edit groups of pixels rather than objects or shapes. Because bitmap graphics can represent subtle gradations of shade and color, they are appropriate for continuous-tone images such as photographs or artwork created in painting programs. A disadvantage of bitmap graphics is that they contain a fixed number of pixels. As a result, they can lose detail and appear jagged when scaled up onscreen or printed at a lower resolution than they were created for.

Vector graphics are made up of lines and curves defined by mathematical objects called *vectors*. These graphics retain their crispness whether they are moved, resized, or have their color changed. Vector graphics are appropriate for illustrations, type, and graphics such as logos that may be scaled to different sizes.

 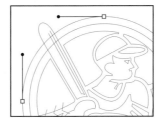

Logo drawn as vector art

Logo rasterized as bitmap art

# About paths and the Pen tool

In Photoshop, the outline of a vector shape is a *path*. A path is a curved or straight line segment you draw using the Pen tool, Freeform Pen tool, or a shape tool. The Pen tool draws paths with the greatest precision; shape tools draw rectangles, ellipses, and other shape paths; the Freeform Pen tool draws paths as if you were drawing with a pencil on paper.

Paths can be open or closed. An open path (such as a wavy line) has two distinct endpoints. A closed path (such as a circle) is continuous. The type of path you draw affects how it can be selected and adjusted.

Paths that have no fill or stroke do not print when you print your artwork. This is because paths are vector objects that contain no pixels, unlike the bitmap shapes drawn by the Pencil tool and other painting tools.

---

*Julieanne Kost is an official Adobe Photoshop evangelist.*

## Tool tips from the Photoshop evangelist

### Accessing tools quickly

Each tool in the Tools panel has a single-letter keyboard shortcut. Type the letter, get the tool. Press Shift with the shortcut key to cycle though any nested tools in a group. For example, press P to select the Pen tool, and press Shift+P to toggle between the Pen and Freeform Pen tools.

---

# Getting started

Before you begin, you'll view the image you'll be creating—a sign for a fictitious toy company.

1   Start Photoshop, and then immediately hold down Ctrl+Alt+Shift (Windows) or Command+Option+Shift (Mac OS) to restore the default preferences. (See "Restoring default preferences" on page 4.)

2   When prompted, click Yes to delete the Adobe Photoshop Settings file.

**Note:** If Bridge and Mini Bridge aren't installed, you'll be prompted to install them. For more information, see page 3.

**Note:** If you open the 08End.psd file in Photoshop, you might be prompted to update type layers. If so, click Update. You may need to update type layers when files are transferred between computers, especially between operating systems.

3   Choose File > Browse In Mini Bridge to open the Mini Bridge panel. If Bridge isn't running in the background, click Launch Bridge.

4   In the Mini Bridge panel, choose Favorites from the pop-up menu on the left. Double-click the Lessons folder, and then double-click the Lesson08 folder.

5   Select the 08End.psd file, and press the spacebar to see it in full-screen view.

To create this sign, you'll work with an image of a toy spaceship, and practice making paths and selections using the Pen tool. As you create the background shapes and type, you'll learn more about shape layers and vector masks as well as ways to use Smart Objects.

6   When you've finished looking at 08End.psd, press the spacebar again. Then double-click the 08Start.psd file to open it in Photoshop.

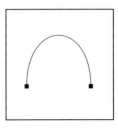 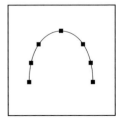

7   Choose File > Save As, rename the file **08Working.psd**, and click Save. Click OK in the Photoshop Format Options dialog box.

## Using paths with artwork

You'll use the Pen tool to select the toy spaceship. The spaceship has long, smooth, curved edges that would be difficult to select using other methods.

You'll draw a path around the spaceship, and create another path inside it. You'll convert the paths to selections, and then subtract one selection from the other so that only the spaceship and none of the background is selected. Finally, you'll make a new layer from the spaceship image, and change the image that appears behind it.

When drawing a freehand path using the Pen tool, use as few points as possible to create the shape you want. The fewer points you use, the smoother the curves are—and the more efficient your file is.

Correct number of points       Too many points

# Creating paths with the Pen tool

You can use the Pen tool to create paths that are straight or curved, open or closed. If you're unfamiliar with the Pen tool, it can be confusing to use at first. Understanding the elements of a path and how to create them with the Pen tool makes paths much easier to draw.

To create a straight path, click the mouse button. The first time you click, you set the starting point. Each time that you click thereafter, a straight line is drawn between the previous point and the current point. To draw complex straight-segment paths with the Pen tool, simply continue to add points.

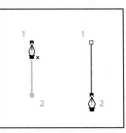

*Creating a straight line*

To create a curved path, click to place an anchor point, drag to create a direction line for that point, and then click to place the next anchor point. Each direction line ends in two direction points; the positions of direction lines and points determine the size and shape of the curved segment. Moving the direction lines and points reshapes the curves in a path.

Smooth curves are connected by anchor points called *smooth points*. Sharply curved paths are connected by *corner points*. When you move a direction line on a smooth point, the curved segments on both sides of the point adjust simultaneously, but when you move a direction line on a corner point, only the curve on the same side of the point as the direction line is adjusted.

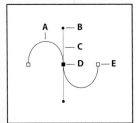

**A.** *Curved line segment*
**B.** *Direction point*
**C.** *Direction line*
**D.** *Selected anchor point*
**E.** *Unselected anchor point*

Path segments and anchor points can be moved after they're drawn, either individually or as a group. When a path contains more than one segment, you can drag individual anchor points to adjust individual segments of the path, or select all of the anchor points in a path to edit the entire path. Use the Direct Selection tool to select and adjust an anchor point, a path segment, or an entire path.

Creating a closed path differs from creating an open path in the way that you end it. To end an open path, click the Pen tool in the Tools panel. To create a closed path, position the Pen tool pointer over the starting point, and click. Closing a path automatically ends the path. After the path closes, the Pen tool pointer appears with a small x, indicating that your next click will start a new path.

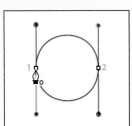

*Creating a closed path*

As you draw paths, a temporary storage area named Work Path appears in the Paths panel. It's a good idea to save work paths, and it's essential if you use multiple discrete paths in the same image file. If you deselect an existing Work Path in the Paths panel and then start drawing again, a new work path will replace the original one, which will be lost. To save a work path, double-click it in the Paths panel, type a name in the Save Path dialog box, and click OK to rename and save the path. The path remains selected in the Paths panel.

# Drawing with the Pen tool

You'll use the Pen tool to connect the dots from point A to point S, and then back to point A. You'll set straight segments, smooth curve points, and corner points.

The first step is to configure the Pen tool options and the work area. Then you'll trace the outline of a spaceship using a template.

1  Double-click the Mini Bridge tab to close the panel and free up more of the workspace.

2  In the Tools panel, select the Pen tool (✐).

3  In the options bar, select or verify the following settings:

   •  Choose Path from the Tool Mode pop-up menu.

   •  In the Pen Options menu, make sure that Rubber Band is not selected.

   •  Make sure that the Auto Add/Delete option is selected.

**A.** Tool Mode menu  **B.** Pen Options menu

4  Click the Paths tab to bring that panel to the front of the Layers panel group.

The Paths panel displays thumbnail previews of the paths you draw. Currently, the panel is empty, because you haven't started drawing.

5  If necessary, zoom in so that you can easily see the lettered points and red dots on the shape template. Make sure you can see the whole template in the image window, and be sure to reselect the Pen tool after you zoom.

6  Click point A (the blue dot at the top of the spaceship), and release the mouse. You've set the first anchor point.

**7** Click point B, and drag the cursor to the red dot labeled b. Release the mouse. You've set the direction of the curve.

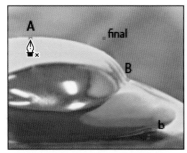

Creating the first anchor point at A

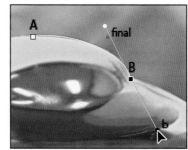

Setting a smooth point at B

At the corner of the cockpit (point B), you'll need to convert the smooth point to a corner point to create a sharp transition between the curved segment and the straight one.

**8** Alt-click (Windows) or Option-click (Mac OS) point B to convert the smooth point into a corner point and remove one of the direction lines.

**9** Click point C, and drag to the red dot labeled c. Do the same for points D and E.

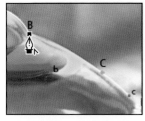

Converting the smooth point

Adding a segment

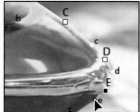

Rounding the corner to a corner point

If you make a mistake while you're drawing, choose Edit > Undo to undo the step. Then resume drawing.

## Completing the outline

You've used the basic techniques that you'll need to draw the entire outline Now, continue around the spaceship until you reach the starting point.

**1** Click point F, and release the mouse without dragging a handle.

**2** Click point G, and drag over from point G to its red dot.

**3** Click point H, and drag up to its dot. Then Alt-click or Option-click to create another corner point at point H.

**4** Click point I, and drag up to its dot in the yellow area. Then Alt-click or Option-click to create a corner point at point I.

**5** Click point J, and drag to its dot. Then create a corner point at point J.

**6** Click point K, and drag to its dot; click point L and drag to its dot; and then create a corner point at point L.

**7** Click point M, drag to its dot, create a corner point at point M, and then click point N, and drag to its dot.

**8** Click points O and P, leaving straight lines. Click Point Q, and drag the handle to the corresponding red dot to create the curve around the tail of the fin.

**9** Click at points R and S without dragging to create straight lines.

**10** Move the pointer over point A so that a small circle appears in the pointer icon, indicating that you are about to close the path. (The small circle may be difficult to see.) Drag from point A to the red dot labeled "final," and then release the mouse button to draw the last curved line.

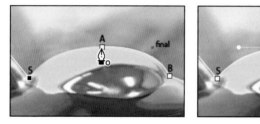

**11** In the Paths panel, double-click Work Path, type **Spaceship** in the Save Path dialog box, and click OK to save it.

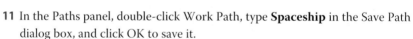

**12** Choose File > Save to save your work.

## Converting selections to paths

Now you'll create a second path using a different method. First you'll use a selection tool to select a similarly colored area, and then you'll convert the selection to a path. (You can convert any selection made with a selection tool into a path.)

1  Click the Layers tab to display the Layers panel, and then drag the Template layer to the Delete button at the bottom of the panel. You no longer need this layer.

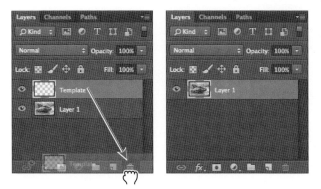

2  Select the Magic Wand tool (✦) in the Tools panel, hidden under the Quick Selection tool.

3  In the options bar, make sure the Tolerance value is **32**.

4  Carefully click the green area inside the spaceship's vertical fin.

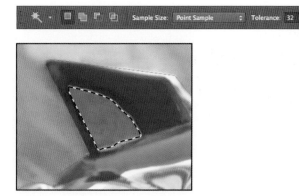

**5**  Click the Paths tab to bring the Paths panel forward. Then, click the Make Work Path From Selection button (⟡) at the bottom of the panel.

The selection is converted to a path, and a new work path is created.

**6**  Double-click the path named Work Path, name it **Fin**, and then click OK to save the path.

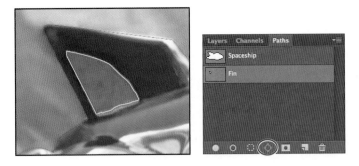

**7**  Choose File > Save to save your work.

## Converting paths to selections

Just as you can convert selection borders to paths, you can convert paths to selections. With their smooth outlines, paths let you make precise selections. Now that you've drawn paths for the spaceship and its fin, you'll convert those paths to a selection and apply a filter to the selection.

**1**  In the Paths panel, click the Spaceship path to make it active.

**2**  Choose Make Selection from the Paths panel menu, and then click OK to convert the Spaceship path to a selection.

▶ **Tip:** You can also click the Load Path As Selection button at the bottom of the Paths panel to convert the active path to a selection.

Next, you'll subtract the Fin selection from the Spaceship selection so that you can see the background through the vacant areas in the fin.

**3** In the Paths panel, click the Fin path to make it active. Then, from the Paths panel menu, choose Make Selection.

**4** In the Operation area of the Make Selection dialog box, select Subtract From Selection, and click OK.

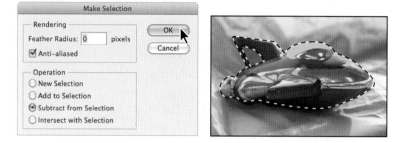

The Fin path is simultaneously converted to a selection and subtracted from the Spaceship selection.

Leave the paths selected, because you'll use them in the next exercise.

## Converting the selection to a layer

Now you'll see how creating the selection with the Pen tool can help you achieve interesting effects. Because you've isolated the spaceship, you can create a duplicate of it on a new layer. Then, you can copy it to another image file—specifically, to the image that's the background for the toy-store sign.

**1** Make sure that you can still see the selection outline in the image window. If you can't, repeat the previous exercise, "Converting paths to selections."

**2** Choose Layer > New > Layer Via Copy.

**3** Click the Layers tab to bring the Layers panel to the front.

A new layer appears in the Layers panel, called Layer 2. The Layer 2 thumbnail shows that the layer contains only the image of the spaceship, not the background of the original layer.

**4** In the Layers panel, rename Layer 2 **Spaceship**, and press Enter or Return.

**5** Choose File > Open, and double-click the 08Landscape.psd file in the Lessons/ Lesson08 folder.

The 08Landscape.psd file contains the landscape that you'll use as the background for the spaceship.

**6** Choose Window > Arrange > 2 Up Vertical so that you can see both the open files. Click the 08Working.psd image to make it active.

**7** Select the Move tool (✛), and drag the spaceship from the 08Working.psd image window to the 08Landscape.psd image window so that the spaceship appears to be hovering over the planet.

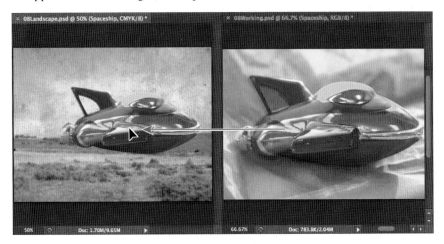

**8** Close the 08Working.psd image without saving changes, leaving the 08Landscape.psd file open and active.

Now you'll position the spaceship more precisely over the background.

**9** Select the Spaceship layer in the Layers panel, and choose Edit > Free Transform.

A bounding box appears around the spaceship.

● **Note:** If you accidentally distort the spaceship instead of rotating it, press Esc and start over.

**10** Position the pointer near any corner handle until it turns into the rotate cursor (↻), and then drag to rotate the spaceship until its angle is about -12 degrees. For precise rotation, you can enter the value in the Rotate box in the options bar. When you're satisfied, press Enter or Return.

**11** Make sure the Spaceship layer is still selected, and then use the Move tool to drag the ship so that it grazes the top of the planet, as in the third image.

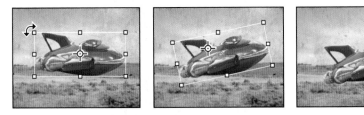

**12** Choose File > Save As, rename the file **08B_Working.psd**, and click Save. Click OK in the Photoshop Format Options dialog box.

# Creating vector objects for the background

Many signs are designed to be scalable, either up or down, while retaining a crisp appearance: a good use for vector shapes. Next, you'll create vector shapes with paths, and use masks to control what appears on the sign. Because they're vectors, the shapes can be scaled in future design revisions without a loss of quality or detail.

## Drawing a scalable shape

You'll begin by creating a white kidney-shaped object for the background of the sign.

1   Choose View > Rulers to display the horizontal and vertical rulers.

2   Drag the tab for the Paths panel out of the Layers panel group so that it floats independently.

Since you'll be using the Layers and Paths panels frequently in this exercise, it's convenient to have them separated.

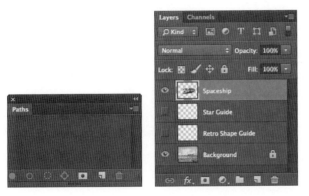

3   Toggle the eye icons in the Layers panel to show the Retro Shape Guide and Background layers, and to hide the other two layers. Select the Background layer to make it active.

The guide layer will serve as a template as you draw the kidney shape.

**4** In the Tools panel, select the Pen tool (✐).

**5** In the options bar, choose Shape from the pop-up menu, and then click the Fill color. Select white for the fill color.

● **Note:** If you have trouble, open the spaceship image again and practice drawing the path around the spaceship shape until you get more comfortable with drawing curved path segments. Also, be sure to read the sidebar "Creating paths with the Pen tool."

**6** Create the shape by clicking and dragging as follows:

- Click point A, drag a direction line up to point B, and then release.

- Click point C, drag a direction line to point D, and then release.

- Continue to draw curved segments in this way around the shape until you return to point A, and then click point A to close the path. Don't worry if the shape flips in on itself; it will right itself as you continue.

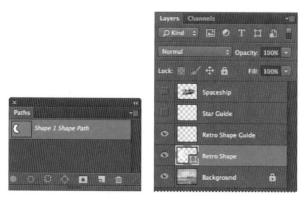

Notice that as you drew, Photoshop automatically created a new layer, Shape 1, just above the active layer (the Background layer) in the Layers panel.

**7** Double-click the Shape 1 layer name, rename the layer **Retro Shape**, and press Enter or Return.

**8** Hide the Retro Shape Guide layer in the Layers panel.

## Deselecting paths

You may need to deselect paths to see the appropriate options in the options bar when you select a vector tool. Deselecting paths can also help you view certain effects that might be obscured if a path is highlighted.

Notice that the border between the white kidney shape and the background has a grainy quality. What you see is actually the path itself, which is a nonprinting item. This is a visual clue that the Retro Shape layer is still selected. Before proceeding to the next exercise, you'll make sure that all paths are deselected.

1  In the Paths panel, click in the empty area beneath the path to deselect all paths.

2  Choose File > Save to save your work.

## Changing the fill color of a shape layer

You created the shape with a white fill so that it was easy to see. But for the sign, you'll change the color of the shape to blue.

1  Make sure the Retro Shape layer is selected in the Layers panel.

2  Select the Pen tool in the Tools panel, if it's not already selected.

3  In the options bar, click the Fill color. Select the Light Cyan Blue color.

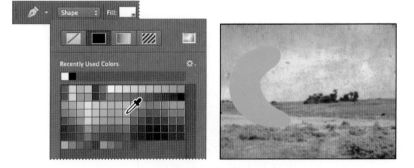

The fill color of the shape changes to the blue you selected.

## Subtracting shapes from a shape layer

After you create a shape layer (vector graphic), you can set options to subtract new shapes from the vector graphic. You can also use the Path Selection tool and the Direct Selection tool to move, resize, and edit shapes. You'll add some interest to the retro shape by subtracting a star shape from it, allowing the background to show through. To help you position the star, you'll refer to the Star Guide layer, which has been created for you. Currently, that layer is hidden.

1  In the Layers panel, show the Star Guide layer, but leave the Retro Shape layer selected. The Star Guide layer is now visible in the image window.

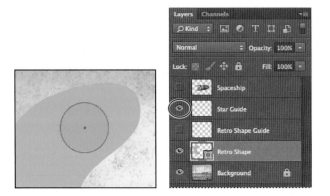

2  In the Paths panel, select the Retro Shape shape path.

3  In the Tools panel, select the Polygon tool (⬤), hidden under the Rectangle tool (▭).

4  On the options bar, do the following:

- For Sides, type **11**.

- From the Path Operations pop-up menu, choose Subtract Front Shape. The pointer now appears as cross-hairs with a small minus sign (✚).

- Click the Settings icon to the left of the Sides option to display the Polygon Options window. Select Star, and type **50%** in the Indent Sides By box. Then click an empty area of the options bar to close the window.

**5** Click on the orange dot in the center of the orange circle in the image window, and drag outward until the tips of the star rays touch the circle's perimeter.

● **Note:** As you drag, you can rotate the star by dragging the pointer to the side.

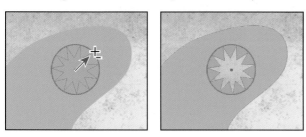

When you release the mouse button, the star shape becomes a cutout, allowing the sky to show through.

Notice that the star has a grainy outline, reminding you that the shape is selected. Another indication that the shape is selected is that the Retro Shape shape path is selected in the Paths panel.

**6** In the Layers panel, hide the Star Guide layer.

Notice that the thumbnails in both the Layers panel and Paths panel show the retro shape with the star-shaped cutout.

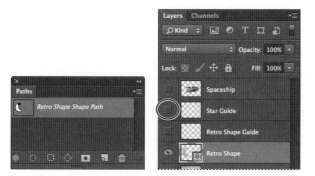

**7** Click in the area beneath the path in the Paths panel to deselect the path.

The path is now deselected, and the grainy path lines have disappeared, leaving a sharp edge between the blue areas and the sky. Also, the Retro Shape shape path is no longer highlighted in the Paths panel. That shape is pretty bright, though, and may overpower the spaceship. You'll make the shape semitransparent.

**8** In the Layers panel, reduce the opacity of the Retro Shape layer to **40**%.

**9** Choose File > Save to save your work.

# Working with defined custom shapes

Another way to use shapes in your artwork is to draw a custom or preset shape. Doing so is as easy as selecting the Custom Shape tool, picking a shape from the Custom Shape Picker, and dragging in the image window. You'll do just that to add checkerboard patterns and clumps of grass to the background of your sign for the toy store.

**1** Make sure the Retro Shape layer is selected in the Layers panel. Then click the New Layer button (⬒) to add a layer above it. Rename the new layer **Pattern**, and then press Enter or Return.

**2** In the Tools panel, select the Custom Shape tool (🧩), which is hidden under the Polygon tool (⬢).

**3** In the options bar, choose Pixels from the Tool Mode menu.

In Pixels drawing mode, you paint rasterized (non-vector) shapes directly on the existing layer.

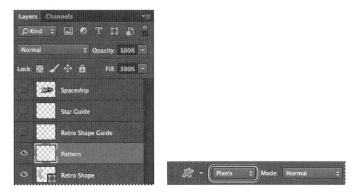

**4** In the options bar, click the arrow next to the Shape option to open the Custom Shape Picker.

**5** Double-click the checkerboard preset in the Custom Shape Picker (you may need to scroll or drag the corner of the picker to see it) to select it and close the picker.

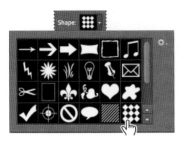

**6** Change the foreground color to white. Then press Shift, and drag diagonally in the image window to draw a shape that is about 2 inches square.

**Note:** The options in the options bar change depending on what you choose from the Tool Mode menu. When you work in Shape mode, you can select a fill or stroke in the options bar; in Pixels mode, those options aren't available.

Pressing Shift constrains the shape to its original proportions.

**7** Add four more checkerboards of various sizes until your image resembles the figure below.

**8** In the Layers panel, reduce the opacity of the Pattern layer to **75%**.

**9** In the Layers panel, show the Spaceship layer so you can see the whole composition.

You'll use the Custom Shape tool to add clumps of grass to the background. You can apply a fill and stroke to shapes when you work in Shape mode.

▶ **Tip:** You can choose categories from the options menu in the Custom Shape Picker to add more shapes.

**10** With the Custom Shape tool still selected, open the Custom Shape Picker, and double-click the clump of grass (called Grass 2).

**11** Choose Shape from the Tool Mode menu. Then, select Dark Yellow Green for the Fill color, select Darker Green Cyan for the Stroke color, and enter **.75** for the stroke width.

**12** Press Shift as you draw four clumps of grass in the lower left corner of the background and an additional clump in the lower right corner.

● **Note:** If the clumps of grass are on separate layers, you weren't holding down the Shift key as you drew them. Delete the grass, and repeat steps 12–13.

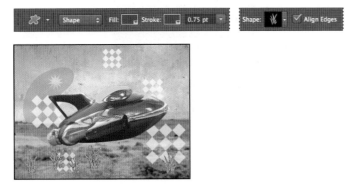

Pressing Shift as you draw ensures that all the shapes are on the same layer.

**13** Select the Path Selection tool (⬉) in the Tools panel, and then Shift-select all five clumps of grass.

**14** Choose Distribute Widths from the Path Alignment menu in the options bar.

Photoshop distributes the grass clumps evenly across the bottom of the background.

**15** Rename the layer **Grass**, change its opacity to **60%**, and drag the layer just above the Background layer in the Layers panel.

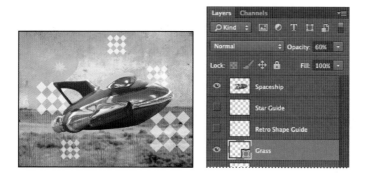

**16** Deselect the layer, and then choose File > Save to save your work so far.

## Working with Photoshop files in Illustrator

In this lesson, you're importing vector artwork that was created in Illustrator to use as the logo in your sign. You can also open, place, or paste Photoshop files in Illustrator.

While you can create and edit vector graphics in Photoshop, its primary purpose is to edit bitmap images. Likewise, you can work with bitmaps in Illustrator, but its strength is to create and edit vector artwork. Depending on the nature of your project, you may want to use both applications to take advantage of features that are available in one but the other.

Illustrator supports most Photoshop data, including layer comps, layers, editable text, and paths. This means that you can transfer files between Photoshop and Illustrator without losing the ability to edit the artwork. In cases where Illustrator must convert the Photoshop data, it displays a warning message so you'll know what you're losing in the process.

# Importing a Smart Object

Smart Objects are layers that you can edit in Photoshop nondestructively; that is, changes you make to the image remain editable and don't affect the actual image pixels, which are preserved. Regardless of how often you scale, rotate, skew, or otherwise transform a Smart Object, it retains its sharp, precise edges.

You can import vector objects from Adobe Illustrator as Smart Objects. If you edit the original object in Illustrator, the changes will be reflected in the placed Smart Object in your Photoshop image file. You'll work with a Smart Object now by placing text created in Illustrator into the toy-store sign.

## Adding the title

The toy-store name was created in Illustrator. You'll add it to the sign now.

1   Select the Move tool (⊹) in the Tools panel. Then select the Spaceship layer, and choose File > Place. Navigate to the Lessons/Lesson08 folder, select the Title.ai file, and click Place. Click OK in the Place PDF dialog box that appears.

The Retro Toyz text is added to the middle of the composition, inside a bounding box with adjustable handles. A new layer, Title, appears in the Layers panel.

2   Drag the Retro Toyz object to the upper left corner of the sign, and then press Shift and drag a corner to make the text object proportionally larger—large enough that it fills the top portion of the image, as in the following figure. When you've finished, either press Enter or Return, or click the Commit Transform button (✔) in the options bar.

When you commit to the transformation, the layer thumbnail icon changes to reflect that the title layer is a Smart Object.

As with any shape layer or Smart Object, you can continue to edit its size and shape if you'd like. Simply select the layer, choose Edit > Free Transform to access the control handles, and drag to adjust them. Or, select the Move tool (▶⊕), and select Show Transform Controls in the options bar. Then adjust the handles.

## Adding a vector mask to a Smart Object

For a fun effect, you'll turn the center of each letter "O" in the title into a star that matches the cutout you created earlier. You'll use a vector mask, which you can link to a Smart Object in Photoshop.

1 Select the Title layer, and then choose Layer > Vector Mask > Reveal All.

2 Select the Polygon tool (⬤), hidden beneath the Custom Shape tool (🎨). The options you used earlier to create the star should still be in effect: settings for an 11-sided star with a 50% indent.

The Polygon tool holds your settings until you change them again.

3 Choose Path from the Tool Mode menu in the options bar. Make sure Subtract Front Shape is still selected from the Path Operations menu. Then select the vector mask thumbnail in the Title layer.

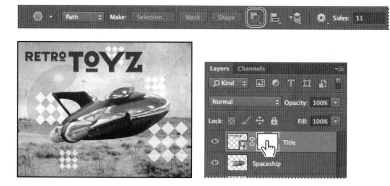

4 Click in the center of the "O" in "Toyz," and drag the cursor outward until the star covers the center of the "O."

5 Repeat step 4 to add a star in the small "O" in Retro. Then deselect the Title Vector Mask path in the Paths panel.

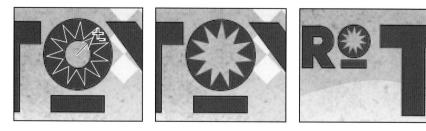

## Rotating the canvas (OpenGL only)

You've been working with the image with "Retro Toyz" at the top of the work area and the ground at the bottom. But if your video card supports OpenGL, you can rotate the work area to draw, type, or position objects from a different perspective. You'll rotate the view as you add a copyright statement along the side of the image. (If your video card doesn't support OpenGL, skip this section.)

First, you'll type the text.

1   Choose Window > Character to open the Character panel. Select a serif font such as Myriad Pro with a small size such as 10 pt, and set the color to white.

2   Select the Horizontal Type tool, and then click in the lower left corner of the image. Type **Copyright YOUR NAME Productions**, substituting your own name.

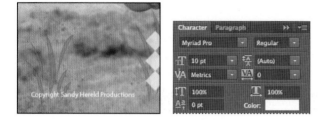

You want the copyright to run along the left side of the image. You'll rotate the canvas to make it easier to place.

3   Select the Rotate View tool (⟳), hidden beneath the Hand tool (✋).

4   Press the Shift key as you drag the tool in an arc to rotate the canvas 90 degrees clockwise. Pressing the Shift key restrains the rotation to 45-degree increments.

▶ **Tip:** You can also enter a value in the Rotation Angle box in the options bar.

**5** Select the Copyright text layer, and then choose Edit > Transform > Rotate 90° CCW.

**6** Use the Move tool to align the text along the top edge of the image, which will be the left edge when it is in its usual position.

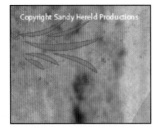

**7** Select the Rotate View tool again, and then click Reset View in the options bar.

**8** Choose File > Save to save your work.

## Finishing up

As a final step, clean up the Layers panel by deleting your guide template layers.

**1** Make sure that the Copyright, Title, Spaceship, Pattern, Retro Shape, Grass, and Background layers are the only visible layers in the Layers panel.

**2** Choose Delete Hidden Layers from the Layers panel menu, and then click Yes to confirm the deletion.

**3** Choose File > Save to save your work.

Congratulations! You've finished the sign. It should look similar to the following image.

# Extra credit

## Using Photoshop files in InDesign

Adobe InDesign supports native Photoshop files. You can place PSD files, and then easily return to Photoshop to edit them, automatically updating the linked file in InDesign.

### Placing images

You'll place the image of the sign that contains the spaceship and the store logo into an InDesign stationery template. Then you'll make changes in Photoshop to adapt the image for this use.

1   In Photoshop, choose File > Save As. Save the file as Final_spaceship.psd. Click OK in the Photoshop Format Options dialog box.

2   Open InDesign, and choose File > Open. Double-click the Lesson08/Extra_Credit/08_Stationery.indd file to open it.

3   In InDesign, choose Normal mode at the bottom of the Tools panel so that you can see the object frames in the template.

4   With the Selection tool, select the frame at the top of the letterhead.

5   Choose File > Place, and double-click the Lesson08/Final_spaceship.psd file.

The image appears in the frame you selected. Frame-fitting options were already applied to the frame in the template, so the image places proportionally, with the bottom half cut off.

6   Repeat steps 4–5 to place the same image in the postcard and the business card.

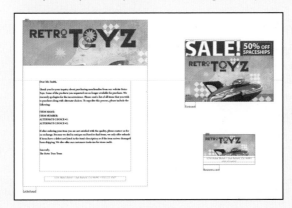

*(continues on next page)*

# Extra credit (continued)

### Editing images

You'll make some changes to the linked image so that it fits the stationery template better. You'll adjust the location of the spaceship and the copyright text, and you'll remove the distracting background pattern. The full image won't fit in each of the object frames, but you'll be able to see more of the spaceship and the copyright information.

1 In InDesign, choose Window > Links to display the Links panel.

2 Select the Final_spaceship.psd (3), and then click the Edit Original button at the bottom of the Links panel.

The Final_spaceship.psd file opens in Photoshop.

3 In Photoshop, select the Spaceship layer, and then use the Move tool to nudge it closer to the Retro Toyz name.

4 Hide the Pattern layer.

5 Select the Copyright layer, and use the Move tool to move it to the upper right corner. Then choose Edit > Transform > Rotate 180°.

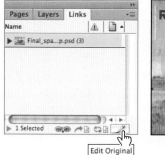 

6 Choose File > Save in Photoshop, and then return to InDesign.

The linked images automatically reflect the changes you made in Photoshop. If you don't see the changes, click the Update Link button at the bottom of the Links panel in InDesign.

## Review questions

1 How can the Pen tool be useful as a selection tool?

2 What is the difference between a bitmap image and a vector graphic?

3 What is a shape layer?

4 What tools can you use to move and resize paths and shapes?

5 What are Smart Objects, and what is the benefit of using them?

## Review answers

1 If you need to create an intricate selection, it can be easier to draw the path with the Pen tool and then convert the path to a selection.

2 Bitmap, or raster, images are based on a grid of pixels and are appropriate for continuous-tone images such as photographs or artwork created in painting programs. Vector graphics are made up of shapes based on mathematical expressions and are appropriate for illustrations, type, and drawings that require clear, smooth lines.

3 A shape layer is a vector layer that contains either a shape (including fill and stroke), pixels, or a path.

4 You use the Path Selection tool and the Direct Selection tool to move, resize, and edit shapes. You can also modify and scale a shape or path by choosing Edit > Free Transform Path.

5 Smart Objects are vector objects that you can place and edit in Photoshop without a loss of quality. Regardless of how often you scale, rotate, skew, or otherwise transform a Smart Object, it retains sharp, precise edges. A great benefit of using Smart Objects is that you can edit the original object in the authoring application, such as Illustrator, and the changes will be reflected in the placed Smart Object in your Photoshop image file.

# 9 ADVANCED COMPOSITING

## Lesson overview

In this lesson, you'll learn how to do the following:

- Apply and edit Smart Filters.

- Apply color effects to selected areas of an image.

- Apply filters to create various effects.

- Record and play back an action to automate a series of steps.

- Create a conditional action.

- Upscale a low-resolution image for high-resolution printing.

- Blend images to create a panorama.

This lesson will take about 90 minutes to complete. Download the Lesson09 project files from the Lesson & Update Files tab on your Account page at www.peachpit.com, if you haven't already done so. As you work on this lesson, you'll preserve the start files. If you need to restore the start files, download them from your Account page.

The curse of FRANK & STEIN

Monster makeup imagery courtesy of Russell Brown, with illustration by John Connell

PROJECT: MONSTER MOVIE POSTER DESIGN

Filters can transform ordinary images into extraordinary digital artwork. Smart Filters let you edit those transformations. Photoshop includes many features to help you vary the look of your artwork. With actions, you can perform repetitive tasks quickly so you can spend more time working creatively.

# Getting started

In this lesson, you'll create publicity materials for a monster movie. You'll assemble a montage of images for a poster, and then stitch together a panorama to create a web banner. First, look at the final projects to see what you'll be creating.

1. Start Photoshop, and then immediately hold down Ctrl+Alt+Shift (Windows) or Command+Option+Shift (Mac OS) to restore the default preferences. (See "Restoring default preferences" on page 4.)

2. When prompted, click Yes to delete the Adobe Photoshop Settings file.

3. Choose File > Browse In Bridge.

**Note:** If Bridge isn't installed, you'll be prompted to install it when you choose Browse In Bridge. For more information, see page 3.

4. In Bridge, choose Favorites from the menu on the left, and then double-click the Lessons folder. Double-click the Lesson09 folder.

5. View the 09A_End.psd thumbnail. Move the slider on the bottom of the Bridge window if you need to zoom in to see the thumbnail more clearly.

This file is a movie poster that comprises a background, a monster image, and several smaller images. Each image has had one or more filters or effects applied to it.

The monster is composed of an image of a perfectly normal (though slightly threatening) guy with several ghoulish images applied. These monstrous additions are courtesy of Russell Brown, with illustration by John Connell.

6. Now view the 09B_End.jpeg thumbnail.

This file is a web banner with a panoramic image and text. You'll create the poster with multiple images first. You'll start by combining several layers in Photoshop to assemble the monster.

**7** In Bridge, navigate to the Lesson09/Monster-Makeup folder, and open it.

**8** Shift-click to select all the files in the Monster-Makeup folder, and then choose Tools > Photoshop > Load Files Into Photoshop Layers.

Photoshop imports all the selected files as individual layers in a new Photoshop file. The visibility icon is labeled red in the layers that create the monster's look.

**9** In Photoshop, choose File > Save As. Choose Photoshop for the Format, and name the new file **09Working.psd**. Save it in the Lesson09 folder. Click OK in the Photoshop Format Options dialog box.

## Arranging layers

Your image file contains eight layers, imported in alphabetical order. In their current positions, they don't make a very convincing monster. You'll rearrange the layer order and resize their contents as you start to build your monster.

**1** Zoom out or scroll so that you can see all the layers on the artboard.

**2** In the Layers panel, drag the Monster_Hair layer to the top of the layer stack.

**3** Drag the Franken layer to the bottom of the layer stack.

**4** Select the Move tool, and then move the Franken layer (the image of the person) to the bottom of the page.

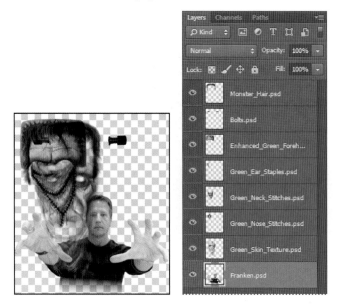

**5** In the Layers panel, Shift-select every layer except the Franken layer, and choose Edit > Free Transform.

**6** Press the Shift key as you drag down from a corner of the selection to resize all the selected layers to about 50% of their original size. (Watch the width and height percentages in the options bar.)

**7** With the resized layers still selected, move them over the head of the Franken layer. Then press Enter or Return to commit the transformation.

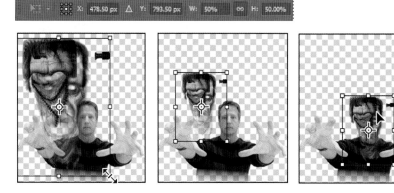

**8** Zoom in to see the head area clearly.

**9** Hide all layers except the Green_Skin_Texture and Franken layers.

**10** Select only the Green_Skin_Texture layer, and use the Move tool to center it over the face.

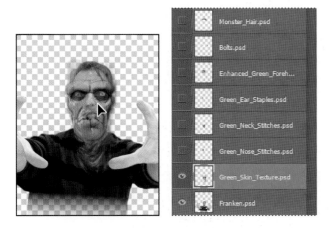

**11** Choose Edit > Free Transform again to adjust the fit of the texture to the face. Use the side handles to adjust the width, the bottom and top handles to adjust the height, and arrow keys to nudge the entire layer into position. Use the eyes and mouth as a guide. When you've positioned the skin texture, press Enter or Return to commit the transformation.

**12** Save your file.

# Using Smart Filters

Unlike regular filters, which permanently change an image, Smart Filters are nondestructive: They can be adjusted, turned off and on, and deleted. However, you can apply Smart Filters only to a Smart Object.

## Applying the Liquify filter

You'll use the Liquify filter to tighten the eye openings and change the shape of the monster's face. Because you want to be able to adjust the filter settings later, you'll use the Liquify filter as a Smart Filter. So you'll first need to convert the Green_Skin_Texture layer to a Smart Object.

1 Make sure the Green_Skin_Texture layer is selected in the Layers panel, and then choose Convert To Smart Object from the Layers panel menu.

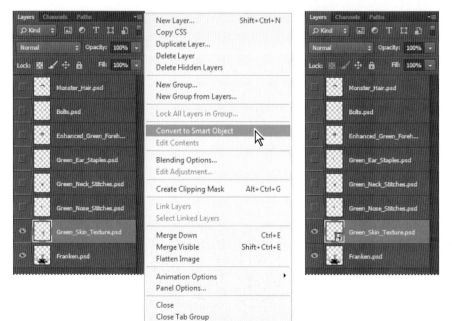

2 Choose Filter > Liquify.

Photoshop displays the layer in the Liquify dialog box.

3 In the Liquify dialog box, select Advanced Mode to see additional options.

4 Select Show Backdrop, and then choose Behind from the Mode menu. Set the Opacity to **75**.

5 Select the Zoom tool (🔍) from the Tools panel on the left side of the dialog box, and zoom in to the eye area.

**6** Select the Forward Warp tool (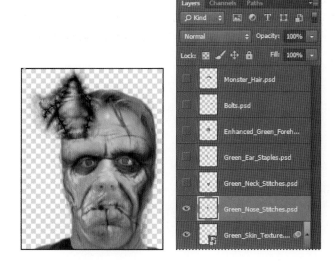)(the first tool).

The Forward Warp tool pushes pixels forward as you drag.

**7** In the Tool Options area, set the Brush Size to **150** and Brush Pressure to **75**.

**8** With the Forward Warp tool, pull the right eyebrow down to close the eye opening. Then pull up from under the eye.

**9** Repeat step 8 on the left eyebrow and under-eye area.

**10** When you've closed the gap around the eyes, click OK.

Because you've applied the Liquify filter as a Smart Filter, you can return later to make additional changes to the face.

## Positioning other layers

Now that you've got the skin texture in place, you'll move the other layers into position, working up from the lowest layers in the Layers panel.

**1** Make the Green_Nose_Stitches layer visible, and select it in the Layers panel.

**2** Choose Edit > Free Transform, and then position the layer over the nose, resizing it as necessary. Press Enter or Return to commit the transformation.

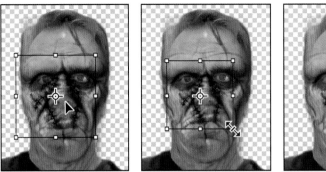

**3** Repeat steps 1–2 to position the following layers:

- Move the Green_Neck_Stitches layer over the neck.

- Move the Green_Ear_Staples layer over the left ear.

- Move the Enhanced_Green_Forehead layer over the forehead.

- Move the Bolts layer so that the bolts are on either side of the neck.

- Move the Monster_Hair layer over the top of the forehead.

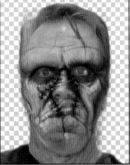

**4** Save your work so far.

## Editing a Smart Filter

With all the layers in position, you can further refine the eye openings and experiment with the bulges in the eyebrows. You'll return to the Liquify filter to make those adjustments.

**1** In the Layers panel, double-click Liquify, listed under Smart Filters in the Green_Skin_Texture layer.

Photoshop opens the Liquify dialog box again. This time, all the layers are visible in Photoshop, so when Show Backdrop is selected, you see them all. Sometimes it's easier to make changes without a backdrop to distract you. Other times, it's useful to see your edits in context.

**2** Zoom in to see the eyes more closely.

**3** Select the Pucker tool (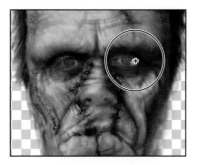) in the Tools panel, and click on the outer corner of each eye.

The Pucker tool moves pixels towards the center of the brush as you click or drag, for a puckering effect.

**4** Select the Bloat tool ( ), and click the outer edge of an eyebrow to expand it; do the same for the other eyebrow.

The Bloat tool moves pixels away from the center of the brush as you click or drag.

**5** Experiment with the Pucker, Bloat, and other tools in the Liquify filter to customize the monster's face. Remember that you can change the brush size and other settings. You can undo individual steps, but if you want to start over, it's easiest to click Cancel, and then return to the Liquify dialog box.

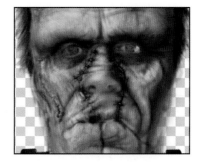

**6** When you're happy with your monster's face, click OK.

## Painting a layer

There are many ways to paint objects and layers in Photoshop. One of the simplest is to use the Color blending mode and the Brush tool. You'll use this method to paint the exposed skin green on your monster.

**1** Select the Franken layer in the Layers panel.

**2** Click the Create A New Layer button at the bottom of the Layers panel.

Photoshop creates a new layer, named Layer 1.

**Tip:** To learn more about blending modes, including a description of each one, see "Blending modes" in Photoshop Help.

**3** With Layer 1 selected, choose Color from the Blending Mode menu at the top of the Layers panel.

The Color blending mode combines the luminance of the base color (the color already on the layer) with the hue and saturation of the color you're applying. It's a good blending mode to use when you're coloring monochrome images or tinting color images.

**4** Select the Brush tool ( ). In the options bar, select a **60**-pixel brush with a hardness of **0**.

**5** Press Alt or Option to temporarily switch to the Eyedropper tool. Sample a green color from the forehead. Then release the Alt or Option key to return to the Brush tool.

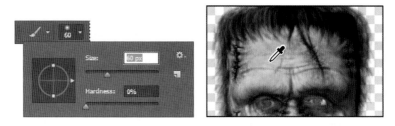

**6** Ctrl-click or Command-click the thumbnail in the Franken layer to select its contents.

**Tip:** To change the brush size as you paint, press the bracket keys on your keyboard. The Left Bracket key ([) decreases the brush size; the Right Bracket (]) increases it.

**7** Make sure Layer 1 is still selected in the Layers panel, and then use the Brush tool to paint over the hands and arms. Be careful not to paint outside the skin where it abuts the shirt colors. You can be less careful where the skin is at the edge of the selection because painting outside the selection has no effect.

8 Paint any areas of the face or neck where the original flesh color shows through the Green_Skin_Texture layer.

9 When you're happy with the green skin, choose Select > Deselect. Save your work.

# Adding a background

You've got a good-looking monster. Now it's time to put him in his spooky environment. To easily move the monster onto a background, you'll first merge the layers.

1 Make sure all the layers are visible. Then choose Merge Visible from the Layers panel menu.

Photoshop merges all the layers into one, named Layer 1.

2 Rename Layer 1 **Monster**.

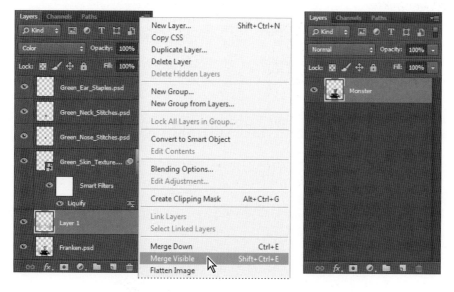

3 Choose File > Open. Navigate to and open the Backdrop.psd file in the Lesson09 folder.

4 Choose Window > Arrange > 2-Up Vertical to display both the monster and backdrop files.

5 Click the 09Working.psd file to make it active.

**6** Select the Move tool (✛), and then drag the Monster layer onto the Backdrop.psd file. Position the monster so his hands are just above the movie title.

**7** Close the 09Working.psd file, saving the changes when prompted.

**8** Choose File > Save As, and save the file with the name **Movie-Poster.psd**. Click OK in the Photoshop Format Options dialog box.

## Automating a multistep task

An *action* is a set of one or more commands that you record and then play back to apply to a single file or a batch of files. You can even create conditional actions that change their behavior based on criteria you define. In this exercise, you'll create actions to apply filters to images of gravestones, and then use a conditional action to determine how those actions are applied.

Using actions is one of several ways that you can automate tasks in Adobe Photoshop. To learn more about recording actions, see Photoshop Help.

## Recording an action

You'll start by recording an action that applies a series of filters to an image. You use the Actions panel to record, play, edit, and delete individual actions. You also use the Actions panel to save and load action files.

1  Choose File > Browse In Mini Bridge to open the Mini Bridge panel.

2  Navigate to the Lesson09 folder, double-click it, and then double-click the Tombstones folder.

3  Double-click T1.psd to open it.

4  In the Tools panel, click the Default Foreground And Background Colors button (◘) to return the foreground color to black.

5  Choose Window > Actions to open the Actions panel.

6  In the Actions panel, click the Create New Action (◪) button.

7  In the New Action dialog box, name the action **Blue Filter**, and click Record.

Don't let the fact that you're recording rush you. Take all the time you need to do this procedure accurately. The speed at which you work has no influence on the amount of time required to play a recorded action.

**8** Choose Filter > Render > Difference Clouds.

**9** Choose Filter > Noise > Add Noise.

**10** In the Add Noise dialog box, set the Amount to **3**%, select Gaussian, and select Monochromatic. Then click OK.

● **Note:** The Lighting Effects filter is unavailable if Use Graphics Processor is not selected in the Performance Preferences dialog box. If your video card does not support the Use Graphics Processor option, skip steps 11–16.

**11** Choose Filter > Render > Lighting Effects.

**12** In the options bar, choose Flashlight from the Presets menu.

**13** In the Properties panel, click the Color swatch, and select a light blue color.

**14** In the image window, drag the light source to the upper third of the tombstone, centered over the letters "RIP."

**15** In the Properties panel, change the Ambience to **46**.

**16** Click OK in the options bar to accept the Lighting Effects settings.

**17** Click the Stop button (■) at the bottom of the Actions panel to stop recording.

The action you just recorded is now saved in the Actions panel. Click the arrows to expand different sets of steps. You can examine each recorded step and the specific selections you made.

## Improving performance with filters

Some filter effects can be memory-intensive, especially when applied to a high-resolution image. You can use these techniques to improve performance:

- Test filters and settings on a small portion of an image.

- Apply the effect to individual channels—for example, to each RGB channel—if the image is large and you're having problems with insufficient memory. (Note, however, that some filters may produce different results when you apply them to individual channels rather than the composite image, especially if the filter randomly modifies pixels.)

- Free up memory before running the filter by using the Purge commands in the Edit menu.

- Close other open applications to free more memory for Photoshop. If you're using Mac OS, allocate more RAM to Photoshop.

- Try changing settings to improve the speed of memory-intensive filters such as Lighting Effects, Cutout, Stained Glass, Chrome, Ripple, Spatter, Sprayed Strokes, and Glass. For example, with the Stained Glass filter, you might increase cell size. With the Cutout filter, try increasing Edge Simplicity, decreasing Edge Fidelity, or both.

- If you plan to print to a grayscale printer, convert a copy of the image to grayscale before applying filters. However, applying a filter to a color image and then converting to grayscale may not have the same effect as applying the filter to a grayscale version of the image.

## Playing an action

Let's test the action you just recorded! Because you didn't save the changes you made, you can revert to the original image easily. Then, play the action, and see the results.

**1** Choose File > Revert.

The changes you made to the tombstone are gone, but the action remains in the Actions panel.

**2** In the Actions panel, select the Blue Filter action, and then click the Play button (▶).

The tombstone almost instantly looks cloudy, with the same lighting effects you applied earlier. You'll create a second action based on the first, applying settings to this same tombstone. So, once again, you'll revert to the original image.

**3** Choose File > Revert.

## Using filters

As you consider which filter to use and the effect it might have, keep in mind the following:

- The last filter chosen appears at the top of the Filter menu.
- Filters are applied to the active, visible layer.
- Filters cannot be applied to bitmap-mode or indexed-color images.
- Some filters work only on RGB images.
- Some filters are processed entirely in RAM.
- See "Using filters" in Photoshop Help for a list of filters that can be used with 16- and 32-bit-per-channel images.
- Photoshop Help provides specific information on individual filters.

## Copying and amending an action

You'll create another action that applies the same filters, but adds a different color effect. Rather than recording the entire action from scratch, you can copy the original action, and then add to it.

**1** In the Actions panel, drag the Blue Filter action onto the Create New Action button.

**2** Rename the Blue Filter copy action **Green Filter**. You may need to scroll down or extend the Actions panel to see the new filter.

**3** Expand the steps in the Green Filter action, if they're not already visible.

**4** Select the Lighting Effects step, and then click the Record button to start recording from that point.

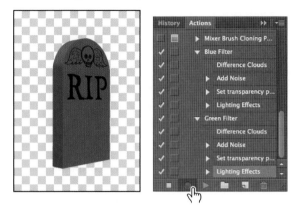

**5** Choose Image > Adjustments > Hue/Saturation.

**6** In the Hue/Saturation dialog box, select Colorize. Enter **120** for Hue. Then click OK.

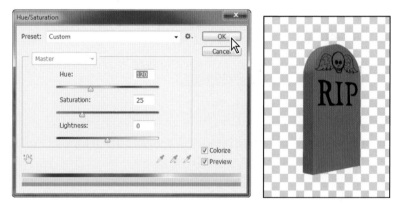

**7** Click the Stop button at the bottom of the Actions panel to stop recording.

**8** Choose Edit > Undo Hue/Saturation to reverse the color in the image so you can test your action.

**9** Select the Green Filter action, and then click the Play button (▶).

All the textures and filters from the first filter have been applied, plus a green hue.

**10** Choose File > Revert again.

## Creating a conditional action

A conditional action applies actions based on criteria such as file orientation, pixel depth, color mode, open status, layer attributes, and more. You've created two actions: One creates a slightly blue cast and one adds a strong green cast. You'll create a conditional action to apply the Green Filter action to tombstones that are horizontal (in landscape orientation) and the Blue Filter action to all others (portrait or square orientations).

1   Click the Create New Action button. Name the new action **Color Select**, and then click Record.

2   Click the Stop button at the bottom of the Actions panel immediately, because you don't actually want to record anything.

3   With the Color Select action selected, choose Insert Conditional from the Actions panel menu.

4   In the Conditional Action dialog box, browse the options in the If Current menu. These are the criteria you can use in a conditional action.

5   Choose Document Is Landscape from the If Current menu.

6   Choose Green Filter from the Then Play Action menu.

7   Choose Blue Filter from the Else Play Action menu, and click OK.

## Batch-playing an action

Applying actions is a timesaving process for performing routine tasks on files, but you can streamline your work even further by applying actions to multiple files at once. You'll apply the conditional action to all five tombstone images, and then add them to your poster.

1 Choose File > Automate > Batch.

2 In the Play area of the Batch dialog box, choose Color Select from the Action menu, and choose Folder from the Source menu.

3 In the Source area of the dialog box, click Choose, navigate to the Lesson09/ Tombstones folder, and click OK or Choose.

4 In the Destination area of the dialog box, choose Folder from the Destination menu, click Choose, navigate to the same Lesson09/Tombstones folder, and click OK or Choose.

5 In the File Naming area of the dialog box, make sure the first box says Document Name. In the box that follows, type **final**.

6 For the next box (the one below "Document Name"), click the arrow to open the pop-up menu, and choose Extension (lower-case). The filename will include the file extension.

7 Click OK.

Photoshop runs the Color Select action on all five of the files in the Tombstone folder, naming each edited file with the word "final" appended to the original file name.

8   In Mini Bridge, Ctrl-select or Command-select all five files that end with the word "final."

9   Drag the selected files to the center of the composition, and then press Enter or Return five times to accept all five placements.

10  Double-click the Mini Bridge tab to close it.

11  Select the Move tool (▶✛). Then, in the options bar, select Auto Select, and choose Layer from the Auto Select menu.

With the Auto Select option selected and Layer chosen, you can move individual objects without first selecting their layers in the Layers panel.

12  Drag the individual tombstones to the bottom of the poster, making sure their bottom edges are cut off by the bottom edge of the poster. You can arrange the tombstones in any way you like.

13  Save your work.

# Upscaling a low-resolution image

Low-resolution images are fine—even desirable—for web pages and social media. If you need to enlarge them, though, they may not contain enough information for high-quality printing. To scale an image up in size, Photoshop needs to resample it. That is, it needs to create new pixels where none existed, approximating their values. A new algorithm in Photoshop CC improves this process tremendously, so you can upscale low-resolution images with much better results.

In your movie poster, you want to use a low-resolution image that was posted on a social media site. You'll need to resize it without compromising quality for your printed poster.

1  Choose File > Open, navigate to the Lesson09 folder, and open the Faces.jpg file.

2  Zoom in to 300%, so you can see the pixels.

3  Choose Image > Image Size.

4  Change the width and height measurements to Percent, and then change their values to **400**%.

The width and height are linked by default, so that images resize proportionally. If you need to change the width and height separately for a project, click the link icon to unlink the values.

5  Pan in the preview window so that you can see the glasses.

6  Make sure Resample is selected, and choose Preserve Details (Enlargement) from the Resample menu.

The image is much sharper, but the sharpening has introduced some noise.

7  Move the Reduce Noise slider to **50**% to smooth the image.

8  Click and hold on the preview window to see the before image, so you can compare it to the altered image.

9  Click OK.

The final image quality is softer, but it holds up well, considering you've quadrupled the image size and made a low-resolution image usable for print. You'll paste the image into a feathered selection on the poster.

**10** Choose Select > All, and then choose Edit > Copy.

**11** Select the Movie-Poster.psd tab to bring it to the front, and then select the Elliptical Marquee tool (◯), hidden beneath the Rectangular Marquee tool (⬚).

**12** In the options bar, enter **50 px** for Feather.

**13** Draw an oval in the upper right corner of the poster, above the monster's head. The oval should overlap the window and fire escape.

**14** Choose Edit > Paste Special > Paste Into. Click OK if you see the Paste Profile Mismatch dialog box.

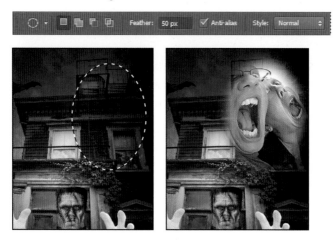

**15** Select the Move tool (⊕), and center the pasted image in the feathered area.

**16** In the Layers panel, choose Luminosity from the Blending Mode menu, and move the Opacity slider to **50%**.

**17** Choose File > Save. Then close the Faces.jpg file without saving it.

# Saving the image for four-color printing

If you plan to have a Photoshop file professionally printed with a four-color press, change the image to CMYK color mode using the Mode command. Because some filters and effects work only in RGB mode, make all the changes to the file before you convert it.

Many professional printers prefer to receive PDF files, so you'll save this file in Photoshop PDF format. It's a good idea to talk with your printer about the settings they require before saving as PDF.

For more information about converting between color modes, see Photoshop Help.

1   Choose File > Save As, and save the file as **Poster_CMYK.psd**. Click OK if you see a Photoshop Format Options dialog box.

It's a good idea to save a copy of your original file before changing color modes, so that you can make changes in the original later, if necessary.

2   Choose Image > Mode > CMYK Color. Click Rasterize to preserve the appearance of Smart Objects. Click Merge to merge the layers when prompted. Finally, click OK if you see a color-management profile warning.

If you were preparing this image for a real publication, you'd want to confirm that you were using the appropriate CMYK profile. See Lesson 14, "Producing and Printing Consistent Color," to learn about color management.

3   Choose File > Save As. In the Save As dialog box, choose Photoshop PDF from the Format menu.

4   Leave the default name (Poster_CMYK.pdf), and click Save. Click OK in the informational dialog box.

5   In the Save Adobe PDF dialog box, choose High Quality Print from the Adobe PDF Preset menu.

▶ **Tip:** Most images include more than one layer. Choose Layer > Merge Visible before you change the color mode to ensure that all the changes you made are included in the CMYK image.

Presets are collections of settings that are appropriate for different purposes. In many cases, the High Quality Print preset will produce the best printed results. However, your print service provider may ask you to customize the settings.

6   Click Save PDF. Click Yes if you see a warning about the Preserve Photoshop Editing Capabilities option.

7   Close the Poster_CMYK.pdf file.

Your poster is ready for printing! Next you'll create a web banner to help publicize the movie.

## Matching color schemes across images

You'll be combining seven images of a cemetery into a panorama for the web banner. To provide continuity in the panorama, you'll harmonize the color schemes in the images by matching the target image to the dominant colors in a source. You can use Match Color with any source file to create interesting and unusual effects. The Match Color feature is also useful for certain color corrections (such as skin tones) in some photographs. The feature can also match the color between different layers in the same image. See Photoshop Help for more information.

You'll create an action so you that you can make the changes to files quickly.

1   Open the Mini Bridge panel, and navigate to the Lesson09/Panorama folder. Double-click the folder name to see its contents.

There are seven sequentially numbered images in the same folder. You'll match the colors for these files.

2   In the Mini Bridge panel, double-click the IMG_7437.jpg file to open it, and then double-click the IMG_7436.jpg file to open it too.

3   Choose Window > Arrange > 2-Up Vertical to see both images.

The IMG_7436.jpg file is overexposed in some areas, and a little washed out. You'll use the Match Color feature to match its colors to those in the IMG_7437.jpg.file. Then you'll sharpen it. Because you'll need to perform the same steps for all of the files in the folder, you'll create an action.

**4** Select the IMG_7436.jpg tab to ensure it's the active file.

**5** Choose Window > Actions to open the Actions panel.

**6** Click the Create New Action button, name the action **Match Color and Sharpen**, and click Record.

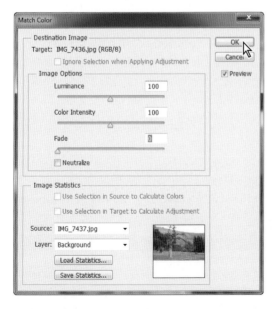

**7** Choose Image > Adjustments > Match Color. In the Match Color dialog box, do the following:

- Select the Preview option, if it's not already selected.

- Choose IMG_7437.jpg from the Source menu.

- Choose Background from the Layer menu. You can select any layer in the source image, but this image has only one layer.

- Experiment with the Luminance, Color Intensity, and Fade settings if you want to. We left them at their default settings.

- When the color scheme unifies the colors in the images, click OK.

**8** Choose Filter > Sharpen > Unsharp Mask.

**9** In the Unsharp Mask dialog box, change the Radius to **1.5**, leave the other settings unchanged, and click OK.

**10** Choose File > Save As. Choose JPEG for the Format, use the same name (IMG_7436.jpg), and save it to a new folder called **Ready For Panorama**. Then click Save.

**11** In the JPEG Options dialog box, choose Maximum from the Quality menu, select Baseline ("Standard"), and click OK.

**12** Close the IMG_7436.jpg file.

**13** Click the Stop button (■) in the Actions panel to stop recording.

**14** Close the IMG_7437.jpg file. Then choose File > Open, select IMG_7431.jpg, IMG_7432.jpg, IMG_7433.jpg, 7434.jpg, 7435.jpg, and 7437.jpg, and click Open.

It may seem silly to close IMG_7437.jpg only to open it again, but the color-matching step in the action requires that 7437.jpg be open, so it needs to be the last tab open in Photoshop.

**15** Choose File > Automate > Batch.

**16** In the Batch dialog box, choose Match Color and Sharpen from the Action menu. Choose Opened Files from the Source menu. Then choose None from the Destination menu, and click OK.

You don't need to specify a destination in the Batch dialog box, because it's included in the action. As soon as you click OK, Photoshop runs the action on all seven files, saving them to the Ready For Panorama folder, and closing them.

**17** Double-click the Mini Bridge tab to close the panel.

# Stitching a panorama

The files have been color matched, sharpened, and saved to prevent unsightly inconsistencies in your panorama. Now you're ready to stitch the images together! Then, you'll add the monster and title to complete the web banner.

**1** With no files open in Photoshop, choose File > Automate > Photomerge.

**2** In the Layout area of the dialog box, select Auto. Then, in the Source Files area, click Browse, and navigate to the Lesson09/Ready For Panorama folder. Shift-select all the images in the folder, and click OK or Open.

**3** At the bottom of the Photomerge dialog box, select Blend Images Together, Vignette Removal, and Geometric Distortion Correction. Then click OK.

Photoshop creates the panorama image. It's a complex process, so you may have to wait several minutes while Photoshop works. When it's finished, you should see an image that looks similar to the one below, with seven layers in the Layers panel—one for each of the images. Photoshop has found the overlapping areas of the images and matched them, correcting any angular discrepancies. In the process, it left some empty areas. You'll make the panorama tidy by cropping the image.

**4** Select all the layers in the Layers panel, and then choose Layer > Merge Layers.

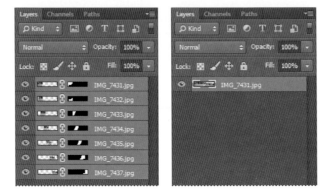

**5** Choose File > Save As. Choose Photoshop for the Format, and name the file **09B_Working.psd**. Save the file in the Lesson09 folder. Click Save, and then click OK in the Photoshop Format Options dialog box.

**6** Select the Crop tool (⊟). In the options bar, make sure the width, height, and resolution boxes are empty, and that Delete Cropped Pixels is selected. Then drag the crop box to crop out all the transparent areas, retaining as much of the image as possible. When you are satisfied with your cropped area, press Enter or Return, or click the Commit Current Crop Operation button (✓) in the options bar.

**7** Choose File > Save to save your work so far.

# Finishing the image

You'll use the Adaptive Wide Angle filter to correct the perspective. Then you'll apply some lighting effects for drama, and add elements from the movie poster for the final touch.

## Using the Adaptive Wide Angle filter

The panorama looks great, but because of the wide angle, some of the lines are a little off. For example, the slope on the right side of the image is greater than it is in real life. You'll adjust that with the help of the Adaptive Wide Angle filter.

**1** Choose Filter > Adaptive Wide Angle.

**2** In the Adaptive Wide Angle dialog box, select the Constraint tool ().

The Constraint tool lets you define the straight areas in the image; the filter adjusts the rest of the image to match the perspective you specify.

**3** Click a point on the black tombstone about a third of the way in from the right, and then click another point in the center of the tree on the right, effectively drawing a straight line.

> **Note:** The Adaptive Wide Angle filter is available only if Use Graphics Processor is selected in the Performance Preferences dialog box. If your video card does not support this option, skip this exercise.

> **Tip:** If transparent areas appear along the edge of the image, use the Scale option in the Adaptive Wide Angle filter to scale the image.

As you release the mouse from the second point, the filter adjusts the perspective of the image slightly. You'll make the adjustment more pronounced.

**4** Hover over the handle on the right side of the circle until you see a rotation arrow. Then click and drag upward slightly, raising the right side of the image.

**5** Change the scale to **135**% to remove the resulting transparency. Depending on the angle you used, you may need to scale up a little higher.

You can continue to adjust the rotation and scaling until you close the filter dialog box.

**6** When you're satisfied, click OK to accept the changes and apply the filter to the image.

## Adding a photo filter

The cemetery looks a little tame. You'll add some drama with a cool blue photo filter that makes it appear the photo was taken at night. Using the Gradient tool, you'll deepen the effect.

*Julieanne Kost is an official Adobe Photoshop evangelist.*

# Tool tips from the Photoshop evangelist

### Using filter shortcuts

These powerful shortcuts can save time when working with filters:

- To reapply the most recently used filter with its last values, press Ctrl+F (Windows) or Command+F (Mac OS).

- To display the dialog box for the last filter you applied, press Ctrl+Alt+F (Windows) or Command+Option+F (Mac OS).

- To reduce the effect of the last filter you applied, press Ctrl+Shift+F (Windows) or Command+Shift+F (Mac OS).

1 Click the Photo Filter button in the Adjustments panel to create an adjustment layer.

2 In the Properties panel, choose Deep Blue from the Filter menu, move the Density slider to **80**%, and deselect Preserve Luminosity.

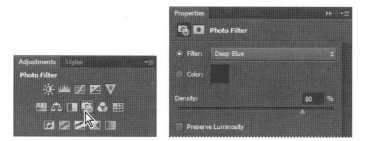

The photo filter creates a blue cast over the entire scene, but the sky is still a little bright. You'll add a gradient to darken it.

3 In the Tools panel, change the foreground color to black, and then select the Gradient tool.

4 In the options bar, open the Gradient Picker, and select the second option (Foreground To Transparent).

5 Select the IMG_7431.jpg layer in the Layers panel. Then click about half an inch above the center of the image, and drag about three-quarters of the way down the image.

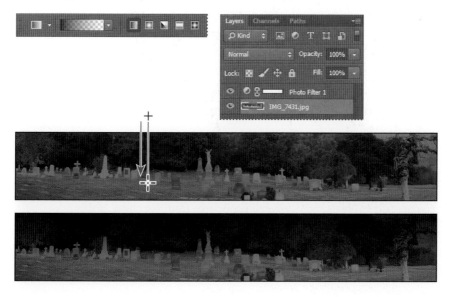

6 Save the file.

## Preparing the file for the web

The web banner needs only the movie poster elements to be complete. However, the movie poster elements are higher resolution. You'll use the Save for Web feature to ensure the final web banner is compact enough for fast downloading. You'll learn more about the Save For Web dialog box in Lesson 13, "Preparing Files for the Web."

1   Choose File > Open, and open the Movie-Poster.psd file.

2   Choose Window > Arrange > 2-Up Vertical so you can see both the panorama and the movie poster. Click the Movie-Poster.psd file to make it active.

3   Ctrl-select or Command-select the Title and Monster layers, and then drag them onto the 09B_Working.psd file's image window.

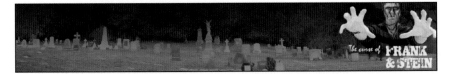

4   Close the Movie-Poster.psd file without saving it, and then use the Move tool to drag the imported monster and title to the right side of the panorama image.

5   In the Layers panel, drag the Photo Filter 1 adjustment layer below the Title and Monster layers so that it affects only the panorama (IMG_7431.jpg) layer.

6   Choose File > Save For Web.

7   In the Save For Web dialog box, choose JPEG High from the Preset menu.

8   In the Image Size area, enter 1024 pixels for the width. Because the height and width are linked by default, the height value changes automatically.

9   Click Save.

10  In the Save Optimized As dialog box, choose Images Only from the Format menu. Then name the file **Banner.jpg**, and save it to the Lesson09 folder. Click Save.

11  Open the Banner.jpg file in Photoshop to see your final web banner. It's ready to hand off to a web designer.

You created a montage of several images, and you blended images into a panorama. You're ready to create montages and panoramas from your own images.

# Review questions

1  What are the differences between using a Smart Filter and a regular filter to apply effects to an image?

2  What do the Bloat and Pucker tools in the Liquify filter do?

3  What is an action? How do you create one?

4  How can you create a panorama?

# Review answers

1  Smart Filters are nondestructive: They can be adjusted, turned off and on, and deleted at any time. In contrast, regular filters permanently change an image; once applied, they cannot be removed. Smart Filters can be applied only to a Smart Object layer.

2  The Bloat tool moves pixels away from the center of the brush; the Pucker tool moves pixels toward the center of the brush.

3  An *action* is a set of one or more commands that you record and then play back to apply to a single file or a batch of files. To create one, click the Create New Action button in the Actions panel, name the action, and click Record. Then perform the tasks you want to include in your action. When you've finished, click the Stop Recording button at the bottom of the Actions panel.

4  To create a panorama, take multiple photos to be stitched together. Then, in Photoshop, choose File > Automate > Photomerge. Select options in the Photomerge dialog box, select the images you want to stitch together, and then click OK.

# 10 EDITING VIDEO

## Lesson overview

In this lesson, you'll learn how to do the following:

- Create a video timeline in Photoshop.
- Add media to a video group in the Timeline panel.
- Add motion to video clips and still images.
- Animate type and effects using keyframes.
- Apply a Smart Filter to a video clip.
- Add transitions between video clips.
- Include audio in a video file.
- Render a video.

This lesson will take about 90 minutes to complete. Download the Lesson10 project files from the Lesson & Update Files tab on your Account page at www.peachpit.com, if you haven't already done so. As you work on this lesson, you'll preserve the start files. If you need to restore the start files, download them from your Account page.

PROJECT: FAMILY VIDEO FROM MOBILE PHONE

You can edit video files in Photoshop using many of the same effects you use to edit image files. You can create a movie from video files, still images, Smart Objects, audio files, and type layers; apply transitions; and animate effects using keyframes.

**Note:** Features covered in this lesson require Mac OS 10.7 or later, or Windows 7 or later. For more complete Photoshop CC system requirements, visit www.adobe.com/ products/photoshop/ tech-specs.html"

**Note:** If Bridge isn't installed, you'll be prompted to install it when you choose Browse In Bridge. For more information, see page 3.

# Getting started

In this lesson, you'll edit a video that was shot using a camera phone. You'll create a video timeline, import clips, add transitions and other video effects, and render the final video. First, look at the final project to see what you'll be creating.

1   Start Photoshop, and then immediately hold down Ctrl+Alt+Shift (Windows) or Command+Option+Shift (Mac OS) to restore the default preferences. (See "Restoring default preferences" on page 4.)

2   When prompted, click Yes to delete the Adobe Photoshop Settings file.

3   Choose File > Browse In Bridge.

4   In Bridge, select the Lessons folder in the Favorites panel. Then, double-click the Lesson10 folder in the Content panel.

5   Double-click the 10End.mp4 file to open it in QuickTime or Windows Media Player.

6   Click the Play button to view the final video.

The short video is a compilation of clips from a day at the beach. It includes transitions, layer effects, animated text, and a musical track.

7   Close QuickTime or Windows Media Player, and return to Bridge.

8   Double-click the 10End.psd file to open it in Photoshop. Click Play, or move the playhead to view different parts of the movie.

Photoshop displays the Timeline panel, and there are guidelines across the document window. The guidelines identify the area that would be visible if you broadcast the video. The Timeline panel includes all the video clips and the audio track.

9   When you've finished exploring the end file, close it, but leave Photoshop open.

# Creating a new video project

Working with video is a little different from working with still images in Photoshop. You may find it easiest to create the project first, and then import the assets you'll be using. You'll choose the video preset for this project, and then add nine video and image files to include in your movie.

## Creating a new file

Photoshop includes several film and video presets for you to choose from. You'll create a new file and select an appropriate preset.

**1** Choose File > New.

**2** Name the file **10Start.psd**.

**3** Choose Film & Video from the Preset menu.

**4** Choose HDV/HDTV 720p/29.97 from the Size menu.

**5** Accept the default settings for the other options, and click OK.

> ● **Note:** The video in this lesson was shot using an Apple iPhone, so one of the HDV presets is appropriate. The 720P preset provides good quality without providing too much data for easy streaming online.

**6** Choose File > Save As, and save the file in the Lesson10 folder.

## Importing assets

Photoshop provides tools specifically for working with video, such as the Timeline panel. The Timeline panel may already be open because you previewed the end file earlier. You use the Timeline panel to arrange layers in a video, animate their properties, set the start and end points for each layer, and apply transitions. To ensure you have access to the resources you need, you'll select the Motion workspace and organize your panels before you import files for the video.

1 Choose Window > Workspace > Motion.

2 Pull the top edge of the Timeline panel up so that the panel occupies the bottom half of the workspace.

3 Select the Zoom tool ($\mathcal{Q}$), and then click Fit Screen in the options bar so that you can see the entire canvas within the top half of the screen.

4 In the Timeline panel, click Create Video Timeline. Photoshop creates a new video timeline, including two default tracks: Layer 0 and Audio Track.

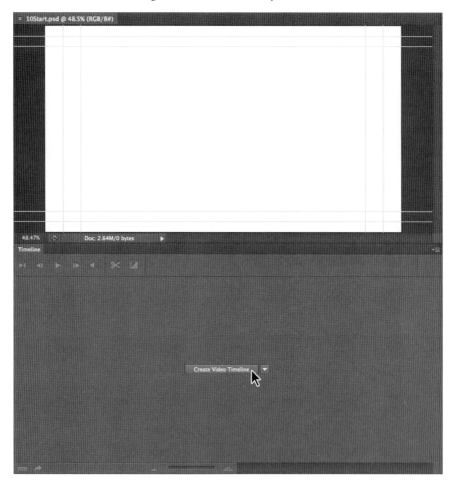

**5** Click the Video menu in the Layer 0 track, and choose Add Media.

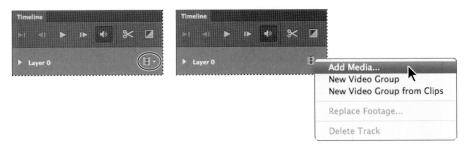

**6** Navigate to the Lesson10 folder.

**7** Shift-select the video and photo assets numbered 1–9, and click Open.

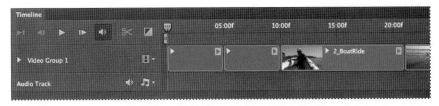

> **Note:** When you use the Add Media button with an unspecified canvas, Photoshop determines the project size based on the size of the first video file it finds—or, if you're importing only images, based on the image size.

Photoshop imports all nine of the assets you selected onto the same track, now named Video Group 1, in the Timeline panel. It displays still images with a purple background and video clips with a blue background. In the Layers panel, the assets appear as individual layers in the layer group named Video Group 1. You don't need the Layer 0 layer, so you'll delete it.

**8** Select Layer 0 in the Layers panel, and click the Delete Layer button at the bottom of the panel. Click Yes to confirm the deletion.

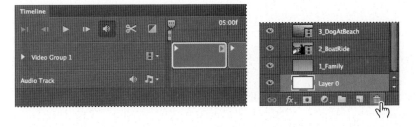

## Changing the duration of clips in the timeline

The clips are of very different lengths, meaning they'd play for different amounts of time. For this video, you want all the clips to be the same length, so you'll shorten them all to 3 seconds. The length of a clip (its *duration*) is measured in seconds and frames: 03:00 is 3 seconds; 02:25 is 2 seconds and 25 frames.

**Note:** You're shortening each clip to the same length here, but you can have clips of varying lengths, depending on what's appropriate for the project.

1   Drag the Control Timeline Magnification slider to the right at the bottom of the Timeline panel to zoom in on the timeline. You want to be able to see a thumbnail of each clip and enough detail in the time ruler that you can accurately change the duration of each clip.

2   Drag the right edge of the first clip (1_Family) to 03:00 on the time ruler. Photoshop displays the end point and the duration as you drag so that you can find the right stopping point.

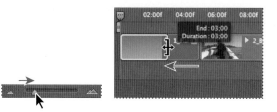

3   Drag the right edge of the second clip (2_BoatRide) to a duration of 03:00.

Shortening a video clip doesn't compress it; it removes part of the clip from the video. In this case, you want to use the first three seconds of each clip. If you wanted to use a different portion of a video clip, you might want to shorten the clip from each end. As you drag the end point of a video clip, Photoshop displays a preview so you can see which part of the clip is included.

**Tip:** To quickly change the duration of a video clip, click the arrow in the upper right corner, and then type a new Duration value. This option isn't available for still images.

4   Repeat step 3 for each of the remaining clips so that each has a duration of 3 seconds.

The clips are now the right duration, but some of the images are the wrong size for the canvas. You'll resize the first image before continuing.

5   Select the 1_Family layer in the Layers panel. The clip is also selected in the Timeline panel.

**6** Click the triangle in the upper right corner of the 1_Family clip in the Timeline panel to open the Motion panel.

**7** Choose Pan & Zoom from the menu, and make sure Resize To Fill Canvas is selected. Then click an empty area of the Timeline panel to close the Motion panel.

**Tip:** The arrow on the left side of a clip (next to the clip's thumbnail) reveals the attributes you can animate using keyframes. The arrow on the right side of a clip opens the Motion panel.

The image resizes to fit the canvas, which is what you wanted. However, you don't actually want to pan and zoom. You'll remove the effect.

**8** Open the Motion panel from the 1_Family clip again, and choose No Motion from the menu. Click an empty area of the Timeline panel to close the Motion panel.

**9** Choose File > Save. Click OK in the Photoshop Format Options dialog box.

## Animating text with keyframes

Keyframes let you control animation, effects, and other changes that occur over time. A keyframe marks the point in time where you specify a value, such as a position, size, or style. To create a change over time, you must have at least two keyframes: one for the state at the beginning of the change and one for the state at the end. Photoshop interpolates the values for the positions in between so that the change takes effect smoothly over the specified time. You'll use keyframes to animate a movie title (Beach Day) from left to right over the opening image.

**1** Click the Video pop-up menu in the Video Group 1 track, and choose New Video Group. Photoshop adds Video Group 2 to the Timeline panel.

**2**  Select the Horizontal Type tool (T), and then click on the left edge of the image, about halfway down from the top.

Photoshop creates a new type layer, named Layer 1, in the Video Group 2 track.

**3**  In the options bar, select a sans serif font such as Myriad Pro, set the type size to **600 pt**, and select white for the type color.

**4**  Type **BEACH DAY**.

The text is large enough that it doesn't all fit on the image. That's okay; you'll animate it to move across the image.

**5**  In the Layers panel, change the opacity for the BEACH DAY layer to **25%**.

**6**  In the Timeline panel, drag the end point of the type layer to 03:00 so that it has the same duration as the 1_Family layer.

**7**  Click the arrow next to the thumbnail in the BEACH DAY clip to display the clip's attributes.

**8**  Make sure the playhead is at the beginning of the time ruler.

**9**  Click the stopwatch icon next to the Transform property to set an initial keyframe for the layer.

The keyframe appears as a yellow diamond in the timeline.

**10** Select the Move tool (⊕), and then use it to drag the type layer over the canvas so that the top of the letters align with the lower of the two top guidelines. Drag it to the right so that only the left edge of the letter "B" in the word "BEACH" is visible on the canvas.

**11** Move the playhead to the last frame of the first clip (02:29).

**12** Press the Shift key as you drag the type layer to the left over the canvas so that only the right edge of the "Y" in the word "DAY" is visible. Pressing the Shift key ensures the type remains level as you move it across.

▶ **Tip:** Photoshop displays the playhead's location in the lower left corner of the Timeline panel.

Because you've changed the position, Photoshop creates a new keyframe.

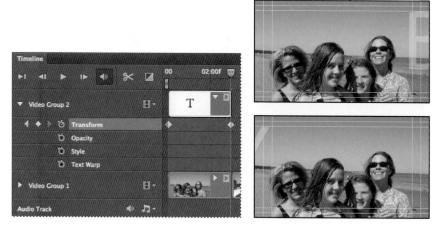

**13** Move the playhead across the first three seconds of the time ruler to preview the animation. The title moves across the image.

**14** Close the clip's attributes, and then choose File > Save to save your work so far.

# Creating effects

One of the benefits of working with video files in Photoshop is that you can create effects using adjustment layers, styles, and simple transformations.

## Adding adjustment layers to video clips

You've used adjustment layers with still images throughout this book. They work just as well on video clips. When you apply an adjustment layer in a video group, Photoshop applies it only to the layer immediately below it in the Layers panel.

1   Select the 3_DogAtBeach layer in the Layers panel.

2   In the Timeline panel, move the playhead to the beginning of the 3_DogAtBeach layer so you can see the effect as you apply it.

● **Note:** If you had imported the video file using the Place command, so that it was not in a video group, you would need to create a clipping layer to limit the adjustment layer to a single layer.

3   In the Adjustments panel, click the Black & White button.

4   In the Properties panel, leave the default preset, and select Tint. The default tint color creates a sepia effect that works well for this clip. You can experiment with the sliders and the tint color to modify the black-and-white effect to your taste.

5   Move the playhead across the 3_DogAtBeach clip in the Timeline panel to preview the effect.

## Animating a zoom effect

Even simple transformations become interesting effects when you animate them. You'll use animation to zoom in on the 4_Dogs clip.

1   Move the playhead to the beginning of the 4_Dogs clip in the Timeline panel (09:00).

2   Click the arrow in the 4_Dogs clip to display the Motion panel.

3   Choose Zoom from the pop-up menu, and choose Zoom In from the Zoom menu. On the Zoom From grid, select the upper left corner to zoom in from that point. Make sure Resize To Fill Canvas is selected, and then click an empty area of the Timeline panel to close the Motion panel.

4   Drag the playhead across the clip to preview the effect.

You'll enlarge the image in the last keyframe to make the zoom more dramatic.

5   Click the arrow on the left side of the 4_Dogs clip to reveal the attributes for the clip.

There are two keyframes, one for the beginning of the Zoom In effect, and one for the end.

6   Click the right arrow next to the Transform attribute to move the playhead to the last keyframe if it's not already there, and choose Edit > Free Transform. Then enter **120%** for the Width and Height in the options bar. Press Enter or Return to confirm the transformation.

▶ **Tip:** You can move to the next keyframe by clicking the right arrow next to the attribute in the Timeline panel. Click the left arrow to move to the previous keyframe.

7   Drag the playhead across the 4_Dogs clip in the time ruler to preview the animation again.

8   Choose File > Save.

## Adding a Smart Filter to a video clip

You can apply Smart Filters nondestructively to Smart Objects, including Smart Objects in a video project. You'll convert the video clip of the boat ride to a Smart Object, and then add an interactive blur to it. Because you'll add the blur as a Smart Filter, you'll be able to edit or remove the blur at any point in the future.

1   Move the playhead to 12:00, the first frame of the clip named 5_BoatRide2, and select the clip in the Timeline panel.

2   With the 5_BoatRide2 layer selected in the Layers panel, choose Convert To Smart Object from the Layers panel menu.

The icon for the layer in the Layers panel changes to indicate that it's a Smart Object.

3 Choose Filter > Blur > Iris Blur.

The workspace changes to display the Blur Gallery, with the Blur Tools and Blur Effects panels open.

4 Drag the center pin to the woman's shoulder, so that the focus is on the people and the dog, with the rest of the scene blurred. Then click OK.

5 Scrub through the clip to preview the blur effect.

As the video moves, the area of focus remains stationary. By 14:20, the dog is out of focus, as he's moved into the blurred area. You'll adjust the effect to widen the focus. Because it's a Smart Filter, you can edit the blur easily.

6 Double-click Blur Gallery in the Layers panel to adjust the filter settings. Extend the ellipse handles and the feather handles to increase the focus area to include the people and dog throughout the clip. Then click OK.

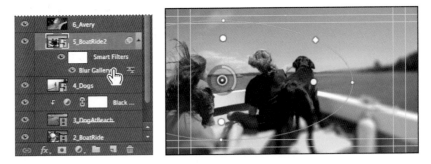

7 Scrub through the clip to preview the edited filter.

The change you made applies to the entire clip, even though the playhead was in a different position when you made it.

## Animating style effects

You can apply layer styles to clips in the Timeline panel. You'll add an interesting effect to the image of the girl in sunglasses. First, you'll resize it to fit the canvas. Then you'll apply a style and remove it, twice, so that it appears to blink on and off in the video.

1 Move the playhead to the beginning of the 6_Avery clip (15:00).

The image is too large for the canvas.

2 Open the Motion panel for the clip, and choose Pan & Zoom from the pop-up menu. Make sure Resize To Fill Canvas is selected. Then click an empty area of the Timeline panel to close the Motion panel and resize the image.

3 Open the Motion panel again, and choose No Motion from the pop-up menu, since you don't actually want to pan and zoom in this image. Click an empty area of the Timeline panel to close the panel.

4 Choose Window > Styles to open the Styles panel.

5 Click the arrow next to the thumbnail in the 6_Avery clip to show its attributes in the Timeline panel, and then click the stopwatch icon for the Style keyframe.

6 Move the playhead about a quarter of the way through the clip. Then, in the Styles panel, select the Negative Image style.

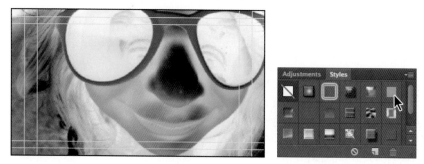

Photoshop adds a keyframe.

7 Move the playhead to the middle of the clip. Select the Default style to remove the effect. Photoshop adds another keyframe.

8 Move the playhead three-quarters of the way through the clip, and apply the Negative Image style again. Photoshop adds a fourth keyframe.

**9** Move the playhead to the end of the clip (17:29), and select the Default style. Photoshop adds a final keyframe for the clip.

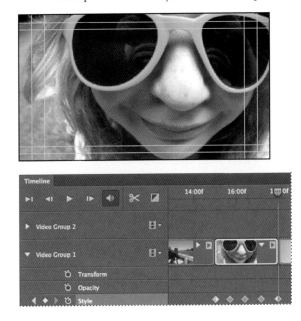

**10** Move the playhead across the time ruler to preview the effect.

## Animating an image to create a motion effect

You'll animate another transformation to create the appearance of motion. You want the image to begin with the diver's legs and end with his hands.

**1** Move the playhead to the end of the 7_jumping clip (20:29), and select the clip. Press Shift while you move the image down so that the hands are near the top of the canvas, putting the diver in the final position.

**2** Display the attributes for the clip, and click the stopwatch icon for the Position attribute to add a keyframe.

**3** Move the playhead to the beginning of the clip (18:00). Press Shift while you move the image up so that the feet are near the bottom of the canvas.

Photoshop adds a keyframe.

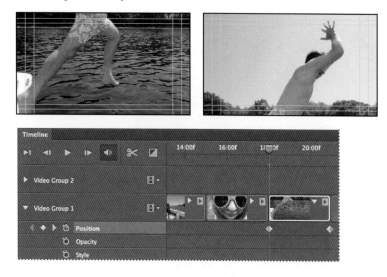

**4** Move the playhead across the time ruler to preview the animation.

**5** Close the clip's attributes. Then choose File > Save to save your work so far.

## Adding pan & zoom effects

You can easily add features similar to the pan and zoom effects used in documentaries. You'll add them to the sunsets to bring the video to a dramatic close.

**1** Move the playhead to the beginning of the 8_Sunset clip.

**2** Open the Motion panel, and choose Pan from the pop-up menu. Make sure Resize To Fill Canvas is selected, and then click an empty area of the Timeline panel to close the Motion panel.

**3** Move the playhead to the beginning of the 9_Sunset2 clip.

4 Open the Motion panel for the clip. Choose Pan & Zoom from the pop-up menu, choose Zoom Out from the Zoom menu, and make sure Resize To Fill Canvas is selected. Then click an empty area of the Timeline panel to close the Motion panel.

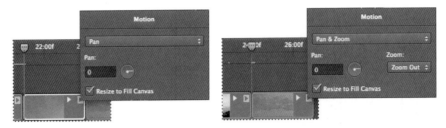

5 Move the playhead across the last two clips to preview the effects.

# Adding transitions

A transition moves a scene from one shot to the next. Simply drag and drop to add transitions to clips in Photoshop.

1 Click the Go To First Frame button (▶ɪ) in the upper left corner of the Timeline panel to return the playhead to the beginning of the time ruler.

2 Click the Transitions button (▧) in the upper left corner of the Timeline panel. Select Cross Fade, and change the Duration value to **.25 s** (for a quarter of a second).

3 Drag the Cross Fade transition between the 1_Family and 2_BoatRide clips.

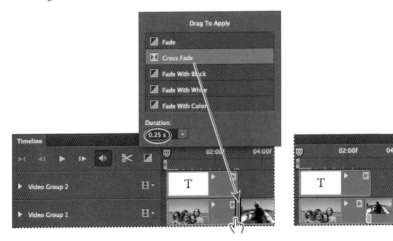

Photoshop adjusts the ends of the clips to apply the transition, and adds a small white icon in the lower corner of the second clip.

**4** Drag Cross Fade transitions between each of the other clips.

**5** Drag a Fade With Black transition onto the end of the final clip.

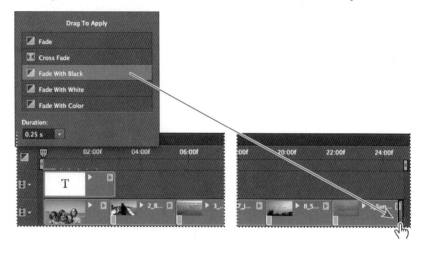

**6** To make the transition smoother, extend the Fade With Black transition by stretching its left side to about one-third the total length of the clip.

**7** Choose File > Save.

# Adding audio

You can add a separate audio track to a video file in Photoshop. In fact, the Timeline panel includes an audio track by default. You'll add an MP3 file to play as the soundtrack for this short video.

▶ **Tip:** You can also add an audio track by clicking the + sign at the far-right end of the track in the Timeline panel.

1  Click the note icon in the Audio Track at the bottom of the Timeline panel, and choose Add Audio from the pop-up menu.

2  Select the beachsong.mp3 file from the Lesson10 folder, and click Open.

The audio file is added to the timeline, but it's much longer than the video. You'll use the Split At Playhead tool to shorten it.

3  Move the playhead to the end of the 9_Sunset2 clip, and then click the Split At Playhead tool.

The audio file is clipped at that point, becoming two audio clips.

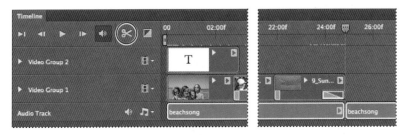

4  Select the second audio file segment, the one that begins after the end of the 9_Sunset2 clip. Press the Delete key on your keyboard to delete the selected clip.

Now the audio file is the same length as the video. You'll add a fade so that it ends smoothly.

**5** Click the small arrow at the right edge of the audio clip to open the Audio panel. Then enter **3** seconds for Fade In and **5** seconds for Fade Out.

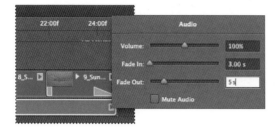

**6** Save your work so far.

# Muting unwanted audio

So far, you've previewed portions of the video by moving the playhead across the time ruler. Now you'll preview the entire video using the Play button in the Timeline panel, and then mute any extraneous audio from the video clips.

**1** Click the Play button (▶) in the upper left corner of the Timeline panel to preview the video so far.

It's looking good, but there is some unwanted background noise from a few of the video clips. You'll mute that extra sound.

**2** Click the small triangle at the right end of the 2_BoatRide clip.

**3** Click the Audio tab to see audio options, and then select Mute Audio. Click an empty area of the Timeline panel to close the panel.

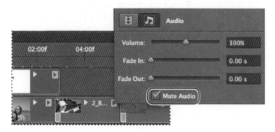

**4** Repeat steps 2–3 for the 3_DogAtBeach layer.

▶ **Tip:** To create a smoother preview, disable the audio playback button in the Timeline panel the first time you play the video. With audio playback disabled, Photoshop can create a more complete cache, resulting in a more accurate preview.

The 5_BoatRide2 clip includes unwanted audio, too. However, because it's a Smart Object, you need to open the Smart Object and mute the audio for it separately.

5  Double-click the 5_BoatRide2 layer thumbnail in the Layers panel to open the Smart Object. Click OK in the informational dialog box.

6  Click the small triangle at the right end of the 5_BoatRide2 clip to open the Motion panel. Then click the Audio tab, and select Mute Audio.

7  Close the 5_BoatRide2 Smart Object, and save when prompted. Photoshop returns to the 10Start.psd file.

8  Play the video again. Now the only sound is the audio file you added.

9  Choose File > Save to save your work so far.

## Rendering video

You're ready to render your project to video. Photoshop provides several rendering options. You'll select options appropriate for streaming video to share on the Vimeo website. For information about other rendering options, see Photoshop Help.

1  Choose File > Export > Render Video, or click the Render Video button (⤴) in the lower left corner of the Timeline panel.

2  Name the file **10Final.mp4**.

3  Click Select Folder, and then navigate to the Lesson10 folder, and click OK or Choose.

4  From the Preset menu, choose Vimeo HD 720p 25.

5  Click Render.

| Render Video | |
|---|---|
| **Location** | Render |
| Name: 10Final.mp4 | Cancel |
| (Select Folder...) Main Drive:Users:...:Lessons:Lesson10 Folder: | |
| ☐ Create New Subfolder: | |
| Adobe Media Encoder ⬍ | |
| Format: H.264 ⬍ | |
| Preset: Vimeo HD 720p 25 ⬍ | |

Depending on your system, this may take a while.

Photoshop displays a progress bar as it exports the video. Depending on your system, the rendering process may take several minutes.

6  Locate the 10Final.mp4 file in the Lesson10 folder in Bridge. Double-click it to view the video you made.

## Review questions

1 What is a keyframe, and how do you create one?

2 How do you add a transition between clips?

3 How do you render a video?

## Review answers

1 A keyframe marks the point in time where you specify a value, such as a position, size, or style. To create a change over time, you must have at least two keyframes: one for the state at the beginning of the change and one for the state at the end. To create an initial keyframe, click the stopwatch icon next to the attribute you want to animate for the layer. Photoshop creates additional keyframes each time you change the values of that attribute.

2 To add a transition, click the Transition icon in the upper left corner of the Timeline panel, and then drag a transition onto a clip.

3 To render a video, choose File > Export > Render Video, or click the Render Video button in the lower left corner of the Timeline panel. Then select the video settings that are appropriate for your intended output.

# 11 PAINTING WITH THE MIXER BRUSH

## Lesson overview

In this lesson, you'll learn how to do the following:

- Customize brush settings.

- Clean the brush.

- Mix colors.

- Use an erodible tip.

- Create a custom brush preset.

- Use wet and dry brushes to blend color.

 This lesson will take about an hour to complete. Download the Lesson11 project files from the Lesson & Update Files tab on your Account page at www.peachpit.com, if you haven't already done so. As you work on this lesson, you'll preserve the start files. If you need to restore the start files, download them from your Account page.

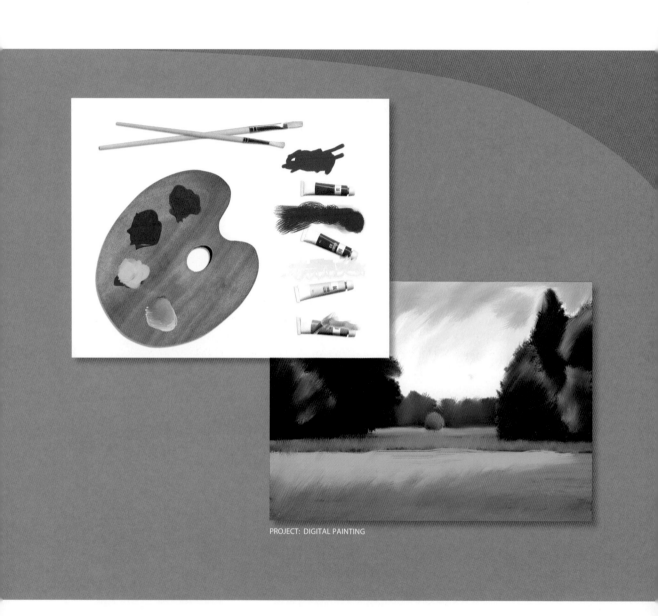

PROJECT: DIGITAL PAINTING

The Mixer Brush tool gives you flexibility, color-mixing abilities, and brush strokes as if you were painting on a physical canvas.

# About the Mixer Brush

In previous lessons, you've used brushes in Photoshop to perform various tasks. The Mixer Brush is unlike other brushes in that it lets you mix colors with each other. You can change the wetness of the brush and how it mixes the brush color with the color already on the canvas.

Photoshop brushes have realistic bristles, so you can add textures that resemble those in paintings you might create in the physical world. While this is a great feature in general, it's particularly useful when you're using the Mixer Brush. You can also use an erodible tip to achieve the effects you might get with charcoal pencils and pastels in the physical world. Combining different bristle settings and brush tips with different wetness, paint-load, and paint-mixing settings gives you opportunities to create exactly the look you want.

# Getting started

In this lesson, you'll get acquainted with the Mixer Brush as well as the brush tip and bristle options available in Photoshop CC. Start by taking a look at the final projects you'll create.

1   Start Photoshop, and then immediately hold down Ctrl+Alt+Shift (Windows) or Command+Option+Shift (Mac OS) to restore the default preferences. (See "Restoring default preferences" on page 4.)

**Note:** If Bridge isn't installed, you'll be prompted to install it when you choose Browse In Bridge. For more information, see page 3.

2   When prompted, click Yes to delete the Adobe Photoshop Settings file.

3   Choose File > Browse In Bridge to open Adobe Bridge.

4   In Bridge, click Lessons in the Favorites panel. Double-click the Lesson11 folder in the Content panel.

5   Preview the Lesson11 end files.

You'll use the palette image to explore brush options and learn to mix colors. You'll then apply what you've learned to transform the landscape image into a watercolor.

**Note:** If you plan to do a lot of painting in Photoshop, consider using a tablet, such as a Wacom tablet, instead of a mouse. Photoshop can sense the way you hold and use the pen to change the brush width, strength, and angle on the fly.

6   Double-click 11Palette_start.psd to open the file in Photoshop.

7   Choose File > Save As, and name the file **11Palette_working.psd**. Click OK if the Photoshop Format Options dialog box appears.

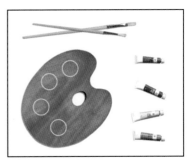

# Selecting brush settings

The image includes a palette and four tubes of color, which you'll use to sample the colors you're working with. You'll change settings as you paint different colors, exploring brush tip settings and wetness options.

1  Select the Zoom tool (🔍), and zoom in to see the tubes of paint.

2  Select the Eyedropper tool (✎), and sample the red color from the red tube.

The foreground color changes to red.

3  Select the Mixer Brush tool (✔), hidden under the Brush tool (✎).

Note: If you have OpenGL enabled, Photoshop displays a sampling ring so you can preview the color you're picking up.

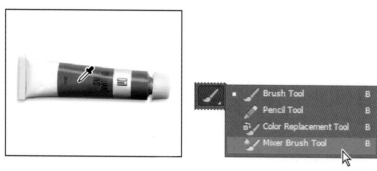

4  Choose Window > Brush to open the Brush panel. Select the first brush.

The Brush panel contains brush presets and several options for customizing brushes.

## Experimenting with wetness options and brushes

The effect of the brush is determined by the Wet, Load, and Mix fields in the options bar. Wet controls how much paint the brush picks up from the canvas. Load controls how much paint the brush holds when you begin painting (as with a physical brush, it runs out of paint as you paint with it). Mix controls the ratio of paint from the canvas and paint from the brush.

You can change these settings separately. However, it's faster to select a standard combination from the pop-up menu.

1　In the options bar, choose Dry from the pop-up menu of blending brush combinations.

When you select Dry, Wet is set to 0%, Load to 50%, and Mix is not applicable. With the Dry preset, you paint opaque color; you cannot mix colors on a dry canvas.

2　Paint in the area above the red tube. Solid red appears. As you continue painting without releasing the mouse, the paint eventually fades and runs out.

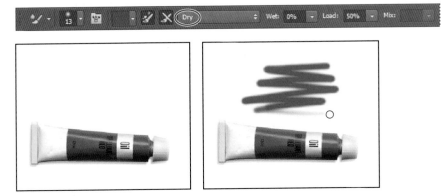

● **Note:** When you Alt-click or Option-click to load paint, the brush picks up color variations in the sample area. To sample only solid colors, select Load Solid Colors Only in the Current Brush Load menu in the options bar.

3　Sample the blue color from the blue tube of paint. You can use the Eyedropper tool or Alt-click (Windows) or Option-click (Mac OS) to sample the color. If you use the Eyedropper tool, return to the Mixer Brush tool after you sample the color.

4　In the Brush panel, select the round fan-shaped brush. Choose Wet from the pop-up menu in the options bar.

**5** Paint above the blue tube. The paint mixes with the white background.

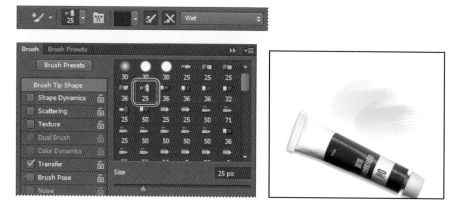

**6** Choose Dry from the menu in the options bar, and then paint again above the blue tube. A much darker, more opaque blue appears, and doesn't mix with the white background.

The bristles from the fan brush you selected are much more apparent than the bristles you used originally. Changing bristle qualities makes a big difference in the texture you paint.

**7** In the Brush panel, decrease the number of bristles to **40%**. Paint a little more with the blue brush to see the change in texture. The bristles are much more obvious in the stroke.

▶ **Tip:** The Live Tip Brush Preview shows you the direction of the bristles as you paint. To show or hide the Live Tip Brush Preview, click the Toggle The Live Tip Brush Preview button at the bottom of the Brush or Brush Presets panel. The Live Tip Brush Preview is available only with OpenGL enabled.

8   Sample the yellow color from the yellow paint tube. In the Brush panel, select the flat-point brush with fewer bristles (the one to the right of the fan brush). Choose Dry from the menu in the options bar, and then paint in the area over the yellow paint tube.

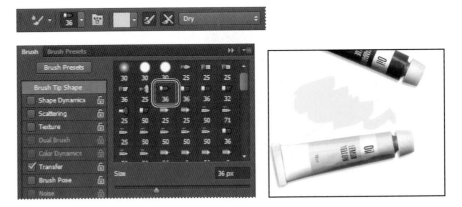

9   Choose Very Wet from the menu in the options bar, and then paint some more. Now the yellow mixes with the white background.

## Using an erodible tip

When you use an erodible tip, the width of the brush changes as you paint. Erodible tips are represented in the Brush panel by pencil icons, because in the physical world, pencils and pastels have erodible tips. You'll experiment with erodible point and triangle tips.

1   Sample the green color from the green paint tube, and choose Dry, Heavy Load in the options bar.

2   Select one of the erodible tips (any tip with a pencil icon), and then choose Erodible Point from the Shape menu. Change the brush's Size to **30 px**, and Softness to **100%**.

The Softness value determines how quickly the tip erodes. A higher value results in faster erosion.

**3** Draw a zig-zag line above the green paint tube.

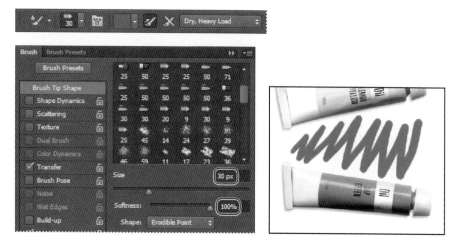

The line gets thicker as the tip erodes.

**4** Click Sharpen Tip in the Brush panel, and then draw a line next to the one you just drew.

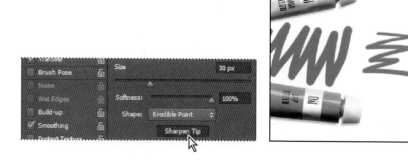

The sharper tip draws a much narrower line.

**5** Choose Erodible Triangle from the Shape menu in the Brush panel, and draw a zig-zag line with it.

You can choose from several erodible tips, depending on the effect you want.

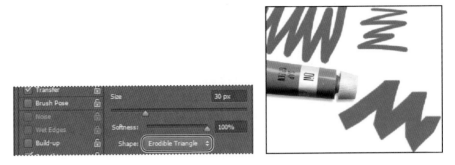

## Mixing colors

● **Note:** Depending on the complexity of your project, you may need to be patient. Mixing colors can be a memory-intensive process.

You've used wet and dry brushes, changed brush settings, and mixed the paint with the background color. Now, you'll focus more on mixing colors with each other as you add paint to the painter's palette.

**1** Zoom out just enough to see the full palette and the paint tubes.

**2** Select the Paint mix layer in the Layers panel, so the color you paint won't blend with the brown palette on the Background layer.

The Mixer Brush tool mixes colors only on the active layer unless you select Sample All Layers in the options bar.

**3** Use the Eyedropper tool to sample the red color from the red paint tube. Select the round blunt brush in the Brush panel (the fifth brush). Then select Wet from the pop-up menu in the options bar, and paint in the top circle on the palette.

**4** Click the Clean The Brush After Each Stroke icon in the options bar to deselect the option.

**5** Use the Eyedropper tool to sample the blue color from the blue paint tube, and then paint in the same circle, mixing the red with the blue until the color becomes purple.

Use the Eyedropper tool to sample the color when the layer that contains the color (in this case, the Background layer) isn't selected.

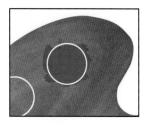 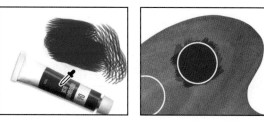

**6** Paint in the next circle. You're painting in purple because the paint stays on the brush until you clean it.

**7** In the options bar, choose Clean Brush from the Current Brush Load pop-up menu. The preview changes to indicate transparency, meaning the brush has no paint loaded.

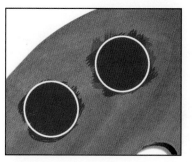

To remove the paint load from a brush, you can choose Clean Brush in the options bar. To replace the paint load in a brush, sample a different color.

If you want Photoshop to clean the brush after each stroke, select the Clean Brush icon in the options bar. To load the brush with the foreground color after each stroke, select the Load Brush icon in the options bar. By default, both of these options are selected.

**8**  Choose Load Brush from the Current Brush Load pop-up menu in the options bar to load the brush with blue, the current foreground color. Paint blue in half of the next circle.

**9**  Sample the yellow color from the yellow paint tube, and paint over the blue with a wet brush to mix the two colors.

**10**  Fill the last circle with yellow and red paint, mixing the two with a wet brush to create an orange color.

**11**  Hide the Circles layer in the Layers panel to remove the outlines on the palette.

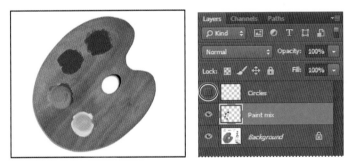

**12**  Choose File > Save.

## Tool tips from the Photoshop evangelist

### Mixer Brush shortcuts

There are no default keyboard shortcuts for the Mixer Brush tool, but you can create your own.

To create custom keyboard shortcuts:

1   Choose Edit > Keyboard Shortcuts.

2   Choose Tools from the Shortcuts For menu.

3   Scroll down to the bottom of the list.

4   Select a command, and then enter a custom shortcut. You can create shortcuts for the following commands:

- Load Mixer Brush
- Clean Mixer Brush
- Toggle Mixer Brush Auto-Load
- Toggle Mixer Brush Auto-Clean
- Toggle Mixer Brush Sample All Layers
- Sharpen Erodible Tips

# Creating a custom brush preset

Photoshop includes numerous brush presets, which are very handy. But if you need to tweak a brush for your project, you might find it easier to create your own preset. You'll create a brush preset to use in the following exercise.

1   In the Brush panel, select the following settings:

- Size: **36** px
- Shape: Round Fan
- Bristles: **35**%
- Length: **32**%
- Thickness: 2%
- Stiffness: **75**%
- Angle: **0**%
- Spacing: **2**%

2   Choose New Brush Preset from the Brush panel menu.

3   Name the brush **Landscape**, and click OK.

4   Click Brush Presets in the Brush panel to open the Brush Presets panel.

The Brush Presets panel displays samples of the strokes created by different brushes. If you know which brush you want to use, it can be easier to find by name. You'll list them by name now, so you can find your preset for the next exercise.

**5** Choose Large List from the Brush Presets panel menu.

**6** Scroll to the bottom of the list. The preset you created, named Landscape, is the last preset in the list.

**7** Close the 11Palette_working.psd file.

# Mixing colors with a photograph

Earlier, you mixed colors with a white background and with each other. Now, you'll use a photograph as your canvas. You'll add colors and mix them with each other and with the background colors to transform a photograph of a landscape into a watercolor.

**1** Choose File > Open. Double-click the 11Landscape_Start.jpg file in the Lesson11 folder to open it.

**2** Choose File > Save As. Rename the file **11Landscape_working.jpg**, and click Save. Click OK in the JPEG Options dialog box.

You'll paint the sky first. Start by setting up the color and selecting the brush.

**3** Click the Foreground color swatch in the Tools panel. Select a medium-light blue color (we chose R=185, G=204, B=228), and then click OK.

**4** Select the Mixer Brush tool (✔), if it isn't already selected. Choose Dry from the pop-up menu in the options bar. Then select the Landscape brush from the Brush Presets panel.

Presets are saved on your system, so they're available when you work with any image.

**5** Paint over the sky, moving in close to the trees. Because you're using a dry brush, the paint isn't mixing with the colors beneath it.

**6** Select a darker blue color (we used R=103, G=151, B=212), and add darker color at the top of the sky, still using the dry brush.

**7** Select a light blue color again, and choose Very Wet, Heavy Mix from the pop-up menu in the options bar. Use this brush to scrub diagonally across the sky, blending the two colors in with the background color. Paint in close to the trees, and smooth out the entire sky.

Adding a darker color with a dry brush          Blending colors with a wet brush

When you're satisfied with the sky, move on to the grass and trees.

8   Select a light green (we used R=92, G=157, B=13). Choose Dry from the pop-up menu in the options bar. Then paint along the top section of the grass to highlight it.

9   Sample a darker green from the grass itself. Choose Very Wet, Heavy Mix in the options bar. Then paint using diagonal strokes to blend the colors in the grass.

▶ **Tip:** Remember that you can Alt-click (Windows) or Option-click (Mac OS) to sample a color instead of using the Eyedropper tool. To sample only solid colors using the keyboard shortcut, choose Load Solid Colors Only from the Current Brush Load pop-up menu in the options bar.

Adding light green with a dry brush

Blending colors with a wet brush

10  Sample a light green, and then use a dry brush to highlight the lighter areas of the trees and the small tree in the middle of the landscape. Then select a dark green (we used R=26, G=79, B=34), and choose Very Wet, Heavy Mix in the options bar. Paint with the wet brush to mix together the colors in the trees.

Highlighting the trees

Mixing the colors

So far, so good. The background trees and the brown grasses are all that remain to be painted.

11  Select a bluer color for the background trees (we used R=65, G=91, B=116). Paint with a dry brush to add the blue at the top. Then choose Wet in the options bar, and paint to mix the blue into the trees.

▶ **Tip:** For different effects, paint in different directions. With the Mixer Brush tool, you can go wherever your artistic instincts lead you.

**12** Sample a brown color from the tall grasses, and then select Very Wet, Heavy Mix in the options bar. Paint along the top of the tall grass with up-and-down strokes for the look of a field. Across the back area, behind the small center tree, paint back and forth to create smooth strokes.

Voilà! You've created a masterpiece with your paints and brushes, and there's no mess to clean up.

## Brush variations

You can go beyond the settings in these projects to explore numerous variations in brush tips and settings. In particular, you may want to play with Brush Pose and Shape Dynamics options.

Brush Pose settings change the tilt, rotation, and pressure of the brush. In the Brush panel, select Brush Pose from the list on the left. Move the Tilt X slider to tilt the brush from left to right. Move the Tilt Y slider to tilt the brush forward and backward. Change the Rotation value to rotate the bristles. (Rotation is more obvious when using a flat fan-shaped brush, for example.) Change the Pressure setting to determine how much effect the brush has on the artwork.

Shape Dynamics settings affect the steadiness of the stroke. Move the sliders up to increase the variability in the stroke.

If you're using a Wacom tablet, Photoshop recognizes the angle and pressure of the pen you're using and applies them to the brush. You can use the pen to control such things as Size Jitter. Choose Pen Pressure or Pen Tilt from the Control menu in the Shape Dynamics settings to determine how the value changes.

There are many more options—some subtle, some not so subtle—to create variety in brush effects. Which options are available depend on the brush tip shape you've selected. For more information about all the options, see Photoshop Help.

# Painting gallery

The painting tools and brush tips in Photoshop CC let you create all kinds of painting effects.

Erodible brush tips give an added realism to your art. The following pages show examples of art created with the brush tips and tools in Photoshop CC.

Image © sholby, www.sholby.net

Image © sholby, www.sholby.net

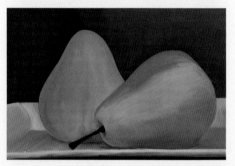

Image © Victoria Pavlov, www.pavlovphotography.com

Image © Lynette Kent, www.LynetteKent.com

## Painting gallery *continued*

Image © Janet Stoppee for m2media.com

Image © John Derry,
www.pixelart.com

Image © sholby, www.sholby.net

Image © John Derry, www.pixelart.com

## Review questions

1 What does the Mixer Brush do that other brushes don't?

2 How do you load a mixer brush?

3 How do you clean a brush?

4 How can you display the names of brush presets?

5 What is the Live Tip Brush Preview, and how can you hide it?

6 What is an erodible tip?

## Review answers

1 The Mixer Brush mixes the color of the paintbrush with colors on the canvas.

2 You can load a mixer brush by sampling a color, either by using the Eyedropper tool or keyboard shortcuts (Alt-click or Option-click). Or, you can choose Load Brush from the pop-up menu in the options bar to load the brush with the foreground color.

3 To clean a brush, choose Clean Brush from the pop-up menu in the options bar.

4 To display brush presets by name, open the Brush Presets panel, and then choose Large List (or Small List) from the Brush Presets panel menu.

5 The Live Tip Brush Preview shows you the direction the brush strokes are moving. It's available if OpenGL is enabled. To hide or show the Live Tip Brush Preview, click the Toggle The Live Tip Brush Preview icon at the bottom of the Brush panel or the Brush Presets panel.

6 An erodible tip erodes, changing thickness, as you paint or draw. It's similar to the way a pencil or pastel tip changes shape as it erodes.

# 12 WORKING WITH 3D IMAGES

## Lesson overview

In this lesson, you'll learn how to do the following:

- Create a 3D shape from a layer.

- Import a 3D object.

- Create 3D text.

- Apply the 3D postcard effect.

- Manipulate 3D objects using the 3D Axis widget.

- Adjust the camera view.

- Set coordinates in the Properties panel.

- Adjust light sources.

- Animate a 3D file.

 This lesson will take about 90 minutes to complete. Download the Lesson12 project files from the Lesson & Update Files tab on your Account page at www.peachpit.com, if you haven't already done so. As you work on this lesson, you'll preserve the start files. If you need to restore the start files, download them from your Account page.

PROJECT: WINERY ADVERTISEMENT

Traditional 3D artists spend hours, days, and weeks creating photo-realistic images. The 3D capabilities in Photoshop let you create sophisticated, precise 3D images easily—and you can change them easily, too.

# Getting started

This lesson explores 3D features, which are available only if your video card has at least 512MB of dedicated vRAM and supports OpenGL 2.0, and if OpenGL 2.0 is enabled on your computer. To learn about your video card, choose Edit > Preferences > Performance (Windows) or Photoshop > Preferences > Performance (Mac OS). Information about your video card is in the Graphics Processor Settings area of the dialog box.

● **Note:** Features covered in this lesson require Mac OS 10.7 or later, or Windows 7 or later, and at least 512MB VRAM. For more complete Photoshop CC system requirements, visit www.adobe.com/ products/photoshop/ tech-specs.html"

In this lesson, you'll create a three-dimensional scene for a wine advertisement. First, you'll view the finished scene.

1 Start Photoshop, and then immediately hold down Ctrl+Alt+Shift (Windows) or Command+Option+Shift (Mac OS) to restore the default preferences. (See "Restoring default preferences" on page 4.)

2 When prompted, click Yes to delete the Adobe Photoshop Settings file.

3 Choose File > Browse In Bridge to open Adobe Bridge.

● **Note:** If Bridge isn't installed, you'll be prompted to install it when you choose Browse In Bridge. For more information, see page 3.

4 In Bridge, click Lessons in the Favorites panel. Double-click the Lesson12 folder in the Content panel.

5 View the 12End.psd file in Bridge. A three-dimensional wine bottle, wine glass, and sale card sit atop a wooden box with 3D lettering.

6 Double-click the 12End.mp4 file to view the movie in which light has been animated to simulate a sunrise. When you're done viewing the movie, exit QuickTime.

7 Double-click the 12Start.psd file to open it in Photoshop.

The file contains an image of a vineyard, a black background layer, and two additional layers.

# Creating a 3D shape from a layer

Photoshop includes several 3D shape presets, representing geometric shapes and the shapes of everyday objects, such as a wine bottle or ring. When you create a 3D shape from a layer, Photoshop wraps the layer onto the 3D object preset. You can then rotate, reposition, and resize the 3D object—you can even light it from various angles with a number of colored lights.

First, you'll create the table for the wine bottle, glass, and card. To make the table, you'll wrap a 3D cube with the layer that contains the image of wood.

1   Choose File > Save As. Navigate to the Lesson12 folder, and save the file as **12Working.psd**. Click OK if the Photoshop Format Options dialog box appears.

2   In the Layers panel, make the Wood layer visible, and then select it.

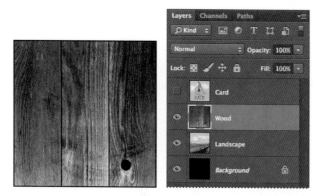

3   Choose 3D > New Mesh From Layer > Mesh Preset > Cube Wrap.

4   Click Yes when asked whether you want to switch to the 3D workspace.

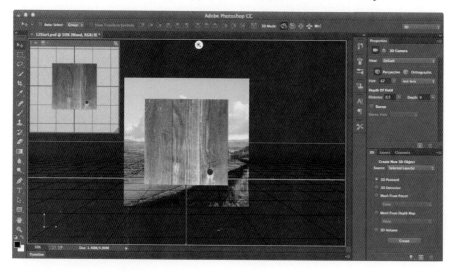

The 3D workspace includes the 3D panel, the Layers panel, and the Properties panel. You'll want to have all of these panels handy as you work with 3D objects. It also displays the ground plane, a grid that reflects the position of the ground relative to the 3D object, and the Secondary View window that lets you see the 3D object from a different perspective.

Photoshop wraps the wood image around a cube. You're viewing the front of the cube. You'll save the file now so you can easily return to this state after you've had a chance to experiment with the 3D tools.

**5**   Choose File > Save to save the file at this point.

## Manipulating 3D objects

The advantage to working with 3D objects is, obviously, that you can work with them in three dimensions. You can also return to a 3D layer at any time to change lighting, color, material, or position without having to re-create a lot of the art. Photoshop includes several basic tools that make it easy to rotate, resize, and position 3D objects. The 3D tools in the options bar manipulate the object itself. The Camera widget in the lower left corner of the application window manipulates the camera so you can view a 3D scene from different angles.

You can use the 3D tools whenever a 3D layer is selected in the Layers panel. A 3D layer behaves like any other layer—you can apply layer styles, mask it, and so on. However, a 3D layer can be quite complex.

Unlike a regular layer, a 3D layer contains one or more *meshes*. A mesh defines the 3D object. In the layer you just created, the mesh is the cube wrap shape. Each mesh, in turn, includes one or more *materials*—the appearance of a part or all of the mesh. Each material includes one or more *maps*, which are the components of the appearance. There are nine typical maps, and there can be only one of each kind; however, you can also use custom maps. Each map contains one *texture*—the image that defines what the maps and materials look like. The texture may be a simple bitmap graphic or a set of layers. The same texture might be used by many different maps and materials. In the layer you just created, the image of the wood composes the texture.

In addition to meshes, a 3D layer also includes one or more *lights*, which affect the appearance of 3D objects and remain in a fixed position as you spin or move the object. A 3D layer also includes *cameras*, which are saved views with the objects in a particular position. The *shader* creates the final appearance based on the materials, object properties, and renderer.

That may all sound complicated, but the most important thing to remember is that the 3D tools in the options bar move an object in 3D space and the Camera widget moves the cameras that view the object.

1  In the Tools panel, select the Move tool (⊹).

All the 3D capabilities are embedded into the Move tool, which recognizes when a 3D layer is selected and enables the 3D tools.

2  Select the Drag The 3D Object tool (✤) in the 3D Mode area of the options bar.

3  Click the edge of the wood, or just outside it, and drag it to move it from side to side or up and down. (If you click the face of the wood, Photoshop recognizes the 3D Axis widget, and switches to the corresponding tool.)

4  Select the Roll The 3D Object tool (⊙) in the options bar, and then click and drag the cube.

5  Experiment with the other tools to see how they affect the object.

When you select a 3D object, Photoshop displays the colorful 3D Axis widget, with green, red, and blue representing different axes. Red represents the x axis, green represents the y axis, and blue represents the z axis. (Hint: Think of RGB color to remember the order.)

If you hover the mouse over the center box until it turns yellow, you can click the box and drag to scale the object uniformly. Click an arrow to move the object along that axis; click the curved handle just before the arrow to rotate on that axis; and click the smaller handle to scale along that axis.

▶ **Tip:** As you move the object, the 3D Axis widget shifts, too. For example, the x and y axis arrows may be available, while the z axis is pointing directly into the scene. The yellow center box may also be obscured by an axis.

**6**  Rotate, scale, and move the cube using the widget.

**7**  Right-click (Windows) or Control-click (Mac OS) the Camera widget in the lower left corner of the application window (it has two axes visible), and choose Top.

Options in the Camera menu determine the angle from which you see the object. The camera angle changes, but the object itself does not. Don't be fooled by its relationship to the background image; that image is not 3D, so Photoshop leaves it in place when it moves the camera for the 3D object.

**8**  Choose other camera views to see how they affect the perspective.

**9**  When you're done experimenting, choose File > Revert. You should see the front view of the wooden cube again.

# Adding 3D objects

The wooden cube is just one of five 3D elements in the scene. You'll create all of the 3D objects, and then merge them onto a single 3D layer, where you can work with them as a group. On one layer, they'll share cameras and lights.

## Creating a 3D postcard

In Photoshop, you can transform a 2D object into a 3D postcard that you can manipulate in perspective in a 3D space. It's called a 3D postcard because it's as if your image became a postcard you could turn over in your hand.

You'll use a 3D postcard to create the card that leans on the wine bottle.

**1**  Click the Layers tab to bring the Layers panel forward.

**2** Make the Card layer visible, and select it.

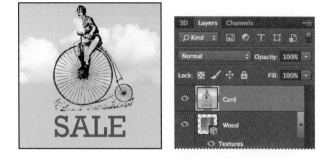

**3** Choose 3D > New Mesh From Layer > Postcard.

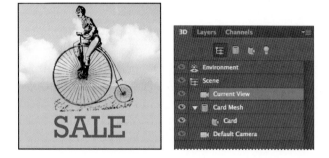

The card doesn't look much different, because you're viewing the front of it. When you manipulate it later, it will be much more obvious that it's a 3D postcard. Meanwhile, you can be sure it's a 3D object because Photoshop switches to the 3D panel, displays the Secondary View window in the upper left corner, enables the 3D tools in the options bar, and displays the Camera widget in the lower left corner of the application window.

## Creating a 3D mesh from a new layer

You used a 3D mesh preset to wrap the wood layer around a cube, but you can also use a mesh preset with a new, empty layer. You'll do that to create a wine bottle.

**1** Bring the Layers panel forward, and make sure the Card layer is selected.

**2** Click the Create A New Layer button (⬛) at the bottom of the Layers panel.

A new layer, named Layer 1, appears above the Card layer.

**3** With Layer 1 selected, choose 3D > New Mesh From Layer > Mesh Preset > Wine Bottle.

A gray wine bottle shape appears in front of the card. Later, you'll apply materials to the shape to make it look like a glass wine bottle.

**4** In the Layers panel, rename the layer **Bottle**.

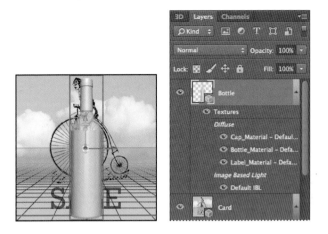

## Importing a 3D file

In Photoshop, you can open and work with 3D files exported from various applications, such as Collada, 3DS, KMZ (Google Earth), or U3D. You can also work with files saved in Collada format, a file interchange format supported by Autodesk, for example. When you add a 3D file as a 3D layer, it includes the 3D model and a transparent background. The layer uses the dimensions of the existing file, but you can resize it.

You'll import a 3D wine glass that was created in another application.

**1** Choose 3D > New 3D Layer From File.

**2** Navigate to the Lesson12/Assets folder, and double-click the WineGlass.obj file.

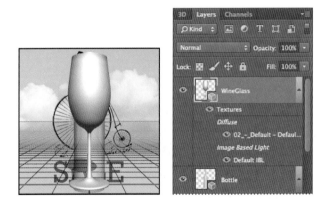

The wine glass shape appears in front of the bottle, centered in the document window.

**3** Choose File > Save to save your work so far.

# Creating 3D text

Even text can be three-dimensional. When you've created 3D text, you can rotate it, scale it, move it, apply materials to it, change its lighting (and the accompanying shadows), and extrude it. You'll create 3D text for the front of the wooden table.

1   Select the Horizontal Type tool (T) in the Tools panel.

2   Drag a marquee across the middle of the window.

3   In the options bar, select a serif font such as Minion Pro, Bold for the font style, and **72 pt** for the font size.

4   Type **HI-WHEEL** in all capital letters.

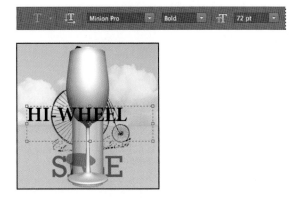

You've created text, but it's not three-dimensional yet. You'll convert it now.

5   Click the Update 3D Associated With This Text button in the options bar.

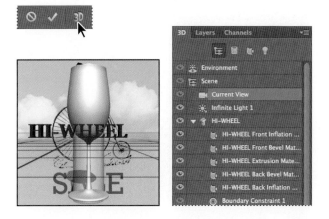

Now the text is 3D, and Photoshop displays its ground plane and the rest of the 3D work environment.

# Merging 3D layers to share the same 3D space

You can include multiple 3D meshes in the same 3D layer. Meshes in the same layer can share lighting effects and be rotated in the same 3D space (also called the *scene*), creating a more realistic 3D effect.

You'll merge the 3D layers you created so that all the 3D objects are part of the same scene.

1   Bring the Layers panel forward.

2   Press Shift while you select the HI-WHEEL, WineGlass, Bottle, Card, and Wood layers.

All five 3D layers are selected. Now you'll merge them. Be sure to press Shift while you merge them in order to retain their alignment.

3   Hold down the Shift key while you choose 3D > Merge 3D Layers.

Photoshop merges the layers into one layer, named Wood. Because you pressed Shift while you merged the layers, the objects' positions are unchanged.

4 Choose File > Save to save your work so far.

▶ **Tip:** If your merged layers don't look like this image, you probably released the Shift key before the layers were merged. Choose Edit > Undo Merge Layers, and try again.

# Positioning objects in a scene

The objects are all there, but it's not a very attractive arrangement. You'll use on-canvas widgets and the Properties panel to resize and reposition each of the 3D objects to compose an appealing scene.

## Changing the camera view

The Secondary View window can show you the scene from different perspectives. You'll use it to see the objects, and then change the camera view to get a better look at them as you reposition them.

1 Pan to see the objects below the wooden block in the Secondary View window in the upper left corner of the document window.

● **Note:** The camera view in the Secondary View window is independent of the camera view for the scene. You can change the view in the Secondary View window to see the scene from different angles without changing its appearance in Photoshop.

The current camera view for the Secondary View window is from the top. The objects you created are in front of the wooden box.

**2**  Click the Select View/Camera button at the top of the Secondary View window, and choose Left.

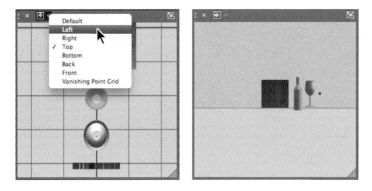

Now you can see the objects clearly. You'll use this camera view for the scene.

**3**  Right-click (Windows) or Control-click (Mac OS) the Camera widget in the lower left corner of the document window, and choose Left.

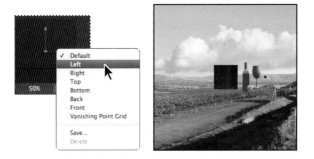

## Moving objects with the 3D Axis widget

The wine glass, wine bottle, and card need to sit atop the wooden table, not beside it. You can manipulate individual 3D objects within a 3D layer by selecting their folders in the 3D panel. You'll use the 3D Axis widget to move the objects on top of the table.

**1**  Bring the 3D panel forward in the Layers panel group.

**2**  Select the Card_Layer folder, and then press the Shift key as you select the Wine_Bottle, and WineGlass_Layer folders.

**3**  Hover the cursor over the tip of the green arrow until you see the Move On Y Axis tool tip.

**4** Click the tip of the green arrow, and drag the objects up until the bottom of the wine bottle is level with the top of the wooden cube.

**5** Click the tip of the blue arrow, and drag the objects to the left until they are centered on the cube. You can use the green arrow to drag the objects up or down again. The positioning doesn't have to be perfect; you'll have the opportunity to make adjustments later.

▶ **Tip:** You can change the size of the 3D Axis widget. Press Shift as you hover the cursor over the yellow scaling cube. Then click and drag to make the 3D Axis widget smaller or larger.

You've moved the card, bottle, and glass. Now you'll move the text, which is currently a small black square off to the side of the box.

**6** In the 3D panel, expand the HI-WHEEL_Layer folder, and select the HI-WHEEL text.

**7** Drag the HI-WHEEL text so that it is just in front of the top of the cube, using the green and blue arrows in the 3D Axis widget. Then, in the 3D panel, collapse the HI-WHEEL_Layer folder to hide its contents.

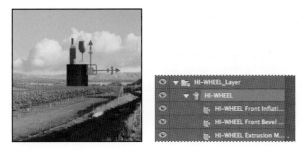

Remember that the camera view is from the left. To move the text in front of the box, it needs to appear to be to the right of the box in this view.

**8** Right-click (Windows) or Control-click (Mac OS) the Camera widget, and choose Default.

The camera angle changes to display the scene from the front.

## Using the Properties panel to position 3D objects

You've done some good work, but the objects aren't in their final positions yet. You'll change coordinates in the Properties panel to move them into place.

**1** Select Scene in the 3D panel.

Changes you make while Scene is selected affect the entire 3D scene. You'll move and rotate all the objects as a group.

▶ **Tip:** Press V to switch between panes in the Properties panel.

**2** In the Properties panel, click the Coordinates button to change the options available.

**3** Type **70** for the X Position value, **70** for the Y Position value, and **17** for the Z position value.

**4** Type **-30** in the Y Rotation box.

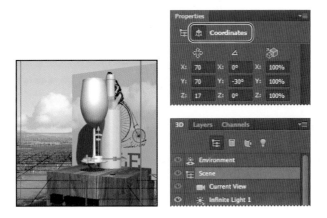

The entire 3D scene rotates 30 degrees against the background. Next, you'll scale the wine glass and align it with the bottle.

5  In the 3D panel, expand the WineGlass_Layer folder, and then select objMesh.

6  In the Properties panel, enter **60%** for the X Scale, Y Scale, and Z Scale values.

7  In the 3D panel, select the Wine_Bottle folder and then Shift-select the WineGlass_Layer folder.

8  Click the Align Bottom Edges button in the Photoshop options bar to align the bottom edges of the two objects (so that they both rest on the cube). If the objects don't rest on the cube, use the green arrow on the 3D Axis widget to move them up or down together as needed.

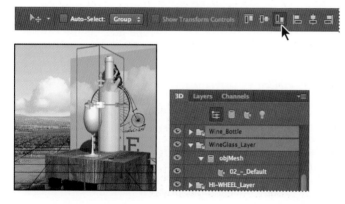

The wine glass is more proportionate with the bottle, and aligned with it. Now you'll move it to the right of the bottle, and then move the bottle over, too. You'll start by entering coordinates that will get you most of the way there, but you may need to adjust the objects' position.

**Tip:** If you'd rather, you can position the wine glass and the bottle using the 3D Axis widget.

9 Select ObjMesh in the WineGlass_Layer folder in the 3D panel. Then enter the following values in the Position boxes in the Properties panel: X: **126**, Y: **123**, and Z: **136**. (Click the Coordinates button if the Position boxes aren't displayed in the Properties panel.)

10 Select the Wine_Bottle folder in the 3D panel. Then enter the following values in the Position boxes in the Properties panel: X: **37**, Y: **229**, and Z: **-97**.

11 In the Properties panel, enter **75%** for the X Scale, Y Scale, and Z Scale.

The coordinates you've entered may not give you the precise results you want, depending on where you positioned the objects originally. You can adjust the objects manually if you need to.

12 Use the widget to nudge the bottle and wine glass so that they're sitting on top of the cube.

13 In the 3D panel, collapse the WineGlass_Layer folder, and then choose File > Save to save your work so far.

## Scaling and rotating objects with widgets

The wine glass and bottle are in position now, but the text and card are still out of place. You'll use the 3D Axis widget to scale and position them appropriately.

1 In the 3D panel, expand the HI-WHEEL_Layer folder, and select the HI-WHEEL text.

2 Use the red arrow on the 3D Axis widget to pull the text back and forth until it's centered on the front of the box. Use the green and blue arrows to move the text up and down, and forward and backward, as needed. Make sure the text is flush against the wooden cube, or even slightly inset.

**3** Hover the mouse over the center of the 3D Axis widget until the center cube turns yellow. Then drag the widget to scale the text so that it fits the width of the cube (about 135% of its original size, as reported in the hint text as you drag).

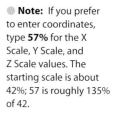

**Note:** If you prefer to enter coordinates, type **57%** for the X Scale, Y Scale, and Z Scale values. The starting scale is about 42%; 57 is roughly 135% of 42.

The text is in place. Now you'll resize and position the card.

**4** In the 3D panel, close the HI-WHEEL folder, and expand the Card_Layer folder.

**5** Select Card Mesh in the 3D panel, and then use the 3D Axis widget to scale it to about 25% of its original size.

**6** Drag the tip of the blue arrow on the 3D Axis widget to move the card forward along the Z axis until the front of the card and the front of the cube are even.

**7** Drag the tip of the green arrow to pull the card down so it rests on the cube.

**8** Use the red handle to move the card in front of the bottle. Then use the blue curved handle to rotate the top of the card back so that it appears to lean against the bottle. Make any further adjustments to the card's position using the blue, green, and red arrows, as necessary.

**Tip:** If the 3D Axis widget behaves unexpectedly or disappears, make sure Card Mesh is selected in the 3D panel, and then try again.

**9** If you need to adjust the bottle or glass further, select the Wine_Bottle folder or the WineGlass_Layer folder in the 3D panel, or both, and move the objects.

Everything's in position!

**10** Collapse any open folders in the 3D panel, and choose File > Save.

# Applying materials to 3D objects

One of the benefits of working with 3D objects is that you can quickly change the appearance of the objects. You'll apply materials to the text to make it stand out. Then you'll make the bottle and wine glass look much more realistic.

## Changing the appearance of 3D text

You'll change the shape of the text, extrude it, and then apply materials to each surface of the 3D text.

1   In the 3D panel, expand the HI-WHEEL_Layer folder, and select the HI-WHEEL text.

2   Press V to change panes in the Properties panel, cycling through the Mesh, Deform, Cap, and Coordinates panels. The on-canvas widgets change for different panes.

3   Click the Deform button (🜨) in the Properties panel to see the Deform properties.

4   In the Properties panel, choose Bevel from the Shape Preset menu. (Bevel is the middle option in the top row.)

▶ **Tip:** When the Deform properties are shown, the on-canvas widget lets you extrude, taper, bend, or twist the selected object mesh.

5   Click the center of the on-canvas Deform widget, and drag until the extrusion depth is approximately 23.

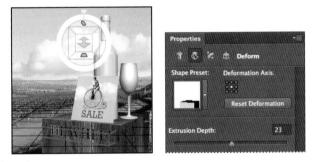

6   Press V to display the Cap properties (🜨) in the Properties panel.

**7** Drag the symbol on the right in the on-canvas widget upwards until the inflation strength is approximately 4.75. (The Strength slider in the Properties panel displays 4 or 5%.)

The bevel looks great. Now you'll apply a material to make the text shiny.

**8** In the 3D panel, Shift-select the five material components of the HI-WHEEL text: HI-WHEEL Front Inflation Material, HI-WHEEL Front Bevel Material, HI-WHEEL Extrusion Material, HI-WHEEL Back Bevel Material, and HI-WHEEL Back Inflation Material.

**9** In the Properties panel, open the Materials picker.

**10** Choose Default from the settings menu. Click OK when you're prompted to replace the materials, and click Don't Save if you're prompted to save the current materials.

**A.** Materials picker
**B.** Settings menu

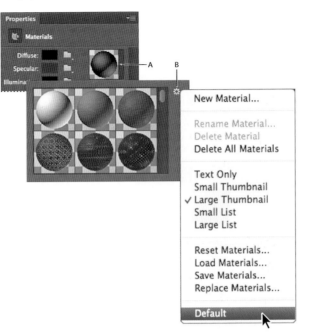

A different set of materials appears in the Materials picker.

**11** In the Materials picker, select Metal Gold, the middle option in the sixth row.

Every aspect of the 3D text is now gold. You'll use the same process to apply materials to the bottle and wine glass.

**12** Hide the contents of the HI-WHEEL_Layer folder in the 3D panel.

## Applying materials to objects

You'll use similar techniques to apply materials to the wine bottle's cap and glass, and then apply an imported label. Then, you'll make the wine glass look much more realistic than it does now.

1 Expand the Wine_Bottle layer in the 3D panel, and select the Cap_Material component.

This material applies only to the cap area of the bottle.

2 In the Properties panel, open the Materials picker, and then select Metal Brass (Solid) from the middle of the fifth row.

The bottle appears to have a foil wrapper around its cork.

3 In the Properties panel, click the Diffuse color swatch. Select a dark blue color (we used R=20, G=66, B=112), and click OK.

▶ **Tip:** When the Color Picker dialog box is open, the pointer becomes an eyedropper tool. You can click anywhere in the image window to select that color.

Now the foil wrapper is blue.

4 Select the Bottle_Material component in the 3D panel, and then select Glass (Smooth) from the Materials picker. Glass (Smooth) is just to the left of Metal Brass (Solid).

5 In the Properties panel, move the Opacity slider to **66%**, so you'll be able to see the colors you apply.

6 Click the Diffuse color swatch in the Properties panel. Select a red so dark it's almost black: At the bottom of the dialog box, enter R=**191**, G=**6**, B=**6**. Then enter **-4** stops for the Intensity slider. Click OK.

When you're assigning properties to 3D objects, Photoshop displays the HDR Color Picker, which includes additional options. You can use the Intensity slider to boost or reduce a color's brightness. The Intensity stops correspond inversely to exposure setting stops.

**7** In the Properties panel, change the Specular color swatch to a dark burgundy (R=**73**, G=**3**, B=**3**), the Illumination color swatch to a dark red that is almost black (R=**191**, G=**4**, B=**4**), and the Ambient color swatch to a dark burgundy (R=**71**, G=**6**, B=**6**). In each case, leave the Intensity slider at 0.

**8** Change the sliders in the Properties panel to the following settings:

- Shine: **47%**

- Reflection: **49%**

- Bump: **0%**

- Refraction: **1.5**

You'll add a label to the bottle next. To see the bottle better, hide the card.

**9** In the 3D panel, click the eye icon to hide the Card_Layer folder.

**10** Select the Label_Material component in the 3D panel, and then click the icon next to the Diffuse swatch in the Properties panel. Choose Replace Texture. Navigate to the Lesson12/Assets folder, and double-click Label.psd. (In Windows, choose Photoshop (*.PSD, *.PDD) from the Files Of Type menu to see the Label.psd file; you may have to scroll up to see the option.)

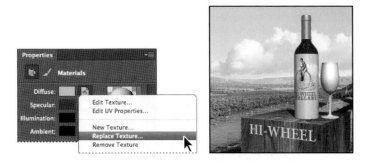

**11** Select the Label mesh in the Wine_Bottle folder in the 3D panel. Then select the Coordinates button at the top of the Properties panel, and change the Y Rotation value to **35** degrees so that the label is more visible.

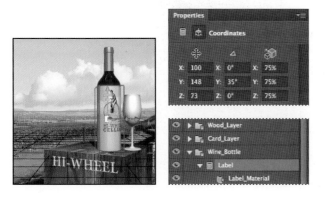

**12** In the 3D panel, click the visibility icon to show the Card_Layer folder again.

**13** In the 3D panel, expand the WineGlass_Layer folder, and then select the 02_Default material component under objMesh.

**14** In the Materials picker, select Glass (Smooth), the first option in the fifth row.

**15** Change the sliders in the Properties panel to apply the following settings:

- Shine: **96**%
- Reflection: **83**%
- Roughness: **0**%
- Bump: **10**
- Opacity: **22**%
- Refraction: **1**

**16** Hide the properties for each of the folders in the 3D panel, and then choose File > Save.

## Lighting a 3D scene

You can adjust the default light for a scene, and add new lights. How you adjust the lights determines the shadows, the highlights, and the mood of the scene.

**1** In the 3D panel, select Infinite Light 1.

By default, Photoshop creates one infinite light when you create a 3D scene. When you select the light, an on-canvas widget appears to help you direct the light. Move the large knob to make sweeping changes; adjust the small knob for more precise lighting shifts.

2   Use the small knob to position the light in the upper left corner (at about the 11:00 position on a clock), so that there's a tall highlight along the center of the neck of the bottle and the bottle color deepens.

Note: The size of the light widget depends on the screen magnification. Yours might be larger or smaller than the one shown here.

3   Right-click (Windows) or Control-click (Mac OS) the light itself (the white round icon above the image) to open the Infinite Light 1 panel. Then change the color to a faint gold color (we used R=251, G=242, B=203). In the Infinite Light 1 panel, change the Intensity to **30%**.

Note: You can make changes in the Infinite Light 1 panel or in the Properties panel.

4   Click the Add New Light To Scene button (💡) at the bottom of the 3D panel, and choose New Infinite Light.

5   With Infinite Light 2 selected, make changes in the Properties panel. Change the color to a light gold color similar to that in the first light. Then change the Intensity value to **30%**.

**6** With Infinite Light 2 still selected in the 3D panel, move the knob on the on-canvas widget to position the light at about the 1:00 position on the clock, so that there's a nice highlight on the edge of the bottle.

**7** Click the Add New Light To Scene button at the bottom of the 3D panel, and choose New Point Light.

**8** Select Point Light 1 in the 3D panel, and then change its Intensity to **30%** in the Properties panel.

**9** Use the on-canvas widget to pull the light onto the center of the wine glass.

**10** Choose File > Save to save your work so far.

# Rendering a 3D scene

As you build a scene in Photoshop, you can get a pretty good idea of what it will look like. But it's only when you render it that you know how realistic the final project will look. You can render small areas of the scene at any time, but wait until you think you're close to done to render the entire scene. Rendering is a time-consuming process, and once you've rendered the scene, every change you makes triggers re-rendering.

You can render the scene now, or, if you're planning to do the Extra Credit project, wait and render the animated scene.

1   Choose File > Save As, and save the file as **12_render.psd**. Click OK if the Photoshop Format Options dialog box appears.

Saving a separate file for rendering ensures that you'll be able to make changes to the original more quickly.

2   In the 3D panel, select Scene to ensure that the entire scene is selected.

3   Click the Render button () at the bottom of the Properties panel.

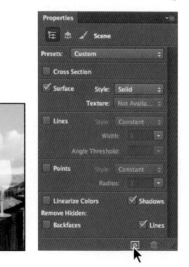

Photoshop renders the file. Depending on your system, this can take anywhere from a few minutes to half an hour or more.

▶ **Tip:** You can change the number of passes Photoshop makes when it renders the scene. Choose Edit > Preferences > 3D (Windows) or Photoshop > Preferences > 3D (Mac OS), and then change the High Quality Threshold value in the Ray Tracer area.

Depending on your system, this may take a while.

▶ **Tip:** If you need to interrupt the rendering, or believe that the quality is sufficient, click anywhere on the image to stop the rendering process.

# Extra credit

## Animating lighting for a 3D scene

You can simulate a time-lapse video of daybreak by setting different states for the lighting and opacity of the background. For more information about animating properties using the Timeline panel, see Lesson 10, "Editing Video."

1 Click the Timeline tab at the bottom of the application window to open the Timeline panel.

2 If the document layers aren't in the timeline, click Create Video Timeline.

3 Shorten the duration of the Wood layer by dragging the end of the clip to the left until it matches the Landscape layer (05:00).

4 Display the properties for the Landscape layer. Move the playhead to the end of the time ruler, and then click the stopwatch for the Opacity property to create a keyframe.

5 Move the playhead to the beginning of the time ruler.

6 Bring the Layers panel forward. In the Layers panel, change the opacity for the Landscape layer to **0**%.

**7** In the Timeline panel, hide the properties for the Landscape layer, expand the properties for the Wood layer, and then expand 3D Lights under the Wood layer.

**8** Move the playhead to the end of the time ruler, and click the stopwatch icons for all three 3D Node properties. Their labels change to Infinite Light 1, Infiinite Light 2, and Point Light 1.

**9** Move the playhead back to the beginning of the time ruler.

**10** Bring the 3D panel forward, and select Infinite Light 1. Use the on-canvas widget to direct the light downward. Then select Infinite Light 2, and move its light downward, too.

**11** Select Point Light 1, and drag its light to the bottom of the scene.

**12** Click Play in the Timeline panel to preview the animation, and then make any adjustments you'd like.

**13** In the 3D panel, select Scene to ensure that the entire scene is selected.

**14** Choose Render Video from the Timeline panel menu.

**15** At the bottom of the Render Video dialog box, choose Interactive from the 3D Quality menu if you have a slower computer; otherwise, choose Ray Traced Draft.

**16** Leave all other options at their default settings, and click Render.

**17** When Photoshop has finished rendering the movie, double-click the 12Working.mp4 file in the Lesson12/Assets folder to view it.

# Review questions

1  How does a 3D layer differ from other layers in Photoshop?

2  How can you change the camera view?

3  How do you apply materials to an object?

4  Which color represents each axis on the 3D Axis widget?

5  How do you render a 3D scene?

# Review answers

1 A 3D layer behaves like any other layer—you can apply layer styles, mask it, and so on. However, unlike a regular layer, a 3D layer also contains one or more meshes, which define 3D objects. You can work with meshes and the materials, maps, and textures they contain. You can also adjust the lighting for a 3D layer.

2 To change the camera view, you can move the Camera widget, or right-click (Windows) or Control-click (Mac OS) the widget to choose a camera view preset.

3 To apply materials, select the material component in the 3D panel, and then select materials and settings in the Properties panel.

4 In the 3D Axis widget, the red arrow represents the X axis; the green arrow represents the Y axis, and the blue arrow represents the Z axis.

5 To render a 3D scene, select Scene in the 3D panel, and then click the Render button at the bottom of the Properties panel.

# 13 PREPARING FILES FOR THE WEB

## Lesson overview

In this lesson, you'll learn how to do the following:

- Slice an image in Photoshop.

- Distinguish between user slices and auto slices.

- Link user slices to other HTML pages or locations.

- Optimize images for the web and make good compression choices.

- Export large, high-resolution files that tile for zooming and panning.

- Copy layer properties to CSS code for use in web design.

 This lesson will take about an hour to complete. Download the Lesson13 project files from the Lesson & Update Files tab on your Account page at www.peachpit.com, if you haven't already done so. As you work on this lesson, you'll preserve the start files. If you need to restore the start files, download them from your Account page.

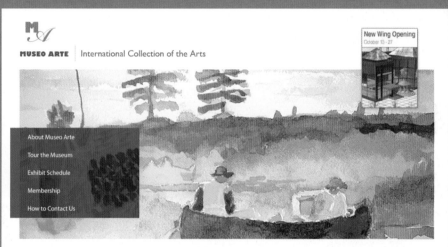

## MUSEO ARTE | International Collection of the Arts

**New Wing Opening**
October 13 - 27

About Museo Arte

Tour the Museum

Exhibit Schedule

Membership

How to Contact Us

### Welcome to Museo Arte : Treasures from South America, Europe & Asia

Museo Arte, founded in 1864, and located in the heart of Madrid's cultural district offers a dazzling array of art works from Spanish masters, as well as from other areas of Europe, and from Asia. The permanent collection at Museo Arte includes paintings, drawings, ceramics, and sculptural works.

**Current Exhibits**
Museo Arte is currently showing a travelling exhibit of Watercolors by Spanish Contemporary Artists Other current exhibits include a Sculpture Show in the Sculpture Garden Courtyard, and Road to Morrisy: An Installation by Jaime Nelson For more information on exhibits at Museo Arte, visit Exhibits.

**Special Events**
Museo Arte holds special events throughout the year for general public, as well as special groups. Facilities are also available for charity events, weddings, and private gatherings.

PROJECT: MUSEUM WEBSITE

Web users expect to click linked graphics to jump to another site or page, and to activate built-in animations. You can prepare a file for the web in Photoshop by adding slices to link to other pages or sites.

# Getting started

For this lesson, you will need to use a web browser application such as Firefox, Internet Explorer, Safari, or Chrome. You do not need to connect to the Internet.

You'll fine-tune graphics for the home page of a Spanish art museum's website. You'll add hypertext links to the topics, so that website visitors can jump to other prebuilt pages on the site.

First, you'll explore the final HTML page that you will create from a single Photoshop file.

1 Start Photoshop, and then immediately hold down Ctrl+Alt+Shift (Windows) or Command+Option+Shift (Mac OS) to restore the default preferences. (See "Restoring default preferences" on page 4.)

2 When prompted, click Yes to delete the Adobe Photoshop Settings file.

3 Choose File > Browse In Bridge.

**Note:** If Bridge isn't installed, you'll be prompted to install it when you choose Browse In Bridge. For more information, see page 3.

4 In Bridge, click Lessons in the Favorites panel. Double-click the Lesson13 folder in the Content panel, double-click the 13End folder, and finally, double-click the Site folder.

The Site folder contains the contents of the website that you'll be working with.

5 Right-click (Windows) or Control-click (Mac OS) the home.html file, and choose Open With from the context menu. Choose a web browser to open the HTML file.

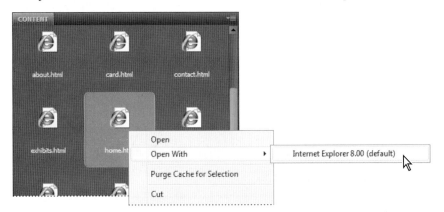

6 Move the pointer over the topics on the left side of the web page and over the images. When the pointer hovers over a link, it changes from an arrow to a pointing hand.

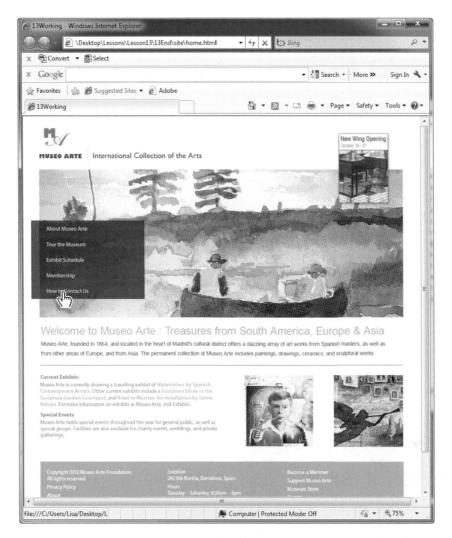

**Note:** Depending on the settings in your browser, it may display security warnings. You are working with files on your hard disk, not on the Internet, so you can safely display the content.

**7** Click the image of the angel in the lower right area of the page. The Zoomify window opens. Click the Zoomify controls to see how they change the magnification and reposition the image.

**8**  To return to the home page, close the Zoomify tab or window.

**9**  Click the image of the boy with the lightbulb to get a closer look at it in its own window. Close its browser window when you have finished.

**10** On the home page, click the topics on the left side to jump to their linked pages. To return to the home page, click the "Museo Arte" text just below the logo in the upper left corner of the window.

**11** When you have finished viewing the web page, quit the web browser, and return to Bridge.

**12** In Bridge, click the Lesson13 folder in the breadcrumbs (the navigation path) at the top of the window to display the folder contents. Double-click the 13Start folder in the Content panel, and then double-click the 13Start.psd thumbnail to open the file in Photoshop. Click OK if you see the Missing Profile dialog box.

**13** Choose File > Save As, and rename the file **13Working.psd**. Click OK in the Photoshop Format Options dialog box.

In the preceding steps, you clicked links that were created from slices (the topics on the left side of the page) and images (the boy and the angel). *Slices* are rectangular areas in an image that you define based on layers, guides, or precise selections in the image, or by using the Slice tool. When you define slices in an image, Photoshop creates an HTML table or Cascading Style Sheet (CSS) layers to contain and align the slices. You can generate and preview an HTML file that contains the sliced image along with the table or cascading style sheet.

You can also add hypertext links to images. A website visitor can then click the image to open a linked page. Unlike slices, which are always rectangular, images can be any shape.

# Creating slices

When you define a rectangular area in an image as a slice, Photoshop creates an HTML table to contain and align the slice. Once you create slices, you can turn them into buttons, and then program those buttons to make the web page work.

Any new slice you create within an image (a *user slice*) automatically creates other slices (*auto slices*) that cover the entire area of the image outside the user slice.

## Selecting slices and setting slice options

You'll start by selecting an existing slice in the start file. We created the first slice for you.

1   In the Tools panel, select the Slice Select tool (🔪), hidden under the Crop tool (🔳).

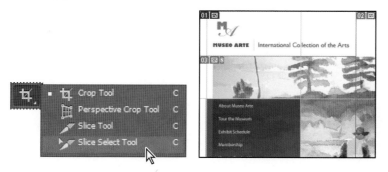

When you select the Slice or Slice Select tool, Photoshop displays the slices, with their slice numbers, on the image.

The slice numbered 01 includes the upper left corner of the image; it also has a small icon, or *badge*, that resembles a tiny mountain. The blue color means that the slice is a user slice—a slice we created in the start file.

Also notice the gray slices—02 to the right, and 03 just below slice 01. The gray color indicates that these are auto slices, automatically created by making a user slice. The symbol indicates that the slice contains image content. See "About slice symbols" for a description.

2   In the upper left corner of the image, click the slice numbered 01 with the small blue rectangle. A gold bounding box appears, indicating that the slice is selected.

# About slice symbols

The blue and gray slice symbols, or *badges*, in the Photoshop image window and Save For Web dialog box can be useful reminders if you take the time to learn how to read them. Each slice can contain as many badges as are appropriate. These badges indicate the following:

- 🔲 The number of the slice. Numbers run sequentially from left to right and top to bottom of the image.

- 🔲 The slice contains image content.

- 🔲 The slice contains no image content.

- 🔲 The slice is layer-based; that is, it was created from a layer.

- 🔲 The slice is linked to other slices (for optimization purposes).

3 Still using the Slice Select tool, double-click slice 01. The Slice Options dialog box appears. By default, Photoshop names each slice based on the filename and the slice number—in this case, 13Start_01.

**Note:** You can set options for an auto slice, but doing so automatically promotes the auto slice to a user slice.

Slices aren't particularly useful until you set options for them. Slice options include the slice name and the URL that opens when the user clicks the slice.

4 In the Slice Options dialog box, name the slice **Logo**. For URL, type #.

The pound sign (#) lets you preview a button's functionality without programming an actual link. It's very helpful in the early stages of website design, when you want to see how a button will look and behave.

**5** Click OK to apply the changes.

| Slice Options | | |
|---|---|---|
| Slice Type: | Image ▾ | OK |
| Name: | Logo | Cancel |
| URL: | | |
| Target: | | |

## Creating navigation buttons

Now you'll slice the navigation buttons on the left side of the page. You could select one button at a time and add navigation properties to it. But you can do the same thing a faster way.

**1** In the Tools panel, select the Slice tool (✂), or press Shift+C. (The Crop tool, Perspective Crop tool, Slice tool, and Slice Select tool share the C key as their keyboard shortcut. To change which of the four tools is selected, press Shift+C.)

Notice the guides above and below the words on the left side of the image.

**2** Using the guides on the left side of the image, drag the Slice tool diagonally from the upper left corner above the first line of text, to the bottom guide below the last line of text, so that all five lines are enclosed.

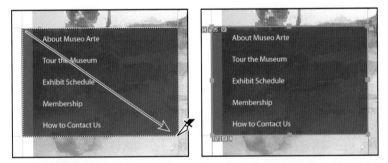

A blue rectangle, similar to the one for slice 01, appears in the upper left corner of the slice you just created, numbered slice 05. The blue color tells you that this is a user slice, not an auto slice. The gold bounding box indicates the bounds of the slice and that it's selected.

The original gray rectangle for auto slice 03 remains unchanged, but the area included in slice 03 is smaller, covering only a small rectangle above the text. Another auto slice, numbered 07, appears below the slice you created.

**3**  With the Slice tool still selected, press Shift+C to toggle to the Slice Select tool (🖋).

The options bar above the image window changes to include a series of alignment buttons. Now you'll slice your selection into five separate buttons.

**4**  Click the Divide button in the options bar.

**5**  In the Divide Slice dialog box, select Divide Horizontally Into, and type **5** for Slices Down, Evenly Spaced. Click OK.

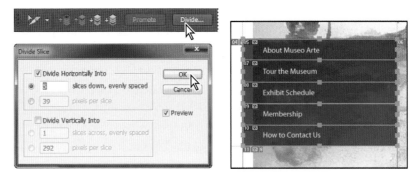

You'll name each slice and add a corresponding link.

**6**  Using the Slice Select tool, double-click the top slice (containing the words "About Museo Arte").

**7**  In the Slice Options dialog box, name the slice **About**; type **about.html** for URL; and type **_self** for Target. (Be sure to include the underscore before the letter *s*.) Click OK.

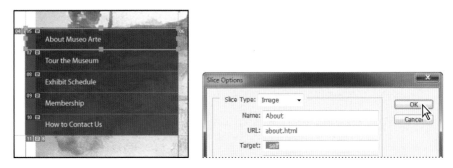

The Target option controls how a linked file opens when the link is clicked. The _self option displays the linked file in the same frame as the original file.

**Note:** Type the HTML filenames in the URL box exactly as shown, to match the names of the existing pages to which you will link the buttons.

8  Repeat steps 6 and 7 for the remaining slices in turn, starting from the second slice, as follows:

- Name the second slice **Tour**; type **tour.html** for URL; and type **_self** for Target.

- Name the third slice **Exhibits**; type **exhibits.html** for URL; and type **_self** for Target.

- Name the fourth slice **Members**; type **members.html** for URL; and type **_self** for Target.

- Name the fifth slice **Contact**; type **contact.html** for URL; and type **_self** for Target.

9  Choose File > Save to save your work so far.

**Tip:** If you find the indicators for the auto slices distracting, select the Slice Select tool and then click the Hide Auto Slices button in the options bar. You can also hide the guides by choosing View > Show > Guides, because you won't need them again in this lesson.

## About creating slices

Here are other methods for creating slices that you can try on your own:

- You can create No Image slices, and then add text or HTML source code to them. No Image slices can have a background color and are saved as part of the HTML file. The primary advantage of using No Image slices for text is that the text can be edited in any HTML editor, saving you the trouble of having to go back to Photoshop to edit it. However, if the text grows too large for the slice, it will break the HTML table and introduce unwanted gaps.

- If you use custom guides in your design work, you can instantly divide up an entire image into slices with the Slices From Guides button on the options bar. Use this technique with caution, however, because it discards any previously created slices and any options associated with those slices. Also, it creates only user slices, and you may not need that many of them.

- When you want to create identically sized, evenly spaced, and aligned slices, try creating a single user slice that precisely encloses the entire area. Then, use the Divide button on the Slice Select options bar to divide the original slice into as many vertical or horizontal rows of slices as you need.

- If you want to unlink a layer-based slice from its layer, you can convert it to a user slice. Select it with the Slice Select tool, and then click Promote in the options bar.

## Creating slices based on layers

In addition to using the Slice tool, you can create slices based on layers. The advantage of using layers for slices is that Photoshop creates the slice based on the dimensions of the layer and includes all its pixel data. When you edit the layer, move it, or apply a layer effect to it, the layer-based slice adjusts to encompass the new pixels.

1  In the Layers panel, select the New Wing layer. If you can't see all of the contents of the Layers panel, drag the panel from its dock, and expand it by dragging the lower right corner downward.

2  Choose Layer > New Layer Based Slice. In the image window, a slice numbered 04, with a blue badge, appears over the image announcing the new wing. It is numbered according to its position in the slices, starting from the top left corner of the image.

3  Using the Slice Select tool (✐), double-click the slice, and name it **New Wing**. For URL, type **newwing.html**. Type **_blank** for Target. The _blank Target option opens the linked page in a new instance of the web browser. Click OK.

Be sure to enter these options exactly as indicated, to match the pages you'll be linking the slices to.

Now you'll create slices for the Image 1 and Image 2 layers.

4  Repeat steps 1–3 for the remaining images, as follows:
   - Create a slice from the Image 1 layer (the image of the boy). Name it **Image 1**; for URL, type **image1.html**; and type **_blank** for Target. Click OK.
   - Create a slice from the Image 2 layer. Name it **Card**; type **card.html** for URL, and type **_blank** for Target. Click OK.

You may have noticed that the dialog box contains more options than the three you specified for these slices. For more information on how to use these options, see Photoshop Help.

5   Choose File > Save to save your work so far.

# Exporting HTML and images

You're ready to make your final slices, define your links, and export your file so that Photoshop creates an HTML page that will display all of your slices as one unit.

It's important to keep web graphics as small (in file size) as possible, so that web pages open quickly. Photoshop has built-in tools to help you gauge how small each exported slice can be without compromising image quality. A good rule of thumb is to use JPEG compression for photographic, continuous-tone images and GIF compression for broad areas of color—in the case of this lesson's site, all of the areas around the three main art images on the page.

You'll use the Save For Web dialog box to compare settings and compression options for different image formats.

1   Choose File > Save For Web.

2   Select the 2-Up tab at the top of the Save For Web dialog box.

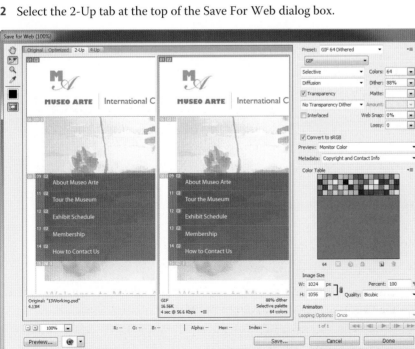

# Fonts for the web

In the past, typography for the web was challenging. You either had to stick with a handful of "web-safe" fonts or include potentially cumbersome images of text on your website. Today, Adobe Typekit gives you access to more than 25,000 professional font choices for your site—and they'll work on both desktop computers and mobile devices. Because the fonts are hosted through Typekit, web pages download faster, and you don't have to worry about browser compatibility.

If you have a paid Creative Cloud membership, you have access to the full Typekit font library. With a free membership, you get the Typekit Free Plan, which gives you a subset of the fonts available.

To use Typekit, log in using your Adobe ID. Browse or search the font library, and create a "kit" of the fonts you want to use on a particular website. Typekit produces the code you need to add to your site, and can also help write some of the CSS code for your new type styles. You type in the places you want the type to go (paragraph, headers, tables, etc.), and click Add. Click Publish, and use a CSS editor like Dreamweaver to add your new fonts to your site.

Learn more about Typekit at http://html.adobe.com/edge/typekit/.

*Select fonts from the library to create a kit for your website.*

*Specify where you want the font to be used (tables, headers, etc.), and Typekit creates the code for you.*

**3** Use the Hand tool (🖐) in the dialog box to move the image within the window so that you can see the portrait of the boy.

**4** Choose the Slice Select tool (✂) in the dialog box, and select slice 17 (the portrait of the boy) from the slices in the image on the left. Note the file size displayed beneath the image.

**5** On the right side of the dialog box, choose JPEG Medium from the Preset pop-up menu. Notice the file size displayed beneath the image; the file size changes dramatically when you choose JPEG Medium.

Now you'll look at a GIF setting for the same slice in the image on the right.

**6** With the Slice Select tool, select slice 17 in the image on the right. On the right side of the dialog box, choose GIF 32 No Dither from the Preset pop-up menu.

Notice that the color area in the portrait in the lower image looks flatter and more posterized, but the image size is roughly the same.

Based on what you've just learned, you will choose which compression settings to assign to all of the slices on this page.

7 Select the Optimized tab at the top of the dialog box, and zoom out so you can see the entire page.

8 With the Slice Select tool, Shift-click to select the images of the boy, the angel, and the new wing announcement in the preview window. From the Preset menu, choose JPEG Medium.

9 Shift-click to select all of the remaining slices in the preview window, and then choose GIF 64 Dithered from the Preset menu.

10 Click Save. In the Save Optimized As dialog box, navigate to the Lesson13/13Start/Museo folder, which contains the rest of the site, including the pages that your slices will link to.

11 For format, choose HTML And Images. Use the default settings, and choose All Slices from the Slices menu. Name the file **home.html**, and click Save.

**12** In Photoshop, choose File > Browse In Bridge to switch to Bridge. Click Lessons in the Favorites panel. Double-click the Lesson13 folder in the Content panel, double-click the 13Start folder, and then double-click the Museo folder.

**13** Right-click (Windows) or Control-click (Mac OS) the home.html file, and choose Open With from the context menu. Choose a web browser to open the HTML file.

**14** In your web browser, move around the HTML file:

- Position your mouse over some of the slices you created. Notice that the pointer turns into a pointing finger to indicate a button.

- Click the portrait of the boy to open a new window with the full image.

- Click the New Wing Opening link to open its window.

- Click the text links on the left to jump to other pages in the site.

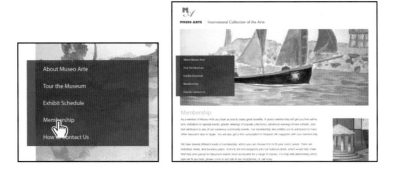

**15** When you have finished exploring the file, close the browser.

# Using the Zoomify feature

With the Zoomify feature, you can publish high-resolution images on the web that viewers can pan and zoom to see more detail. The standad-size image downloads in the same time as an equivalent-size JPEG file. Photoshop exports the JPEG files and HTML file that you can upload to your website. The Zoomify capabilities work with any web browser.

**1** In Bridge, click the 13Start folder in the breadcrumbs at the top of the window. Then, double-click the card.jpg file to open it in Photoshop. Click OK if you see the Embedded Profile Mismatch dialog box.

The card is a large bitmap image that you'll export to HTML using the Zoomify feature. You'll convert the angel image into a file that will be linked to one of the links that you've just created in the home page.

# Optimizing images for the web

*Optimizing* is the process of selecting format, resolution, and quality settings to make an image efficient, visually appealing, and useful for web pages. Simply put, it's balancing file size against good looks. No single collection of settings can maximize the efficiency of every kind of image file; optimizing requires human judgment and a good eye.

Compression options vary according to the file format used to save the image. JPEG and GIF are the two most common formats. The JPEG format is designed to preserve the broad color range and subtle brightness variations of continuous-tone images such as photographs. It can represent images using millions of colors. The GIF format is effective at compressing solid-color images and images with areas of repetitive color, such as line art, logos, and illustrations with type. It uses a panel of 256 colors to represent the image and supports background transparency.

Photoshop offers a range of controls for compressing image file size while optimizing the onscreen quality. Typically, you optimize images before saving them in an HTML file. Use the Save For Web dialog box to compare the original image to one or more compressed alternatives, adjusting settings as you compare. For more on optimizing GIF and JPEG images, see Photoshop Help.

2   Choose File > Export > Zoomify.

3   In the Zoomify Export dialog box, click Folder, select the Lesson13/13Start/Museo folder, and click OK or Choose. For Base Name, type **Card**. Set the quality to **12**; set the Width to **800**, and set the Height to **600** for the base image in the viewer's browser. Make sure that the Open In Web Browser option is selected.

**4** Click OK to export the HTML file and images. Zoomify opens them in your web browser.

**5** Use the controls in the Zoomify window to zoom in and out of the angel image.

**6** When you have finished, close the browser.

## Using Photoshop images in Dreamweaver

In this lesson, you've designed a website in Photoshop and exported the HTML for it. You can then open that HTML file in Dreamweaver to further develop the site. However, you can also add individual Photoshop images to web pages you create in Dreamweaver.

If you insert a native Photoshop (PSD) file into a web page, Dreamweaver optimizes the file for the web in GIF, JPEG, or PNG format. It then inserts the file as a Smart Object, so it maintains a live connection to the original PSD file. Though the inserted image is linked, you can make changes to it in the Dreamweaver file without affecting the original linked image.

Alternatively, you can copy and paste all or part of an image into a web page in Dreamweaver. However, pasted images are not linked. If you update the original image, you'll need to copy and paste again.

# Extra credit

## Copying layer properties for CSS

In Photoshop CC, you can generate CSS properties from shape and text layers without writing code. For shape layers, the Copy CSS feature captures size, location, fill color (including gradients), stroke color, and drop shadows created with layer styles. For text layers, it also captures font family, font size, font weight, line height, underline, strikethrough, superscript, subscript, and text alignment.

You'll generate CSS properties from the Flyer.psd file and paste them into the site's HTML file.

1   In Photoshop, navigate to the Lesson13/Extra_Credit folder, and open the Flyer.psd file.

2   Select the new_wing layer, and choose Layer > Copy CSS.

Photoshop copies the CSS properties for the new_wing layer to the clipboard.

3   Open Dreamweaver. Then navigate to the Lesson13/Extra_Credit folder, and open the New-Wing_Start.html file.

4   Choose File > Save As, and save the file as **New-Wing_Finished.html** in the Lesson13/Extra_Credit folder.

5   In Dreamweaver, choose View > Code to see the source code if it's not already visible. Then select the entire comment between the <style> and </style> tags ("<! -- Paste your CSS code here -- >"), and choose Edit > Paste.

```
<style type="text/css">

<!-- Paste your CSS code here -->

</style>
```

```
<style type="text/css">

.new_wing {
  font-size: 0.436in;
  font-family: "Trajan Pro";
  color: rgb( 254, 242, 147 );
  text-align: center;
  -moz-transform: matrix( 1.43355542890517, 0, 0, 1.43355542890517, 0, 0);
  -webkit-transform: matrix( 1.43355542890517, 0, 0, 1.43355542890517, 0, 0);
  text-shadow: 0.021in 0.036in 0.069444444444444in rgb( 0, 0, 0 );
  position: absolute;
  left: 1.051in;
  top: 3.88in;
  height: 0.625in;
  z-index: 3;
}

</style>
```

*(continues on next page)*

# Extra credit (continued)

The CSS code Photoshop copied is pasted into your Dreamweaver file. Not all of the boilerplate code may be necessary for a website. In this case, you'll delete some lines you don't need.

6   Delete the lines that specify position, left, top, and height.

7   In Photoshop, select the info layer, and choose Layer > Copy CSS.

8   In Dreamweaver, click beneath the close brace (}) that follows the CSS code you pasted from the new_wing layer, and then choose Edit > Paste to add the CSS code from the info layer.

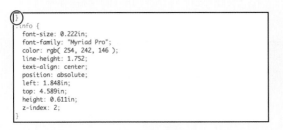

```
.info {
    font-size: 0.222in;
    font-family: "Myriad Pro";
    color: rgb( 254, 242, 146 );
    line-height: 1.752;
    text-align: center;
    position: absolute;
    left: 1.848in;
    top: 4.589in;
    height: 0.611in;
    z-index: 2;
}
```

9   Delete the lines that specify position, left, top, and height. Then, choose File > Save to save the changes to the HTML file.

10   Click the Preview/Debug In Browser button, and then choose a browser.

11   Preview the website. Notice that the text, font size, color, and even the drop shadow were copied from Photoshop.

It's a good idea to preview a website in multiple browsers, as results may vary. You may want to edit the CSS code to specify type size and position, for example.

## Review questions

1  What are slices? How do you create them when you're working with an image in Photoshop?

2  What is image optimization, and how do you optimize images for the web?

3  How can you copy layer properties for use in CSS files?

## Review answers

1  Slices are rectangular areas of an image that you define for individual web optimization. You can add animated GIFs, URL links, and rollovers to slices. You can create image slices with the Slice tool or by converting layers into slices using the Layer menu.

2  Image optimization is the process of choosing file format, resolution, and quality settings for an image to keep it small, useful, and visually appealing when published to the web. Continuous-tone images are typically optimized in JPEG format; solid-color images or those with repetitive color areas are typically optimized as GIF. To optimize images, choose File > Save For Web.

3  To generate CSS code from layer properties, select the layer in Photoshop, and choose Layer > Copy CSS. Then paste the clipboard contents into the CSS file for a web page using Dreamweaver or another application.

# 14 PRODUCING AND PRINTING CONSISTENT COLOR

## Lesson overview

In this lesson, you'll learn how to do the following:

- Define RGB, grayscale, and CMYK color spaces for displaying, editing, and printing images.

- Prepare an image for printing on a PostScript CMYK printer.

- Proof an image for printing.

- Save an image as a CMYK EPS file.

- Create and print a four-color separation.

- Understand how images are prepared for printing on presses.

This lesson will take less than an hour to complete. Download the Lesson14 project files from the Lesson & Update Files tab on your Account page at www.peachpit.com, if you haven't already done so. As you work on this lesson, you'll preserve the start files. If you need to restore the start files, download them from your Account page.

PROJECT: GARDEN PHOTOGRAPHY POSTER

To produce consistent color, you define the color space in which to edit and display RGB images, and the color space in which to edit, display, and print CMYK images. This helps ensure a close match between onscreen and printed colors.

# About color management

● **Note:** One exercise in this lesson requires that your computer be connected to a PostScript color printer. If it isn't, you can do most, but not all, of the exercises.

Colors on a monitor are displayed using combinations of red, green, and blue light (called RGB), while printed colors are typically created using a combination of four ink colors—cyan, magenta, yellow, and black (called CMYK). These four inks are called *process colors* because they are the standard inks used in the four-color printing process.

RGB image with red, green, and blue channels

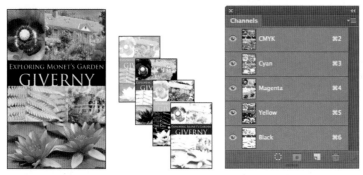

CMYK image with cyan, magenta, yellow, and black channels

Because the RGB and CMYK color models use different methods to display colors, each reproduces a different *gamut*, or range, of colors. For example, RGB uses light to produce color, so its gamut includes neon colors, such as those you'd see in a neon sign. In contrast, printing inks excel at reproducing certain colors that can lie outside the RGB gamut, such as some pastels and pure black.

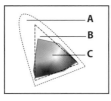
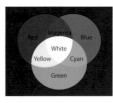

**A.** Natural color gamut
**B.** RGB color gamut
**C.** CMYK color gamut

RGB color model

CMYK color model

But not all RGB and CMYK gamuts are alike. Each monitor and printer model differs, and so each displays a slightly different gamut. For example, one brand of monitor may produce slightly brighter blues than another. The *color space* for a device is defined by the gamut it can reproduce.

## RGB model

A large percentage of the visible spectrum can be represented by mixing red, green, and blue (RGB) colored light in various proportions and intensities. Where the colors overlap, they create cyan, magenta, yellow, and white.

Because the RGB colors combine to create white, they are also called *additive* colors. Adding all colors together creates white—that is, all light is transmitted back to the eye. Additive colors are used for lighting, video, and monitors. Your monitor, for example, creates color by emitting light through red, green, and blue phosphors.

## CMYK model

The CMYK model is based on the light-absorbing quality of ink printed on paper. As white light strikes translucent inks, part of the spectrum is absorbed, while other parts are reflected back to your eyes.

In theory, pure cyan (C), magenta (M), and yellow (Y) pigments should combine to absorb all color and produce black. For this reason, these colors are called *subtractive* colors. But because all printing inks contain some impurities, these three inks actually produce a muddy brown, and must be combined with black (K) ink to produce a true black. (K is used instead of B to avoid confusion with blue.) Combining these inks to reproduce color is called four-color process printing.

The color management system in Photoshop uses International Color Consortium (ICC)-compliant color profiles to convert colors from one color space into another. A color profile is a description of a device's color space, such as the CMYK color space of a particular printer. You specify which profiles to use to accurately proof and print your images. Once you've selected the profiles, Photoshop can embed them into your image files, so that Photoshop and other applications can accurately manage color for the image.

For information on embedding color profiles, see Photoshop Help.

Before you begin working with color management, you should calibrate your monitor. If your monitor doesn't display colors accurately, color adjustments you make based on the image you see on your monitor may not be accurate. For information about calibrating your monitor, see Photoshop Help.

# Getting started

First, start Photoshop and restore its default preferences.

1   Start Photoshop, and then immediately hold down Ctrl+Alt+Shift (Windows) or Command+Option+Shift (Mac OS) to restore the default preferences. (See "Restoring default preferences" on page 4.)

2   When prompted, click Yes to delete the Adobe Photoshop Settings file.

# Specifying color-management settings

In the first part of this lesson, you'll learn how to set up a color-managed workflow in Photoshop. Most of the color-management controls you need are in the Color Settings dialog box.

By default, Photoshop is set up for RGB as part of a digital workflow. If you are preparing artwork for print production, however, you'll want to change the settings to be more appropriate for images that will be printed on paper rather than displayed on a screen.

You'll begin this lesson by creating customized color settings.

1   Choose Edit > Color Settings to open the Color Settings dialog box.

The bottom of the dialog box interactively describes each option.

2   Move the pointer over each part of the dialog box, including the names of areas (such as Working Spaces), the menu names, and the menu options. As you move the pointer, Photoshop displays information about each item. When you've finished, return the options to their defaults.

Now, you'll choose a set of options designed for a print workflow, rather than an online workflow.

3   Choose North America Prepress 2 from the Settings menu. The working spaces and color-management policy options change for a prepress workflow. Then click OK.

# Proofing an image

You'll select a proof profile so that you can view a close onscreen representation of what an image will look like when printed. An accurate proof profile lets you proof on the screen (*soft-proof*) for printed output.

1  Choose File > Open. Navigate to the Lessons/ Lesson14 folder, and double-click the 14Start.tif file. Click OK if you see an embedded profile warning.

An RGB image of a scanned poster opens.

2  Choose File > Save As. Rename the file **14Working.tif**, keep the TIFF format selected, and click Save. Click OK in the TIFF Options dialog box.

Before soft-proofing or printing this image, you'll set up a proof profile. A proof profile (also called a *proof setup*) defines how the document is going to be printed, and adjusts the onscreen appearance accordingly. Photoshop provides a variety of settings that can help you proof images for different uses, including print and display on the web. For this lesson, you'll create a custom proof setup. You can then save the settings for use on other images that will be output the same way.

3  Choose View > Proof Setup > Custom. The Customize Proof Condition dialog box opens. Make sure Preview is selected.

4  From the Device To Simulate menu, choose a profile that represents the final output device, such as that for the printer you'll use to print the image. If you don't have a specific printer, the profile Working CMYK–U.S. Web Coated (SWOP) v2, the current default, is generally a good choice.

5  If you've chosen a different profile, make sure Preserve Numbers is *not* selected.

The Preserve Numbers option simulates how colors will appear without being converted to the output device color space.

> **Note:** The Preserve Numbers option is not available when the U.S. Web Coated (SWOP) v2 profile is selected.

6  Make sure Relative Colorimetric is selected for the Rendering Intent.

A rendering intent determines how the color is converted from one color space to another. Relative Colorimetric, which preserves color relationships without sacrificing color accuracy, is the standard rendering intent for printing in North America and Europe.

**7** If it's available for the profile you chose, select Simulate Black Ink. Then deselect it, and select Simulate Paper Color; notice that selecting this option automatically selects Simulate Black Ink. Click OK.

**Tip:** To display the document with and without the proof settings, choose View > Proof Colors.

Notice that the image appears to lose contrast. Paper Color simulates the dingy white of real paper, according to the proof profile. Black Ink simulates the dark gray that actually prints to most printers, instead of solid black. Not all profiles support these options.

Normal image

Image with Paper Color and Black Ink options selected

# Identifying out-of-gamut colors

Most scanned photographs contain RGB colors within the CMYK gamut, so changing them to CMYK mode converts all the colors with relatively little substitution. Images that are created or altered digitally, however, often contain RGB colors that are outside the CMYK gamut—for example, neon-colored logos and lights.

Before you convert an image from RGB to CMYK, you can preview the CMYK color values while still in RGB mode.

1 Choose View > Gamut Warning to see out-of-gamut colors. Adobe Photoshop builds a color-conversion table, and displays a neutral gray in the image window where the colors are out of gamut.

Because the gray can be hard to spot in the image, you'll convert it to a more visible color.

2 Choose Edit > Preferences > Transparency & Gamut (Windows) or Photoshop > Preferences > Transparency & Gamut (Mac OS).

3 Click the color sample in the Gamut Warning area at the bottom of the dialog box. Select a vivid color, such as purple or bright green, and click OK.

4 Click OK to close the Preferences dialog box.

The bright new color you chose appears instead of the neutral gray as the gamut warning color.

5 Choose View > Gamut Warning to turn off the preview of out-of-gamut colors.

Photoshop will automatically correct these out-of-gamut colors when you save the file in Photoshop EPS format later in this lesson. Photoshop EPS format changes the RGB image to CMYK, adjusting the RGB colors as needed to bring them into the CMYK color gamut.

# Adjusting an image and printing a proof

The next step in preparing an image for output is to make any necessary color and tonal adjustments. In this exercise, you'll add some tonal and color adjustments to correct an off-color scan of the original poster.

So that you can compare the image before and after making corrections, you'll start by making a copy.

1 Choose Image > Duplicate, and click OK to duplicate the image.

2 Choose Window > Arrange > 2 Up Vertical so you can compare the images as you work.

You'll adjust the hue and saturation of the image to move all colors into gamut.

3 Select 14Working.tif (the original image).

4 Choose Select > Color Range.

5 In the Color Range dialog box, choose Out Of Gamut from the Select menu, and then click OK.

The areas that were marked as out of gamut earlier are now selected, so you can make changes that affect only those areas.

6  Choose View > Extras to hide the selection while you work with it.

The selection border can be distracting. When you hide extras, you no longer see the selection, but it's still in effect.

7  Click the Hue/Saturation button in the Adjustments panel to create a Hue/Saturation adjustment layer. (Choose Window > Adjustments if the panel isn't open.) The Hue/Saturation adjustment layer includes a layer mask, created from your selection.

8  In the Properties panel, do the following:

- Drag the Hue slider until the colors look more neutral (we used -5).

- Drag the Saturation slider until the intensity of the colors looks more realistic (we used -50).

- Leave the Lightness setting at the default value (0).

9  Choose View > Gamut Warning. You have removed most of the out-of-gamut colors from the image. Choose View > Gamut Warning again to deselect it.

10  With 14Working.tif still selected, choose File > Print.

**11** In the Print dialog box, do the following:

- Choose your printer from the Printer menu.

- In the Color Management area of the dialog box, choose Printer Manages Colors from the Color Handling menu.

- Choose Hard Proofing from the pop-up menu.

- For Proof Setup, choose Working CMYK.

- If you have a color PostScript printer, click Print to print the image, and compare the color with the onscreen version. Otherwise, click Cancel.

## Saving the image as a CMYK EPS file

You'll save the image as an EPS file in CMYK format.

**Note:** These settings cause the image to be automatically converted from RGB to CMYK when it is saved in the Photoshop Encapsulated PostScript (EPS) format.

**1** With 14Working.tif still selected, choose File > Save As.

**2** In the Save As dialog box, do the following, and then click Save:

- Choose Photoshop EPS from the Format menu.

- Under Color, select Use Proof Setup. Don't worry about the warning icon; you'll save a copy.

- Accept the filename 14Working.eps.

**Save As**

| | |
|---|---|
| Save As: | 14Working.eps |
| Where: | Lesson14 |

| | |
|---|---|
| Format: | Photoshop EPS |
| Save: | ☑ As a Copy    ☐ Notes |
| | ☐ Alpha Channels    ☐ Spot Colors |
| ⚠ | ☐ Layers |
| Color: ⚠ | ☑ Use Proof Setup: U.S. Web Coated (... |
| | ☑ Embed Color Profile: U.S. Web Coated (SWOP) ... |
| ⚠ | File must be saved as a copy with this selection. |

Cancel    Save

**3**   Click OK in the EPS Options dialog box that appears.

**4**   Save and then close the 14Working.tif and 14Working copy.tif files.

**5**   Choose File > Open, navigate to the Lessons/Lesson14 folder, and double-click the 14Working.eps file.

Notice in the image file's title bar that 14Working.eps is a CMYK file.

# Printing

When you're ready to print your image, use the following guidelines for best results:

- Print a *color composite*, often called a *color comp*, to proof your image. A color composite is a single print that combines the red, green, and blue channels of an RGB image (or the cyan, magenta, yellow, and black channels of a CMYK image). This indicates what the final printed image will look like.

- Set the parameters for the halftone screen.

- Print separations to make sure the image separates correctly.

- Print to film or plate.

When you print color separations, Photoshop prints a separate sheet, or *plate*, for each ink. For a CMYK image, it prints four plates, one for each process color.

In this exercise, you'll print color separations.

**1** With the 14Working.eps image open from the previous exercise, choose File > Print.

By default, Photoshop prints any document as a composite image. To print this file as separations, you need to explicitly instruct Photoshop in the Print dialog box.

**2** In the Print dialog box, do the following:

- In the Color Management area, choose Separations from the Color Handling menu.

- Click Print.

**3** Choose File > Close, and don't save the changes.

This lesson has provided an introduction to printing and producing consistent color from Adobe Photoshop. If you're printing on a desktop printer, you can experiment with different settings to find the best color and print settings for your system. If you're preparing images for professional printing, consult with your print service provider to determine the best settings to use. For more information about color management, printing options, and color separations, see Photoshop Help.

# Review questions

1 What steps should you follow to reproduce color accurately?

2 What is a gamut?

3 What is a color profile?

4 What are color separations?

# Review answers

1 To reproduce color accurately, first calibrate your monitor, and then use the Color Settings dialog box to specify which color spaces to use. For example, you can specify which RGB color space to use for online images, and which CMYK color space to use for images that will be printed. You can then proof the image, check for out-of-gamut colors, adjust colors as needed, and—for printed images—create color separations.

2 A gamut is the range of colors that can be reproduced by a color model or device. For example, the RGB and CMYK color models have different gamuts, as do any two RGB scanners.

3 A color profile is a description of a device's color space, such as the CMYK color space of a particular printer. Applications such as Photoshop can interpret color profiles in an image to maintain consistent color across different applications, platforms, and devices.

4 Color separations are separate plates for each ink used in a document. Often, you'll print color separations for the cyan, magenta, yellow, and black (CMYK) inks.

# Appendix: Tools Panel Overview

## Photoshop CC Tools panel

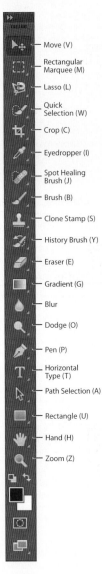

- Move (V)
- Rectangular Marquee (M)
- Lasso (L)
- Quick Selection (W)
- Crop (C)
- Eyedropper (I)
- Spot Healing Brush (J)
- Brush (B)
- Clone Stamp (S)
- History Brush (Y)
- Eraser (E)
- Gradient (G)
- Blur
- Dodge (O)
- Pen (P)
- Horizontal Type (T)
- Path Selection (A)
- Rectangle (U)
- Hand (H)
- Zoom (Z)

**The Move tool** moves selections, layers, and guides.

**The marquee tools** make rectangular, elliptical, single row, and single column selections.

**The lasso tools** make free-hand, polygonal (straight-edged), and magnetic (snap-to) selections.

**The Quick Selection tool** lets you quickly "paint" a selection using an adjustable round brush tip.

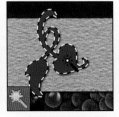

**The Magic Wand tool** selects similarly colored areas.

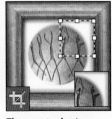

**The crop tools** trim, straighten, and change the perspective of images.

**The Eyedropper tool** samples colors in an image.

**The 3D Material Eyedropper tool** loads selected material from a 3D object.

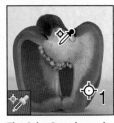

**The Color Sampler tool** samples up to four areas of the image.

**The Ruler tool** measures distances, locations, and angles.

**The Note tool** makes notes that can be attached to an image.

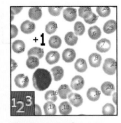

**The Count tool** counts objects in an image.

**The Slice tool** creates slices.

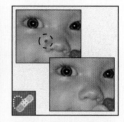

**The Slice Select tool** selects slices.

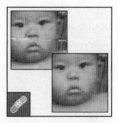

**The Spot Healing Brush tool** quickly removes blemishes and imperfections from photographs with a uniform background.

**The Healing Brush tool** paints with a sample or pattern to repair imperfections in an image.

**The Patch tool** repairs imperfections in a selected area of an image using a sample or pattern.

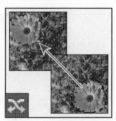

**The Content-Aware Move tool** recomposes and blends pixels to accommodate a moved object.

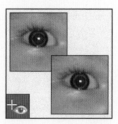

**The Red Eye tool** removes red eye in flash photos with one click.

**The Brush tool** paints brush strokes.

**The Pencil tool** paints hard-edged strokes.

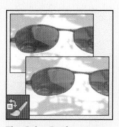

**The Color Replacement tool** substitutes one color for another.

**The Mixer Brush tool** blends sampled color with an existing color.

**The Clone Stamp tool** paints with a sample of an image.

**The Pattern Stamp tool** paints with a part of an image as a pattern.

**The History Brush tool** paints a copy of the selected state or snapshot into the current image window.

**The Art History Brush tool** paints stylized strokes that simulate the look of different paint styles, using a selected state or snapshot.

**The Eraser tool** erases pixels and restores parts of an image to a previously saved state.

**The Background Eraser tool** erases areas to transparency by dragging.

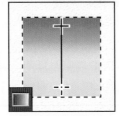

**The Magic Eraser tool** erases solid-colored areas to transparency with a single click.

**The Gradient tool** creates straight-line, radial, angle, reflected, and diamond blends between colors.

**The Paint Bucket tool** fills similarly colored areas with the foreground color.

**The 3D Material Drop tool** drops the material loaded in the 3D Material Eyedropper tool onto the targeted area of a 3D object.

**The Blur tool** blurs hard edges in an image.

**The Sharpen tool** sharpens soft edges in an image.

**The Smudge tool** smudges data in an image.

**The Dodge tool** lightens areas in an image.

**The Burn tool** darkens areas in an image.

**The Sponge tool** changes the color saturation of an area.

**The pen tools** draw smooth-edged paths.

**The type tools** create type on an image.

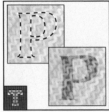

**The type mask tools** create a selection in the shape of type.

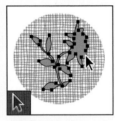

**The path selection tools** make shape or segment selections showing anchor points, direction lines, and direction points.

**The shape tools and Line tool** draw shapes and lines in a normal layer or shape layer.

**The Custom Shape tool** makes customized shapes selected from a custom shape list.

**The Hand tool** moves an image within its window.

**The Rotate View tool** nondestructively rotates the canvas.

**The Zoom tool** magnifies and reduces the view of an image.

# INDEX

3D Axis widget 315, 322, 326
  resizing 323
3D features 312–341
3D files, importing 318
3D layers
  creating 3D postcards 316–317
  creating from imported
      files 318–319
  merging 320
  overview 314
3D objects
  applying materials to 331
  moving 322
  positioning 321–328
  rotating 326
  scaling 326
3D postcards 316
3D scenes
  lighting 334
  rendering 337
3D shape presets 313, 317–318
3D text 319
  extruding 328–329
3D tools 314

## A

actions 246–254
  amending 250–251
  batch-playing 253–254
  conditional 252
  copying 250–251
  overview 246, 267
  playing 250
Actions panel 247–253
  Play button 250
Adaptive Wide Angle
    filter 263–264
Add Audio option 286

Add Layer Mask button 163
Add Media button 273
Add To Path Area option 210
adjustment layers 103–104
  Black & White 58, 278
  Curves 18, 139
  defined 19
  editing 28
  Hue/Saturation 104, 177
  Levels 131, 175, 177
  Photo Filter 265
  using in video 277
  Vibrance 155
Adobe Authorized
    Training Centers 7
Adobe Bridge
  adding favorites 14
  Favorites panel 14
  installing 3
  opening files in Camera Raw
      from 118
  opening files in Photoshop
      from 13–14
  starting 44
Adobe Camera Raw
  adjusting white balance in 119
  Basic panel 121
  Detail panel 124
  dialog box 118
  opening images in 117
  Open Object button 128
  saving files in 129
  synchronizing settings
      across images 125
  workflow 119
Adobe Certified Associate 6
Adobe Certified Expert 7
Adobe Certified Instructor 7
Adobe Dreamweaver, using
    Photoshop files in 360
Adobe Illustrator

Glyphs panel 197
  importing Smart Objects
      from 227
  importing text from 227–228
  using Photoshop files in 226
Adobe InDesign, using
    Photoshop files
    in 231–232
Adobe Photoshop CC
  installing 3
  new features 2
  resetting the default
      preferences for 10
  starting 3, 10
  work area 10–39
*Adobe Photoshop CC
    Classroom in a Book* 1
  accessing lesson files 3
  prerequisites 2
Adobe Photoshop
    Lightroom 136–137
Align Bottom Edges button 325
Aligned option 55
aligning
  layers 110
  objects 325
  slices 350–351
alpha channels 162, 172
  about 164, 174
anchor points 208, 209
animating
  a zoom effect 278
  lighting in a 3D scene
      338–339
  position 282
  style effects 280–281
  text 275
anti-aliasing 70
application frame,
    in Mac OS 12
Apply Layer Comp box 109

arrow keys
  nudging selections
    with 67–68
  using the Shift key with 67
assets
  importing for video 271
  resizing for video 275
audio
  adding to a video
    timeline 286
  fading 287
  muting 287–288
  shortening clips 286
Audio track 286
Auto-Align Layers 110, 151
Auto Enhance option 64
automating tasks 246–254
auto slices 347
  hiding 351
axes, 3D 315

**B**

background layer 82
  converting to regular
    layer 84
  erasing 87
  overview 84
badges, on slices 347, 348
barrel distortion,
    correcting 147
Basic panel
    (in Camera Raw) 121
Batch command 253
bitmap images
  overview 10, 206
  vector graphics vs. 206–207
black and white, converting
    color images
    in Photoshop 58
black point 121
Black & White adjustment
    layer 58, 278
_blank Target option 352
blemishes, removing 49
blending colors with a
    photograph 303
blending modes

achieving different effects
    with 91
  applying to layers 92
  Color 244
  Multiply 92
  Overlay 92
  overview 90
Bloat tool in the Liquify
    filter 243
Blur Gallery 280
blurs
  caused by camera motion,
    removing 144
  interactive 153
  iris blur 153, 280
  surface blur 140
borders
  adding 87, 107
  discarding 46
breadcrumbs 346
Bridge. See Adobe Bridge
bristle tips 292
Browse In Bridge
    command 13
brushes
  loading with color 300
  presets 301
  settings 293
  Shape Dynamics
    options 306
Brush panel 293
Brush Pose settings 306
Brush Presets panel 302–303
Brush tool 22
  setting options 169
buttons, website 349

**C**

calibration, monitor 367
camera lens flaws,
    correcting 147–149
Camera Raw. See Adobe
    Camera Raw
camera raw images
  cameras supported by Adobe
    Camera Raw 117
  creating 117
  file formats for saving 129
  histogram 123

opening 117–118
  overview 117
  proprietary 114
  saving 127–128
  sharpening 124
  white balance and exposure
    adjustment 119–120
Camera Shake Reduction
    filter 144
cameras, in 3D layers 314
  changing the angle of 316
camera views 316, 321
Camera widget 316
canvas, rotating 229
center point, selecting from 74
certification programs,
    Adobe 6
channel masks 164
channels
  adjusting individual
    175–177
  alpha channels 172, 174
  applying filters to
    individual 249
  correcting noise in 146
  loading as selections 176
  overview 162, 172
Channels panel 162
Character panel 31, 96
character styles 197–198
checkerboard
  pattern 222–224
  transparency indicator 87
chromatic aberration 147
Classroom in a Book 1
Clean Brush After Every
    Stroke icon 298
clean brush (Mixer Brush
    tool) 299
Clear Override button 196
clipping masks
  about 164, 183
  creating 185–187
  indicator 187
  in placed video assets 278
  shortcut 186
Clone Stamp tool 52–54
closed paths 207, 209
closing a Photoshop file 13

Clouds filter 94
CMYK color mode,
    converting to 370
CMYK color model 367
  defined 366
  gamut 366
color
  additive 367
  adjusting overall 47
  changing in the Photoshop
    interface 37
  converting to black and
    white 58
  correcting skin tones 258
  default text 185
  editing masks and 178
  managed
    workflow 368–369
  matching across
    images 258–260
  mixing with the
    Mixer Brush 298
  out-of-gamut 370
  previewing CMYK values
    in RGB mode 370
  sampling 293
  selecting by 62
  selecting using the Swatches
    panel 23–24
  softening edge transitions 70
color blending mode 244
color casts, removing 47
color comp 375
color management 368–369
  selecting when printing 374
Color panel 31
color profiles 367
Color Range, Skin Tones
    option 138
color settings
  restoring 5
  saving 4
Color Settings dialog
    box 368–369
color space 367
  device profile 367
combining images in a
    panorama 261–266
Commit Any Current Edits
    button 106

Commit Transform button 227

compression settings 359

conditional actions 252

content-aware fill 52

Content-Aware Move tool 152

Content-Aware Patch tool 54

Content panel, in Bridge 14

context menus 21
annotations 201
type 188, 191
web browser 344

continuous-tone images 359

Contrast slider in Camera Raw 121

Control Timeline Magnification slider 274

converting images to black and white 58

Coordinates in the Properties panel 324

copying
and anti-aliasing 70
at same resolution 77
commands 77
images 108, 372
images, and centering 85
layers 85–87
selections 76, 77
settings in Camera Raw 125

Copy Merged command 77

corner points 209, 211

creases, repairing 49

Create Video Timeline 272

cropping images 45–47, 77–78, 262

cropping shield 46

Crop tool 45, 262

Cross Fade transition 284

CSS, copying properties for 361

curved paths 209, 211–212

Curves adjustment layer 18–19, 139

customizing
keyboard shortcuts 33
user interface 37
workspaces 32

Custom Shape tool 222, 224–225

cutouts 220–221

**D**

defaults
resetting 4, 10
resetting foreground and background color 25

Deform widget 328

Delete Cropped Pixels option 45

depth of field, adding 150

deselecting
paths 221
selections 65

Detail panel in Camera Raw 124

Direct Selection tool 209, 220

discretionary ligatures 199

displaying
document size 108
layers 86
multiple documents 85

distortions, correcting 147–150

DNG file format 129

docking panels 30

document size, displaying 108

Dodge tool 135–136

dragging image files to add layers 95

Drag The 3D Object tool 315

Dreamweaver. See Adobe Dreamweaver

drop shadows 99–100, 102

duplicating
areas of a scene 152
images 372

duration of video clips, changing 274

Dust & Scratches filter 56

**E**

editing
paragraph styles 197

shapes 220

Smart Filters 242

editing images
adjusting highlights and shadows 142–144
correcting distortions 147–149
nondestructively 178
reducing noise 145–147
removing red eye 145–146

Edit In Quick Mask Mode button 168

effects, animating 281–282

Elliptical Marquee tool 17, 62
centering selection 74
circular selections with 66

EPS file format 374

Erase Refinements tool 167

Eraser tool 110

erodible tip 296

exporting
HTML pages 353–355
video 288

extruding 3D text 328–329

Eyedropper tool 21, 293

eye icon, in the Layers panel 83

**F**

Fade With Black transitions 285

fading audio 287

Favorites panel, in Bridge 14

Feather command 70

feathering 70
masks 178

file formats
from Camera Raw 129
transferring images between applications and platforms 129
type 199

file size
compressing for the web 359
flattened vs. unflattened 108
reducing 108

files, saving 20, 108–111

shapes 220

Smart Filters 242

fill, content-aware 52

film. See video

filtering layers in the Layers panel 105

filters
Adaptive Wide Angle 263
adding clouds with 94
Camera Shake Reduction 144
Dust & Scratches 56
improving performance 249
Liquify 240–241
overview 250
shortcuts 264
Smart Sharpen 56

Fit On Screen command 75

Flatten Image command 48

flattening images 108

focus, adjusting 150

fonts
alternates 199
changing in the options bar 23
for use on the web 354
selecting 184

Foreground color
swatch 23, 94
resetting to default 25

four-color printing 257–258, 366

fractions 199

Freeform Pen tool 207

freehand selections 71–72

Free Transform 238, 239

**G**

gamut 366
colors outside of 370–371

Gamut Warning 371–372

GIF compression 353, 355

Go To First Frame button 284

Gradient Picker 98

gradients, listing by name 98

Gradient tool 98

guides
adding 183
for creating slices 351

## H

Hand tool 73
Healing Brush tool 48, 133
hiding
    layers 86
    selection edges 68
High Dynamic Range (HDR)
    images 156
highlights, adjusting 142–144
high-resolution images 43
    filters and 249
histogram, in Camera
    Raw 123
History panel
    changing number
        of states 27
    undoing multiple
        actions 26–29
Horizontal Type tool
    22, 96, 184
HTML pages
    exporting 353–355
    naming 351
hue, adjusting for printing 372
Hue/Saturation adjustment
    layers 18, 170, 177
hypertext links 347
    adding 351, 352

## I

illustrations with type 359
Illustrator. *See* Adobe
    Illustrator
images
    centering and copying 185
    continuous-tone 359
    copying 108
    determining scan
        resolution 43
    duplicating 372
    fitting on-screen 73
    flattening 108–110
    matching color schemes
        258–260
    optimizing for web
        353–355, 359
    resizing for web 127
    resolution 43–44

sharpening 124
size and resolution 43–44
solid-color 359
Image Size command 77
image size, increasing 255
image window 13, 15, 15–16
    fitting image to 75
    scrolling 20
importing
    3D files 318–319
    multiple files from
        Bridge 237
increasing image size 255
InDesign. *See* Adobe
    InDesign
Infinite Light 334
Inner Shadow layer style 187
interactive blurs 153
interface. *See* user interface
Inverse command 18
Invert command 176
Iris Blur filter 153, 280

## J

JPEG file format
    camera raw images and 117
    compression 353, 356
    image degradation and 137

## K

keyboard shortcuts
    creating 33–35
    customizing 301
    duplicating 76
    filters 264
    finding 18
    for tools 17
    Move tool 67
Keyboard Shortcuts And
    Menus dialog box 33–35
keyframes
    appearance of 276
    moving to the next or
        previous 279
    using to animate text 275

## L

Lasso tools 62, 71–72
layer comps 109
layer effects
    adding 99
    updating 105
layer masks
    defined 164
    turning on and off 178
layer properties, copying
    for CSS 361
layers
    3D shapes from 313
    about 82
    adding 94–95
    aligning 110
    background 84
    blending modes 90–91
    converting to
        background 84
    copying 85–87
    copying and centering 85,
        89, 92, 197
    copying and merging 77
    creating by copying 215
    deleting 213
    deleting hidden 230
    duplicating 90
    effects 98–101, 99–102
    erasing 87–89
    filtering in the Layers
        panel 105
    flattening 108, 109
    hiding and showing
        19, 83, 86, 87
    linking 92–94
    locking 83
    matching colors 258
    merging 3D layers 320
    merging visible 108
    opacity 90
    overview 82
    painting 243
    rearranging 88–90
    removing pixels from 87–89
    renaming 85
    resizing 92–94
    rotating 92
    showing 87
    slices from 352
    template 217, 230

thumbnails, hiding
    and resizing 83
transforming 92
transparency 90–91
type 96
Layers panel
    deleting hidden layers 230
    overview 83–84
    Quick Mask mode
        indicator 169
    searching for layers in 105
layer styles
    adding to type 187
    applying 98–101, 99–102
    Drop Shadow 99, 102
    overview 98, 99
    Satin 102–103
    Stroke 101
Layer Via Copy command 215
learning resources for Adobe
    Photoshop CC 5
length of video clips,
    changing 274
Lens Correction filter
    147–149
lesson files, accessing 3
Levels adjustment layers
    47–48, 131, 175, 177
lightness, adjusting for
    printing 373
Lightroom. *See* Adobe
    Photoshop Lightroom
lights, in 3D layers
    adding 335
    animating 338–339
    moving 334
    overview 314
linear gradients 94–96
line art 359
linking masks to layers 178
Liquify filter 240–241
Live Tip Brush Preview 295
Load Files Into Photoshop
    Layers command 237
loading
    brushes with color 300
    channels as selections 176
Load Path As Selection
    option 214
low-resolution images 43

**M**

Mac OS, differences in work area 12

Magic Wand tool 62, 213
combining with other tools 68–69

Magnetic Lasso tool 62, 73–74

magnification 15–16. *See also* Zoom tool

magnifying glass. *See* Zoom tool

Make Selection dialog box 215

Make Work Path From Selection option 214

marquee tools 62

masks
color values for editing 162, 178
creating 163–166
feathering 178
inverting 170
overview 162
refining 164
terminology 164

Masks panel 178

Match Color dialog box 259

materials, in 3D layers 314, 328–331, 331–333

Merge to HDR Pro 156

Merge Visible command 109

merging
3D layers 320
images 110, 150
layers 108
multiple Photoshop files 237

meshes, in 3D layers 314
merging into the same 3D layer 320

Mini Bridge panel 82

mistakes, correcting 25–32

Mixer Brush tool
about 292
cleaning the brush 299

mixing colors 298
with a photograph 303

monitor
calibration 367
resolution 43–44

Motion dialog box 275, 278

Motion workspace 272

Move tool 25, 216
moving selections 65
scissors icon 75

moving
3D objects 316, 322
panels 30
selections 64–65

Multiply blending mode 92

muting audio 287–288


**N**

navigating
using Scrubby Zoom 16
using the Navigator panel 20
with the Zoom tool 15–16

navigation buttons, website 349–351
previewing function 348

Navigator panel 20

Negative Image style 281

New Layer Based Slice command 352

No Image slices 351

noise, reducing 56, 145–147

nondestructive filters 240

Notes panel 193


**O**

opacity, changing 90–91

opening images in Camera Raw 117

Open Object button (in Camera Raw) 128

open paths 207, 209

OpenType file format 182, 199

optimizing images 359

options bar 21
compared to panels 31–32
overview 22–23
setting type options in 23

organizing photos 136–137

out-of-gamut color 370–371

output resolution, determining 44

Overlay blending mode 92

overrides, clearing in text 196


**P**

page layout, preparing images for 257–258

painting
layers 243
wetness options 294
with an erodible tip 296
with the Mixer Brush tool 290–306

pan and zoom effects, adding to video 283–284

panel dock 30

panels
Brush panel 293
compared to options bar 31
docking 30
expanding and collapsing 30–31
floating 217
moving to another group 30
overview 29–30
resizing 31
Styles panel 281
Timeline panel 271
undocking 30
working with 23–25

panning with the Navigator panel 20

panoramas, creating 261–266

Pan & Zoom option 275, 284

Paper Color option 370

paper, simulating white 370

Paragraph panel 31

paragraph styles 194–196
applying 196–197
editing 197

paragraph type 184

Paste Into command 77

pasting
and anti-aliasing 70
at same resolution 77
commands 77

Patch tool 54

paths 207–208
adding type to 187–188
closing 209, 212
converting smooth points to corner 211
converting to selections 213–214, 214–216
deselecting 219–220, 221
drawing curved 209
drawing straight 209
guidelines for drawing 208
naming 214
saving 209, 212

path segments 209

Path Selection tool 220

Paths panel 209, 210
vector mask 220

patterns, creating 222–224

PDF. *See* Photoshop PDF

Pencil tool 207

Pen tool 218
as selection tool 208
drawing paths 208–212
keyboard shortcut 207
overview 207–208, 209
setting options 210–211

perspective, changing 263

photo correction
resolution and size 43–44
retouching strategy 42

Photo Filter adjustment layer 265

Photomerge dialog box 261

photo restoration, manual 50–51

Photoshop EPS file format 371

Photoshop Help 36

Photoshop PDF, saving as 202

Photoshop Raw file format 117

pincushion distortion 147

pixel mask 163

pixels
defined 10, 43, 206
image and monitor 43–44

placing files 227–228

playhead, in the Timeline panel 277

plug-ins 10

Point Light 336

point type 184
- distorting 191–192
- paragraphs vs. 192

Polygonal Lasso tool 62

Polygon tool 220

position, animating
in video 282

positioning 3D objects
321–328
- with the Properties
panel 324

PostScript fonts 182, 199

pound sign (#) in slice
properties 348

preferences
- gamut-warning color 371
- restoring defaults 4, 10

Preserve Numbers option 369

presets
- brush 301
- film and video 271

previewing brush tips 295

Print dialog box 374, 376

printing 365–377
- adjusting tone and
color 372–374
- CMYK model and 366–367
- guidelines 375
- identifying out-of-gamut
color 370–371
- proofing images
on screen 369–372
- proofs 372
- resolution 44
- saving image as
separations 374

printing inks, simulating 370

process colors 42, 366

Proof Colors command 370

proofing images 369–372

Properties panel 18
- using to position 3D
objects 324

PSD format 129
- camera raw images
and 117

Pucker tool in the Liquify
filter 243

Puppet Warp 170

Purge command 249


**Q**

Quick Mask mode 169

quick masks 162, 168
- painting color 169

Quick Selection tool
62, 63–64, 163


**R**

RAM, filters and 249, 250

raster images, overview 206

rasterizing vector masks 178

rectangles, rounded 199

Rectangular Marquee tool
22, 62, 69

Red Eye tool 145–146

Reduce Noise filter 145–147

Refine Edge 70, 173

Refine Mask dialog box 165

Refine Radius tool 166

rendering video 288, 339

repositioning selections 66

resampling to enlarge
images 255

Resize To Fill Canvas
option 275

resizing
- layers 92
- panels 31
- video assets 275

resolution 43–44

retouching/repairing
- by cloning 52–54
- overview 42
- removing blemishes 48–49
- setting correct resolution
43–44
- with the Healing Brush
tool 133
- with the Spot Healing Brush
tool 48, 133–135

RGB color mode, converting
to CMYK 370

RGB color model
366–368, 367

about 367
- gamut 366

right-click menus 21

Roll The 3D Object tool 315

Rotate View tool 229

rotating 216
- 3D objects 316, 326
- selections 72
- the canvas 229

Rounded Rectangle
tool 199–200

ruler guides 183

rulers 184
- displaying 217


**S**

sampling colors 293

Satin layer style 102–103

saturation, adjusting
in Photoshop 135–136

Saturation slider (in Camera
Raw) 121

Save For Web And
Devices dialog box
353–354, 359

saving
- as Photoshop PDF 202
- for the web 266
- images as separations 374
- optimized images 359

scaling 185
- 3D objects 316, 326

scan resolution 43

scene, 3D 320, 324

scrubbing 23

Scrubby Zoom 16

searching for layers in
the Layers panel 105

Secondary View window 321

selecting
- a layer in a multilayer file 65
- from center point 74–75
- high-contrast edges 73–74
- inverse selection 69–70
- layers 87
- overview 62
- skin tones 138
- slices 347
- text 106

selections
- by color 62
- circular 74
- converting to paths 213–214
- copying 77
- copying to another
image 215–216
- duplicating 76
- elliptical 65–73
- feathering existing 70
- freehand 62
- geometric 62
- hiding edges of 68
- inverting 18
- moving 64–65, 67, 75–76, 76
- precise 214
- recognizing 17
- rotating 72–73
- showing edges 68
- softening 70
- subtracting from 69, 215

selection tools 62–63
- Pen tool 208

_self Target option 351

separations
- printing 375–377
- saving image as 374

sepia effect, creating 278

shaders, in 3D layers 314

Shadow/Highlight
adjustment 143–145

shadows
- adjusting 142–144
- creating 172

Shape Dynamics options, for
brushes 306

shape layers 220–221

shapes
- custom 222–225
- editing 220

sharpening images
- in Camera Raw 123–124
- in Photoshop 56–57

shortcut menus 21

shortcuts. See keyboard
shortcuts

shortening video clips 274

Show/Hide Visibility
column 87

Show Transform Controls
option 228

sidecar XMP files  125

Single Column Marquee
    tool  62

Single Row Marquee tool  62

skewing an object  174

skin tones
    correcting  258
    selecting  138

Slice Options dialog box  348

slices  347–354
    aligning  350–351
    creating buttons from  349
    defined  346
    dividing  351
    layer-based  352–353
    methods for creating  351
    naming  350
    optimizing for web  355
    selecting  347
    selection indicator  347
    symbols  347, 348
    targeting  350
    unlinking from layer  351

Slice Select tool  347, 348, 355

Slice tool  349

Smart Filters  240–243
    applying to video
        clips  279–280
    editing  242

Smart Objects
    automatic update
        on editing  227
    converting layers to  240
    layer thumbnail  227
    linking vector
        masks to  228
    overview  227
    Smart Filters and  240

Smart Sharpen filter  56

smooth points  209, 211

soft-proofing  369–372

solid-color images  359

spell checking  188

Split at Playhead button  286

Sponge tool  135–136

Spot Healing Brush tool
    48–49, 133–135

stacking order,
    changing  88–90

Standard mode  168

starting Photoshop  10

status bar  15

Step Backward command  26

sticky notes  193

stopwatch icon in the
    Timeline panel  276

straightening an image  45

Stroke layer style  101

Styles panel  281

styles, paragraph  194–196

Subtract From Selection
    button  69

Surface Blur filter  140

swashes  199

Swatches panel  24–25

swatches, selecting  23

synchronizing settings
    in Camera Raw  125


T

Target option  351

temperature, image  119

template layers  217
    deleting  230

text. See also type
    3D  319, 328
    adding  184
    animating  275
    applying styles  194–196
    creating  22, 96–97
    default color  185
    moving  97
    placing from Adobe
        Illustrator  227–228
    selecting  106

textures, in 3D layers  314

thumbnails
    layer  83
    layer mask  178
    shape layer  221
    Smart Object  227

TIFF (Tagged Image File
    Format)  369
    camera raw images
        and  117
    overview  129

timeline, creating  272

Timeline panel  338–339
    about  271
    changing the
        magnification  274
    returning to the first
        frame  284

tints
    defined  119
    in Black & White adjustment
        layers  278

Tolerance option for the
    Magic Wand tool  68

tone, adjusting  47–48

tools
    Brush tool  22
    Clone Stamp tool  52
    Content-Aware Move
        tool  152
    Crop tool  45
    Eyedropper  293
    Healing Brush tool  48
    Horizontal Type tool  22
    keyboard shortcuts
        for  17, 207
    Lasso tool  71
    Magic Wand tool  68
    Magnetic Lasso tool  71, 73
    Move tool  25
    Patch tool  54
    Polygonal Lasso tool  71
    Quick Selection tool  63, 163
    Rectangular Marquee
        tool  22
    Rounded Rectangle
        tool  199–200
    selecting hidden  16–17
    selection  62–63
    Spot Healing Brush tool  48
    using  14–20

Tools panel
    compared to other
        panels  31–32
    double-column view  15
    selecting and using tools
        from  15–21

tool tips, displaying  15

tracks, in a timeline  272

transformations, freeform
    92–93, 216–217

transforming
    layers  92–94
    Smart Objects  228

transitions
    adding to video  284
    changing the length of  285

transparency
    adjusting  90–91
    indicating  87
    in web-optimized
        images  359

Transparency And Gamut
    dialog box  371

trimming an image  46

TrueType fonts  199

type. See also text
    aligning  184
    clipping mask
        183, 185–187
    creating  184–185
    glyphs  197
    on a path  187–188
    overview  182
    resizing  182
    resolution-independent  182
    setting options  184
    swashes  199
    tricks  188
    true fractions  199
    vertical  200–201
    warping  191–192

typefaces. See fonts
    formats  182
    selecting  184

type layers  96
    creating new  188
    selecting contents  188
    updating  208

Type tool  22–23


U

undocking panels  30

Undo command  26

undoing actions  25–32

upscaling images  255

user interface
    changing settings for  37
    learning  10–12

user slices  347

**V**

vector graphics
    bitmap images vs. 206
    defined 10
    drawing shapes 217–219
    overview 206
    subtracting shapes from
        220–221

vector masks
    converting to layer
        masks 178
    defined 164
    selection indication 221
    unlinking from layers 178

Vertical Type tool 200

Vibrance adjustment layer 155

video
    adding audio to 286
    adding pan and zoom
        effects 283–284
    adding transitions 284–285
    applying Smart Filters
        to 279–280
    exporting 288
    groups 273
    importing assets for 271
    overview 271
    rendering 288, 339
    resizing assets for 275
    using adjustment layers
        in 277

vignetting 147

**W**

Wacom tablets 306

warping
    images with the Liquify
        filter 240
    type 191–192

web
    browsers 344
    color mode for content 42
    optimizing images for
        353–355, 359
    preparing files for 266
    selecting fonts for 354

wetness options, in
    painting 294

white balance,
    adjusting 119–120

White Balance tool (in
    Camera Raw) 120–121

white point 121

widgets, 3D 315, 316, 328,
    334–335

Windows, differences in work
    area 12

work area 10–39

workflows
    color-managed 368–369
    for retouching images 42
    organizing files 136–137
    prepress 368

Work Path
    naming 214
    overview 209

workspaces
    customizing 32–36
    default 11
    Motion 272
    preset 32–33
    saving 36

**X**

x axis 315

XMP files 125

**Y**

y axis 315

**Z**

z axis 315

Zoomify feature 358

zooming
    in to a video through
        animation 278
    in to the Timeline
        panel 274
    out 67

Zoom option in video 278

Zoom tool 15–16
    shortcuts 168
    using Scrubby Zoom 16

# Production Notes

The *Adobe Photoshop CC Classroom in a Book* was created electronically using Adobe InDesign CS6. Art was produced using Adobe InDesign, Adobe Illustrator, and Adobe Photoshop. The Myriad Pro and Warnock Pro OpenType families of typefaces were used throughout this book. For information about OpenType and Adobe fonts, visit www.adobe.com/type/opentype/.

References to company names in the lessons are for demonstration purposes only and are not intended to refer to any actual organization or person.

## Images

Photographic images and illustrations are intended for use with the tutorials.

Lesson 4 pineapple and flower photography © Image Source, www.imagesource.com

Lesson 6 and 7 model photography © Image Source, www.imagesource.com

## Team credits

The following individuals contributed to the development of *Adobe Photoshop CC Classroom in a Book*:

Project Manager: Elaine Gruenke

Writer: Brie Gyncild

Illustrator and Compositor: Lisa Fridsma

Copyeditor and Proofreader: Wendy Katz

Indexer: Brie Gyncild

Keystroker: Megan Ahearn

Cover design: Eddie Yuen

Interior design: Mimi Heft

Art Director: Andrew Faulkner

Designers: Elaine Gruenke and Megan Lee

Adobe Press Executive Editor: Victor Gavenda

Adobe Press Project Editor: Connie Jeung-Mills

Adobe Press Production Editor: Tracey Croom

## Contributors

**Jay Graham** began his career designing and building custom homes. He has been a professional photographer for more than 22 years, with clients in the advertising, architectural, editorial, and travel industries. He contributed the "Pro Photo Workflow" tips in Lesson 5. www.jaygraham.com

**Lisa Farrer** is a photographer based in Marin County, CA. She contributed photography for Lesson 5. www.lisafarrerphoto.com

**Gawain Weaver** has conserved and restored original works by artists ranging from Eadward Muybridge to Man Ray, and from Ansel Adams to Cindy Sherman. He contributed to "Real World Photo Restoration" in Lesson 2. www.gawainweaver.com

## Special Thanks

We offer our sincere thanks to Christine Yarrow, Daniel Presedo, Pete Falco, Stephen Nielson, Russell Brown, and Zorana Gee for their support and help with this project. We couldn't have done it without you!

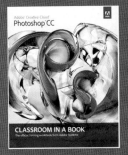